GOVERNING THE AMERICAN STATE

PRINCETON STUDIES IN AMERICAN POLITICS

HISTORICAL, INTERNATIONAL, AND COMPARATIVE PERSPECTIVES

SERIES EDITORS

IRA KATZNELSON, MARTIN SHEFTER, AND THEDA SKOCPOL

A list of titles in this series appear at the back of the book.

GOVERNING THE AMERICAN STATE

CONGRESS AND THE NEW

FEDERALISM, 1877–1929

Kimberley S. Johnson

PRINCETON UNIVERSITY PRESS   PRINCETON AND OXFORD

Library of Congress Cataloging-in-Publication Data
Johnson, Kimberley S., 1966–
Governing the American state : Congress and the new federalism, 1877–1929 /
Kimberley S. Johnson.
    p.   cm. — (Princeton studies in American politics)
Includes bibliographical references and index.
ISBN-13: 978-0-691-11974-8 (alk. paper)
ISBN-10: 0-691-11974-0 (alk. paper)
1. Federal government—United States. 2. United States—Politics and government.
I. Title. II. Series.
JK325.J59 2006
320.473′04909034—dc22   2005037976

British Library Cataloging-in-Publication Data is available

This book has been composed in Palatino

Printed on acid-free paper. ∞

pup.princeton.edu

Printed in the United States of America

10 9 8 7 6 5 4 3 2 1

Contents

List of Figures

List of Tables

Acknowledgments _____

THE PATH to this book, like many works in American politics, has been guided by the recent evolution of political science and by events within contemporary American politics. It has also been profoundly shaped by the input of mentors, fellow scholars, friends, and random interested observers. To all of them I owe a profound debt of gratitude. Most notable in this list is my dissertation committee, Ira Katznelson, Robert Shapiro, Ester Fuchs, and Sharyn O'Halloran. A special thank-you is extended to Ester Fuchs, friend and mentor from undergraduate days until today. A number of people such as Ira Katznelson, Robert Lieberman, and David Robertson have provided supportive advice and counsel along the way. My colleagues at SUNY Stony Brook and especially Barnard College provided a wonderful supportive environment for productive research and writing. I thank the talented Barnard and Columbia students who have provided invaluable research assistance over the years. The Ford Foundation and Columbia University's Center for the Social Sciences provided critical assistance for this project at the dissertation stage. The anonymous reviewers for Princeton University Press provided excellent advice and criticism that has only changed this book for the better. I thank them.

Writing a book does not happen within a vacuum. I thank all of my fellow graduate school travelers who have helped in the writing, especially Marianne Ide, Chauncy Lennon, and Ray Smith. I also extend a heartfelt thanks to family, especially my mother, Kerlene Coote, whose own search for her place in the world has inspired my own. Milo, Aaron, and Liza have been joyous companions of this book from its beginning. Finally but not least, my final thank-you and acknowledgment is to Daniel Marcus, who has been with me from beginning to end, and has given so much of everything, especially when sometimes it has seemed too much.

Introduction _____

The First New Federalism and the Making of the Modern American State

> The characteristic feature and special interest of the American Union is that it shows us two governments covering the same ground, yet distinct and separate in their action. It is like a great factory wherein two sets of machinery are at work, their revolving wheels apparently intermixed, their bands crossing each other, yet each set doing its own work without touching or hampering the other.
> James Bryce, *American Commonwealth*

FOR MANY Americans who worry about the size, complexity, or responsiveness of the American government, the nineteenth century is a lost Eden of Jeffersonian agrarian democracy. In this idealized perspective, nineteenth-century American government was limited and orderly, a great machine overseen by a night watchman state and held in check by an active yeoman citizenry. There were no overlapping lines of authority—the federal structure ensured that the national government and the states each had their respective and limited orbits. Indeed this structure ensured that in the dual machinery of government, the national government, even more so than the states, would remain small and limited. This system of limited governments precluded the emergence of a sprawling regulatory state with a cacophony of competing interest groups, unresponsive bureaucrats, ambitious politicians, and citizen-clients. In short, the idealized image of nineteenth-century federalism reflected a political system that was (thankfully) nothing like contemporary American politics.

As Americans enter a new century, we seem stymied by the intractable problems besetting our political system. Political institutions and public policy appear to be out of our control, dominated by an unholy alliance of career politicians, special interest groups, and government bureaucrats. Each group pursues its own agenda rather than the broader public interest. As a result, the public perceives the government as impervious to citizens' attempts to ensure more account-ability, effectiveness, and efficiency in the cost and delivery of govern-ment services.

The competing voices of today are urging a reordering of govern-mental power to restore accountability and efficacy to our political in-stitutions and public policy. For some conservatives and some liberals, the solutions to these problems lie in decreasing the size of government or devolving its powers—whether to the states, the private sector, or the people. Yet efforts to achieve these solutions are contested, either through the outright opposition of actors with a vested interest in the current political and institutional arrangements, or through political and institutional inertia and rigidity. Both of these factors make less likely the achievement of smaller, decentralized government that is more responsive to the people, than to the interests.

Yet what some Americans admire about nineteenth-century gover-nance—smallness, decentralization—was the bane of many nine-teenth century reformers and critics. To these individuals, the Ameri-can political system was an assemblage of weak legislative institutions dominated by a multitude of powerful interests, and characterized by limited administrative capacity. America's small, bounded, and frag-mented governmental sphere—the coglike machine described by James Bryce, a nineteenth-century analyst of American government—was an impediment to the creation of a "strong" state that could ade-quately address the demands of an industrializing and urbanizing country. For reformers and critics of the American political system from the end of the nineteenth century onward, the solutions of today—smaller government and more decentralization—were the ob-stacles of the moment.

At the beginning of the twentieth century, for these reformers—whom I will refer to as national state builders—better government for American citizens lay in expanding, centralizing, and strengthening existing institutions and policies, and in some cases, creating new ones as well. The goal of many of these state builders was Hamiltonian in its scope—a truly national government with significant powers and re-sources to address what reformers saw as the moral and political ills of the day.

Contesting and checking these statist visions, however, was the American federal system, designed to produce disjointed and weak political and institutional structures. The nineteenth-century federal system enabled a variety of interests and actors who benefited from existing fragmented and limited political and institutional powers to stand in the way of the state builders. To build and then to govern a modern American state, new ways of thinking about the role of the state would have to be developed. New ways of governing would have to be found. Walter Weyl, a Progressive intellectual and journalist, captures the uncertainty of this statebuilding process.

> [T]his movement, because of the heterogeneous character of those who further it, is tentative, conciliatory, compromising, evolutionary, and legal, proceeding with a minimum of friction through a series of partial victories; [it] is influenced and colored by American conditions and traditions, proceeding with but few violent breaks, out of our previous industrial, political, and intellectual development and out of our material and moral accumulations, and utilizing, even while reforming and reconstituting, our economic and legal machinery."[1]

Today a very different institutional, political, and ideological environment faces reformers of all stripes. Near the beginning of the twenty-first century, much like the beginning of the twentieth century, it is perhaps difficult for us to envision a world that strays very far from the boundaries of what is currently known or, because of a veil of nostalgia and wishful thinking for a supposedly better era, to perceive what happened in the past.

Yet as this book will show, change does occur in the American system. It is rarely as logical, coherent, or aesthetically pleasing as reformers would like, but it does happen. Understanding the roles played by ideas, interests, institutions, and history will perhaps provide guidance as well as comfort. We can better understand the political, policy, and administrative contours of the twenty-first-century American state by looking back to the previous century and observing the ways in which competing forces interacted with preexisting institutions. Perhaps we too can find our way to a new American state by understanding the source of one of the most important puzzles of state development in the United States: the disjuncture between institutional strength and coherence, and the disjointed and fragmented nature of public policy. At the beginning of the twentieth century, much like today, efficient and effective government, both by and for the people, seemed to be a wistful dream. This book returns to the beginnings of that dream.

Key Questions

Like many beliefs, the notion that American government was once limited and orderly is more of an ideal type than reality. Even at the time that this picture of ordered government was painted, that order was swiftly becoming unraveled. The great and simple machine of early American government was transformed, by 1929, into a much more complex apparatus, what we now see as the modern American state. Despite the weight and influence of preexisting political and institutional arrangements, during the Gilded Age and Progressive Era something happened to alter the nineteenth-century machine of government, ultimately transforming the American state into something very different from the one that James Bryce surveyed in the late nineteenth century. Understanding, shaping, and ultimately governing this strange new governmental apparatus—the modern state—would be the focus of critics, reformers, politicians, and citizens from its initial appearance until today.

This book seeks to answer three questions about the emergence of the modern American state: How did preexisting political and institutional arrangements shape the preferences and choices available to those interested in centralizing and expanding government? How did forces in favor of a greater centralization and expansion of government establish their vision as a competitive, and eminently viable, option for structuring American politics and policy? Finally, how can understanding the timing and sequence of these changes in the American state help us to understand broader patterns in American politics and policy?

The book examines a period in American history when the answers to these questions can be unearthed. The nearly 60 years that spanned the Gilded Age and Progressive Era are a curious period in American political history. From the perspective of this study, it was an uneasy period when the United States was precariously balanced between a continued dual federal system and a centralized modern state.[2] I call this era the first New Federalism.

Before this story can be told, we must first define "federalism" in order to understand how this national statebuilding process unfolded. Over time, the term *federal* has meant many things to many people. To help clarify this book's argument, I provide the following definitions. *National government* refers to what is commonly called the federal government. The term *intergovernmental policy* refers to laws, policies, or administrative arrangements that alter the relationship between the national government and the states. Finally, *federalism* will be reserved to mean the constitutional relationship between the national government and the states.

While the Civil War decisively ended the notion that the United States was a state subject to the will of its constituent members, the war and its aftermath did not fully take up the implicit nationalization project that a war based on union would predict. By 1877, the leviathan Union government created by Lincoln to win the war had been dismantled; the courts fairly quickly ended any notion of clarifying the promise of national citizenship contained in the text of the Fourteenth Amendment; and the Republican Party with the end of Reconstruction pulled the national government back not only from its governing role in the South, but also as an active force in American life.[3] Nationalization, and even more concretely, centralization of power seemed to be out of the realm of possibility.

By 1929, however, a form of national expansion, though uneasily accepted, had been agreed upon: congressionally enacted policy, with limited national oversight or implementation, matched by some degree of state and local control. The first New Federalism, with its widely accepted, yet at times bitterly contested, constraints on the national government, fell before the onslaught of the Great Depression and the upending of the settled order of American politics and society. The thirty-six-year reign of McKinley-Hoover Republicanism vanished in the 1932 elections. In its place came a new model of federalism, a more centralized national government led by a strong president, aided by an assertive and active national bureaucracy and a compliant legislature and judiciary.

Yet a closer look at this New Deal federalism would reveal a strong resemblance to its first New Federalism forebears. Even before President Franklin Roosevelt put the first phases of the New Deal into place, a state recognizable to modern eyes—in terms of bureaucratic organization, interest group activity, and even legislative oversight—was already established.[4]

The book begins with a curious puzzle: the crisis of Civil War and Reconstruction was not enough to create a centralized state, yet the key elements necessary for a modern state to form were already in place before the crisis of the Great Depression and the response of the New Deal. These key elements would constitute the source of the two problems of the modern American state: the jarring mix of institutional incoherence and strength, and the fragmented and disjointed nature of public policy.

The nearly sixty-year period that spanned the Gilded Age and Progressive Era, but ended prior to the New Deal, I call the first New Federalism. It was in this era, I argue, that the roots of the modern American state grew. The seeds of the modern American state were planted in the struggles of an earlier time, when the dual clockwork of (small) states and (smaller) national government was not simply an image but a hard reality. Yet the state developed during this period was not merely a New Deal state-in-waiting. The first New Federalism reflected and was fundamentally shaped by the partisan, institutional, and ideological struggles of the Gilded Age and Progressive Era.

From 1877 to 1929, Congress joined with bureaucrats, reformers, and interest groups in this paradoxical reshaping of the American state. Legislative and administrative choices made in pursuit of modernization were conditioned by the logic of America's federal structure. Federalism was accommodated, if not overcome, through the enactment and spread of intergovernmental policy.

Enacted by Congress, intergovernmental policy was a series of new policy and administrative innovations—including now familiar instruments such as intergovernmental regulations and grants-in-aid. These instruments would comprise a New Federalism that bridged the dualism of the nineteenth century with the centralization of the twentieth. The intergovernmental policies of the first New Federalism included significant legislation such as the Hatch Act of 1887, which established agricultural experiment stations, and, the Federal Highway Act of 1916, which established the foundation of the Interstate Highway System. The first New Federalism also included the obscure, such as the Standard Barrel acts establishing uniform measures for interstate shipping and commerce, and a grant for the American Printing House for the Blind (1879).

Intergovernmental policy fostered the development of interlocking bureaucracies at the national and state levels. At the same time, it facilitated the growth in networks of interest groups, and the rise of new professions and associations that bridged the divide between bureaucrats and interest groups. Most importantly, the first New Federalism reflected the uneasy balance between Congress's localist representational structure and modernist impulses for greater centralization and nationalization. By focusing on this era in national state development, we can better understand how the hallmarks of modern American politics evolved during this unique period of American federalism.

In this story of American political development I examine the role of ideas (of limited government versus modernization), interests (such as bureaucrats and interest groups), and institutions (such as Congress and federalism), in the creation of a new American state. Using a blend of historical narrative, case study investigation, and quantitative analysis, I trace the emergence and development of the first New Federalism across time and across policy areas as a way to develop a more accurate picture of the contours of national-state relations during the Gilded Age and Progressive Era. This multifaceted approach demonstrates how Congress became the key player in creating a new federalist policy system that would eventually substantively alter the relationship between the national government and the states.

Federalism and American Political Development

The modern American state did not fully emerge out of the crisis of the Great Depression, or for that matter out of the Civil War and Reconstruction. The modern American state—more highly centralized than ever before with unprecedented fiscal and regulatory scope—did not emerge as a logical and fully formed outcome from the minds of the New Deal architects, and through the extension of executive power. Instead, dual processes of path dependency and evolutionary adaptation during the Gilded Age and Progressive Era also powerfully shaped the modern American state.[5] American political institutions responded in a variety of ways to long-term secular changes in American society unleashed by urbanization and industrialization. These institutional responses, themselves conditioned by historical legacy, powerfully shaped the way in which the modern federal state would emerge.

Thus, American state development cannot be seen solely a series of punctuated equilibria, wherein periods of rapid change (stimulated by exogenous shocks) were succeeded (or preceded) by long instances of institutional stasis.[6] While exogenous shocks such as war or economic crisis may create critical junctures in American politics and society, each of these junctures was powerfully shaped by the preceding period of so-called stasis. In the case of the first New Federalism, the expansion of national power was not a sudden or dramatic process; rather it was the slow accretion of administrative ties and the building up of organizational structures, buttressed by a growing network of interest groups and bureaucrats, all overseen by an emergent legislature that eventually brought about a new American state.

Understanding the rise of the new American state entails a reclaiming and recognition of a lost historical and constitutional legacy: federalism. To answer the questions posed in this book, we have to turn our attention to this obvious, yet analytically ignored, aspect of the American political system. Federalism not only shaped the context of political decision making during the first New Federalism; it also shaped the policy responses to the political and institutional challenges and transformations that made up the Gilded Age and Progressive Era polities.

In order to create a modernized, centralized state, the American federal structure of fragmented, decentralized power would have to be weakened if not undone. However, to undertake the development of a strong national government, the political and organizational features of federalism would have to be harnessed and deployed in order to surmount the limitations on national power. The centralization of the national state came at a price: the disjointed and fragmented nature of the federal system was mapped onto the face of the modern American state.

During the era of the first New Federalism, federalism not only acted *on* political institutions and actors, but was also acted *upon* by political institutions and actors. That is, we can think of federalism structuring the incentives and constraints of actors and institutions. These very same actors and institutions could also alter federalism—constitutionally, politically, ideologically, and administratively.[7]

Thus, the first New Federalism was a distinctive period in the development of the American *federal* state. It was an era characterized by a set of institutional arrangements, political structures, and opportunities that were distinctively shaped by a particular constitutional and popular interpretation of federalism. I elaborate on this distinctive period in American federalism in chapter 1.

The first New Federalism was also a specific set of policy innovations and administrative arrangements that evolved in response to the late-nineteenth-century institutional and political arrangements of Congress and American federalism. At the heart of this modernization project, and discussed in greater detail in chapter 2, was intergovernmental policy. Consisting of 131 policies enacted from 1877 to 1929, and ranging from regulations covering food and drugs, to funds for building highways or providing health services to mothers and children, the intergovernmental policies of the first New Federalism created the basis for a new national state based on shared standards, an interlocking array of interest groups and bureaucrats, and a new thinking about the relationship between the national government and the states.

Accompanying the enactment of intergovernmental policy was the development of state or administrative capacity at both the national and the state levels. In the words of early Progressive Era public administration theorist (as well as practitioner) Frank J. Goodnow, state or administrative capacity was the link between "the expression of the will of the state and the execution of that will."[8] Administrative capacity is what government does; it bridges the gap between enactment and enforcement. It thus includes, as Stephen Skowronek would argue, the "governmental forms and procedures necessary for securing order."[9] Order, however, does not spontaneously occur. The creation of order rests upon the ability of policy elites (as well as the people) not only to think up "workable" policies, but also to determine "how to actually implement them."[10] At least in the American case, the creation of administrative capacity at the national and state levels was a process of trial and error: a rapid spreading and adoption of some ideas, and the slower adoption or even rejection of other ideas. With these instruments, the nationalist aspirations of American national state builders could be adapted to the constitutional, political, and ideological realities of late-nineteenth- and early-twentieth-century American government.

The new intergovernmental policy instruments, and the administrative capacity they created, ultimately became the device that accommodated the expression of national interest desired by national-level actors while acknowledging the demands of judicial or state-oriented interests for some degree of state control. For reformers, interest groups, and bureaucrats at the state level, the ability to tap into the fiscal and regulatory authority of the national government via intergovernmental policy helped to strengthen and legitimize emerging government activities. At the level of the national government, I show that intergovernmental policy allowed the national government to amplify and extend its limited administrative capacity into control over policy outcomes at the state and local level. Although this control was restricted to certain policy arenas, it laid the groundwork for shaping future policy decisions. From 1877 until 1929, these policy instruments knit together legislators, bureaucrats, interest groups, reformers, and citizens into ever tighter bonds, and raised the bar of what it was possible for American government, whether at the national or state level, to do. Exactly how these instruments knit a new state is probed through the use of case studies in three policy areas: food and drug regulation, highway building, and maternal and child health services.

Conceptualizing federalism as an institution that structures outcomes as well as one that is responsive to change is a complex, yet necessary, step toward solving the institutional and historical puzzle that the first New Federalism presents. First, we can reconsider the role of federalism in shaping American political development. Federalism is not a dusty constitutional issue largely disconnected from normal politics and policy. Federalism during the first New Federalism was, at the very least, an active force shaping the preferences and institutions that surrounded political actors. At the same time, the federal structure was (and is) not writ in stone. While the judiciary and reigning political beliefs during the Gilded Age and Progressive Era often endorsed a narrow dual federal system, actors and interests looked for ways to subvert these judicial limitations. Thus federalism, in the form of intergovernmental policy, became the means for these subversions.

Congress and the First New Federalism

Connecting broad processes of change to specific policy developments is difficult without specifying a mechanism. Unlike other analyses of American political development, this study emphasizes the role of

Congress as that mechanism. One reason for this emphasis is that in late-nineteenth-century America, neither the executive, here meaning the president, executive branch officials, and the nascent professional bureaucracy, nor elites—reformers or capitalists—had the strength in and of themselves to enact and implement sweeping policy changes, or to create fully developed and effective bureaucratic structures.[11]

Congress was the terrain on which ideas and interests were translated into policy. This translation was not automatic; rather, Congress had to grapple with its own partisan and institutional issues. The conjunction of Congress's own institutional evolution with statebuilding attempts produced a unique administrative and policy response, the first New Federalism. Intergovernmental policy instruments, or IPIs, offered a way for Congress to balance the competing demands and conflicts that it faced, as well as the tensions produced by its own internal development.

Within Congress, intergovernmental policy provided resources that the modernizing Congress needed: the ability to generate electoral support through policies that delivered distributive goods and allowed Congress to claim credit. Because of their deliberately chosen geographically based distributions, IPIs perfectly mapped onto the representational structure of Congress. In addition, intergovernmental policy, with its fragmented authority and multiple lines of accountability, was a comfortable match for the still weak and limited capacity of the national state. Finally, intergovernmental policy offered one way to bridge partisan and sectional divisions within Congress, within the national government, and across the federal system.

Outside of Congress, intergovernmental policy allowed reformers and interest groups to advance their policy aspirations, while allowing experts and bureaucrats to claim, and in some cases reinforce, professional and administrative dominance over particular policy areas. In cases where the assertion of national power was problematic—for constitutional, political, or economic reasons—IPIs allowed state and local interests to be strategically accommodated in order to gain some degree of national power. These claims are discussed and analyzed more fully in chapter 3.

The impact of congressional politics and structure on the enacting and shaping of intergovernmental policy calls into question some current assumptions about American federalism. First, intergovernmental policy was first and foremost a creature of Congress, not the executive. While presidents such as Theodore Roosevelt and Woodrow Wilson were associated with periods of increased enactment of intergovernmental policy, on the whole it was Congress, and not the executive, that was responsible for the ebb and flow of intergovernmental policy. It was Congress, not the executive, that was responsible for the shaping of the administrative structures and procedures that would govern the implementation of intergovernmental policy, and would determine a policy's winners and losers. Finally, while interest groups and their bureaucratic partners are important parts of this national statebuilding story, Congress with its own internal partisan and institutional dynamics played a powerful independent role in shaping the first New Federalism and the modern federal state that would follow.

This emphasis on Congress is not meant to downplay the role of interest groups, entrepreneurial bureaucrats, the president, or even the courts. All of these actors played an important role, as the case studies will demonstrate. While one or several of these actors may have had greater influence over Congress at particular moments, Congress has an important autonomous role in American politics. In the context of Gilded Age and Progressive Era politics, not taking Congress and federalism into account creates a misleading picture of American state development. Congress and federalism played key roles in shaping the policy and administrative basis of the modern American state.

This book differs from executive- and polity-centered studies because it argues that the development of national state capacity, including the development of a national bureaucracy, was heavily influenced by the structural constraints imposed by federalism.[12] Because of federalism, the development of state capacity reflected the organizational and partisan imperatives of Congress rather than the executive. Because of federalism, the ability to develop a strong, highly centralized administrative state in the more familiar European model was essentially checked. The ability of the national state to implement its policies was dependent upon its ability to develop bureaucratic partners in the American states. Although the New Deal with its expansion of executive power and administrative capacity would seemingly overcome these limitations, the institutional legacy of this pre–New Deal era would live on in the United States' disjointed and fragmented system of policy formation and delivery that modern presidents, from Eisenhower to Nixon and to Reagan, each with his "new federalism," have continually attempted to reform.

Beyond the Shadow of the New Deal

The idea of a first New Federalism fundamentally contradicts models of American federalism premised on the New Deal experience of an active and relatively powerful executive presiding over an acquiescent Congress while a submissive judiciary declines to intervene. As a result of this lack of fit with dominant models, the first New Federalism has been underplayed, if not ignored in favor of a simpler developmental model.[13]

This lack of historical knowledge rests in part on the nature of the New Deal, and its impact on research on American federalism. The political and societal impact of the policy "big bang" of the New Deal was so great that the first New Federalism was lost in its corona.[14] By the end of the 1940s, because of the ideological and fiscal changes brought about by New Deal federalism, political scientists and others would openly speculate on the irrelevance of the American states.[15] To the extent that researchers gazed beyond the New Deal to the era that preceded it, their focus was on demonstrating that the centralization of the American state that had occurred in the New Deal was the result of a natural, logical progression of forces. Some scholars, such as Daniel Elazar, cast their eyes back into American history to finds instances of New Deal–type federalist policy.[16] Critics, however, dismissed these historical examples as simplistic and wrongheaded interpretations of past political and policy developments. For these critics, the federal system that had come into being in the New Deal was sui generis; the history of modern federalism began with the New Deal.

It is not surprising, then, that a bifurcated view of American federalism exists, given this analytical legacy. The premodern, dual federalism of limited government is almost always contrasted to modern, cooperative, welfare state federalism. For supporters of the latter, the era of dual federalism is a period of unrelieved weakness of national and state governments, punctuated by instances of corruption and incompetence. Critics of modern welfare state federalism characterize it as an intricate and incoherent administrative structure, supported—or perhaps enabled—by a network of national, state, and local interests solely concerned with a particular policy, rather than a broader public or national interest.

For many observers of American federalism, the source of this incoherence and particularism lies in the emergence of New Deal federalism, and the solutions to these problems point to a return to a simpler dual federal system. The first New Federalism shows that this simple dichotomy with its simple policy answers is wrong. The first New Federalism is the missing, and necessary, link between these two stories of American state development, institutions, and the shaping of public policy.

Plan of the Book

Reexamining and understanding the first New Federalism helps to lay bare one of the most important and yet least appreciated peculiarities of American political development. The rest of this book expands on the relationship between federalism and the development of the modern American state. Interwoven within these chapters will be a discussion of three policies that are emblematic not only of American policy writ large, but specifically of intergovernmental policy. While these three policies—food and drug regulation, highway construction, and maternal and child health programs—were enacted during the first New Federalism, their legislative and administrative influence persisted decades past their first enactment.

In chapter 1, I present a brief overview of the key ideas, interests, and institutions that shaped the unique environment from which the first New Federalism would emerge. States and the judiciary played key roles in determining the constraints and possibilities that state builders would encounter. While states would offer political arenas to advance new policy innovations, economic competition as well as administrative incapacity would limit the spread and effectiveness of these innovations. The courts sent mixed signals to national state builders about the scope of both state and national governments. New and often contradictory voices spoke out both for and against a stronger national state (as well as a continued dualism). Alongside this struggle over ideas emerged a new organizational society and the reformers, experts, and intergovernmental bureaucrats who helped to shape it.

Chapter 2 explores the intergovernmental policies that form the basis of the first New Federalism. I focus on how dozens of policies and programs, governed by an array of new administrative structures and procedures, combined to create the core of administrative structure and capacity upon which rested the new modern state. I first discuss the scope and structure of these intergovernmental policy instruments (IPIs), across time and across policy areas. I then trace the administrative structures and procedures, such as reporting requirements or funding mechanisms, that developed alongside these intergovernmental policy innovations. I show that these structures allowed for the development of more centralized and strengthened government (at the national and state levels). I then introduce two measures of discretionary power in order to trace the national assertions of power (or state maintenance of power) across time and policy areas, again to determine the contours of the first New Federalism.

Chapter 3 provides the first test of the book's argument, that Congress—with its changing partisan and institutional arrangements—played a key role in the enactment and shaping of intergovernmental policy, and consequently the first New Federalism. Statistical analyses model the impact of representational imperatives and the partisan environment of congressional policymaking, as well as the effects of long-term trends in institutionalization, such as member turnover and legislative staff growth, on the enactment and structure of the first New Federalism. I find that the strength of the Republican Party, mediated by factors such as party cohesion, sectionalism, and divided government, determined if the national government enacted intergovernmental legislation or not, and the degree of power asserted by the national government when intergovernmental policy was enacted. On the whole, Republicans' willingness to enact IPIs varied across policy areas. They were more likely to enact IPIs in the distributive and redistributive policy areas than in other areas. The Republicans were more likely to place power in the hands of the national government. By contrast, Democrats—a largely minority party during the first New Federalism—were more willing to enact intergovernmental policy and to share power with the states.

The second part of the book, chapters 4, 5, and 6, consists of three case studies: food and drug regulation, highway development, and maternal and child health care. These in-depth case studies are designed to provide more textured evidence supporting the analytical distinctiveness of the first New Federalism. By examining three distinctive kinds of policies—regulatory, distributive, and redistributive—broad similarities as well as important differences can be analyzed. The goal of these case studies is to situate the usual Progressive Era story of interest groups, reformers, and bureaucrats not only within a policy-specific, but also an institutionally specific, context—the American federal system and, in particular, Congress.

The final chapter, chapter 7, discusses how the continuities and the disjunctures between the first two new federalism(s) of the twentieth century have affected the modern American federal state, and our understanding of American state development.

Chapter One _____

Congress and Statebuilding in a Federal Polity

The principle of the division of powers
between state and federal governments is a
very simple one when stated in its most
general terms. It is that legislatures of the states
ought to have . . . free choice with regard to all
matters of local regulation and development,
and that Congress shall have control only of
such matters as concern the peace and the
commerce of the country as a whole.
    Woodrow Wilson, *Constitutional Government in
the United States*

CONGRESS WAS the key governing institution of the Gilded Age and
Progressive Era. Not only was Congress the initiator of policy; it also
structured the implementation of policy. Although some national state
builders could and did focus on reconstituting executive authority in
order to initiate policy, it was in some ways easier and more logical for
them to focus on Congress, the source of political authority during this
era. The goal of political parties during the middle to late nineteenth
century was the capture and control of political institutions. Because
of the legacy of Jacksonian administration, while the executive branch
was a rich source of patronage, it was never seen as the source of policy
innovation. Unlike the modern era with its "imperial presidency," in
the Gilded Age and Progressive Era, Congress proposed policy and the
executive disposed.[1] Congress and its leaders set the political agenda,
while the president, more or less, acquiesced.

Congress's role as the key governing institution during this period
did not, however, translate into an overt desire for an expanded national state. With some exceptions, in the late nineteenth century, the
party system, and politicians who were its members, focused on spoils
first and policy second. Although both parties would accommodate
the desires of key interests such as the railroads or the trusts, such an
accommodation was seen as a return for favors proffered, not part of
a systematic national or party-building effort. The public's perception

of this system of favors was that Congress, and by extension the American government, had been captured by the "interests."[2]

Given this perception, it is not surprising that even as late as the 1970s, studies of nineteenth-century Congress portrayed the institution as the "weakened spring of American government," in which "in the hands of a passive government the statutes took on whatever meaning interested persons chose for them."[3] The story of nineteenth-century congressional governance was one of public power seized for private ends. The seizing of public power resulted from a "spider web of clogged agendas, cumbersome committees, obsolete procedures, and amateurism" that characterized nineteenth-century congressional government.[4] Yet the occurrence of the first New Federalism belies this claim of a limited, wholly ineffective, and wholly inactive Congress. How and why did it emerge, given the alleged weakness of Congress, and by extension, the national state?

These questions are difficult to answer given the common analysis of nineteenth-century Congress. Corruption and inefficiency certainly plagued Congress during the late nineteenth century, yet to dismiss its activities understates its role as the linchpin of Gilded Age and Progressive Era politics. The American Congress, as Morton Keller argues, is "the representative structure . . . linking decentralized and centralized loci of political power on an ongoing basis." Indeed it is this function, Keller argues, that separates and "distinguishes [Congress] from other national-level institutions."[5]

By looking more closely at the partisan, institutional, and ideological context that nineteenth-century Congresses operated within, we can develop a more analytically useful picture of the American state during the Gilded Age and the Progressive Era. In particular, we can focus on key interests and institutions that pushed Congress (and that Congress pushed) into creating a distinctive American state. These elements together constituted what I call the *federal polity*—a mix of ideas, interests, and institutions rooted in the twin upheavals of industrialization and urbanization during the late nineteenth century that produced a host of new economic and political issues and fissures.[6]

While this federal polity influenced congressional policymaking, it did not define it. Despite its Gilded Age reputation as an institution where the "interests" ran policy, Congress was not a neutral arena, or indeed a unitary actor, in which bargaining among interests took place. As the new institutionalists have argued, Congress, both then and now, is made up of "*structural features* (the division and specialization of labor (committees), leadership organizations, staffing arrangements, party groupings) and *procedures* (rules of debate, amendment, and those regulating other features of daily life" that powerfully shape who wins and who loses.[7] Congress is directed by rules, both formal and informal, that shape preferences as well as outcomes. The rules, procedures, and norms of Congress structure what kinds of policies make it onto the legislative agenda, the consideration of policy alternatives, and the enactment of policies. The presence of these institutions can have a powerful independent effect on policymaking. Congressional institutions shape ideas (promoted by interests) in the sense that an approach ultimately adopted by Congress is not necessarily the best one, or the one preferred by a powerful interest group, but rather an idea that can generate an enacting coalition, within and across chambers and branches, given existing institutional structure and procedures.[8]

During the first New Federalism, intergovernmental policy was an institutional choice made by the national government and specifically by Congress in order to control its exercise of authority. Conceiving of intergovernmental policy as an institutional choice offers analytical leverage, as it rests upon several plausible assumptions. The decision to either share substantive policy authority with the states or to assert national power was made by rational, electorally motivated legislators who weighed the political benefits and costs of enacting specific legislation. Intergovernmental policy offered one way to balance these competing needs.[9] By choosing to share or not to share authority over policy with the states, Congress addressed one of the organizational problems that it faced: the development of enacting coalitions. Congress's choice to use intergovernmental policy instruments was broadly influenced by the need to create majority coalitions, by the need to weigh political uncertainties, and by the restricted administrative options that were available to Gilded Age and Progressive Era policymakers. In short, intergovernmental policy enabled Congress to address its reluctance to expand national power given the perceived constraints of federalism.

In a political environment characterized by sharp inter- and intraparty disputes, sectional divisions, and divided government, intergovernmental policy offered members of Congress a way to put together enacting coalitions in order to pass legislation, facilitate the building of national electoral coalitions, and address the problems of passing legislation in a separation-of-powers system.

In the face of states and courts, intergovernmental policy created the possibility that Congress could overcome the structural hurdles on policymaking imposed by the federal structure. For example, intergovernmental policy allowed states and the national government legislators and party officials to reach strategic accommodations with each other that did not, in a majority of cases, challenge the ideological or judicial boundaries of the day. For national legislators, intergovernmental policy instruments offered a way for individual representatives to satisfy local policy preferences. National goods and services could be directed to congressional districts, and in some cases, control over those goods and services could be maintained in the hands of state and local interests.

National legislators—aided by entrepreneurial bureaucrats, mobilized interest groups, and organized reformers—labored over the structure of intergovernmental policy. This was not an empty or meaningless process for those involved. The structure of intergovernmental policy reflected which interests won and which lost, both at the time of enactment and in the future. Given the institutional and partisan constraints of Congress, choices over the administrative structure of intergovernmental policy mirrored Congress's cautious creation of a discretionary state. Intergovernmental policy was structured to control the actions of bureaucrats, to be responsive to the needs of constituents, and to maintain congressional influence over policy outcomes.[10] This new and growing exercise of congressional power, however, was complicated by its occurring within a federal system with judicially imposed limits on national oversight and implementation powers, and by the logistical problem of overseeing and implementing policy in multiple states.[11]

Congress played a key role in facilitating the development of intergovernmental policy instruments that not only asserted a national role, but responded to local interests as well. Instruments such as intergovernmental regulations and grants-in-aid permitted the development of national administrative capacity while still responding to a constitutional, political, and ideological framework that privileged state interests and favored state control over policy outcomes.

The intergovernmental policies enacted by Congress during the era of the first New Federalism were acquiesced to, with varying degrees of enthusiasm, by the states, and largely unchallenged by the Supreme Court. Over time these policies laid out the framework for a stronger, more centralized national state. New laws knit together the goals of national elites—the creation of a more effective national government, with the hard-edged reality of federalism. In short, the reformers' dreams of greater national administrative capacities came at a price. That price was the establishment of an administrative state that privileged state interests and state control over national policy. While policymaking could occur under the eyes of reformers, professionals, and experts, congressional organization and the influence of state interests ensured that the administration of *national* policy was carried out at the *state* level.

The Federal Polity

Although Congress occupied a preeminent position in the statebuilding process, it did not operate autonomously. Working both with and against Congress was a growing field of interest groups, ranging from functional and economic interests to political and social reformers. They collectively created a new type of politics that linked local, state, and national interests and represented them directly to politicians, sidestepping the political parties.[12] Along with interest groups emerged bureaucrats who advanced their own professional and policy agendas. Like the interest groups with whom they often cooperated, these bureaucrats, again at local, state, and national levels, worked individually, with each other, and with other allies to advance their national statebuilding agenda.

Shaping the strategies and resources of these groups were two preexisting institutional features of the American federal policy: states and courts.[13] For much of the middle to late twentieth century, many political scientists paid perfunctory attention to the notion of state police power and the limited scope of the interstate commerce clause. In the late nineteenth century, both constitutional principles were vital and contentious issues. The extent of these powers, as interpreted by individuals and the courts, would play an important role in shaping the agendas of both the state builders and the supporters of limited national power. The presence of the states, and the varying interpretations of state police power and the interstate commerce clause, would act as both a policymaking opportunity and an impediment for reformers and interest groups. While some benefited from interstate competition and the pressure it induced to keep state governments limited in their regulatory and fiscal scope, others were able to influence state governments to enact their policy preferences.

The courts sent contradictory signals about the scope of both state and national governments. The actors involved in the statebuilding process (both those for and those against) constructed their strategies and goals according to these mixed signals. Although we know now that the conservatism of the courts was somewhat overstated, to statebuilders during the Gilded Age and Progressive Era the laissez-faire constitutionalism of the courts seemed to preclude the development of a strong centralized national state. Statebuilders thus shaped their strategies so as to create policies that would clear the bar set by courts that were perceived as wary of, if not hostile to, any unwarranted expansion in government power.

This federal polity influenced the political incentives of Congress in its decisions to enact intergovernmental policy. Overcoming the constraints of federalism would require a legislature that was generally nationalist in its representation, statist in its collective policy preferences, and capable of administering the implementation of policy. Thus, given the hurdles of a federal structure, the development and growth of intergovernmental policy was a logical—although not necessarily the most efficient—way for Congress to enact policy.

Reformers, Experts, Interests, and the Growth of the American State

The year 1877 marked the beginning of what Robert Wiebe and others would call the "search for order," a period when the social, economic, and political challenges engendered by the United States' rapid industrialization and urbanization were responded to and mediated by an emergent "organizational society" in which "[i]ndustrialism had shifted the context of economic decisions from personal relationships among individuals to competition among well-organized groups."[14]

The dislocations and challenges of the Gilded Age produced a new wave of reformers. These groups were animated by beliefs ranging from a "social gospel," with its avowal of the perfectibility of man, to the "gospel of efficiency" in both business and government.[15] Reformers during the first New Federalism grappled with the effects of modernization on individuals' ability to compete in the new industrial order. They turned their attention to such issues as educational reform, both general and vocational; protective labor legislation for women and children; mother's pensions; and worker's compensation laws.

Women's groups comprised an important segment of reformers concerned with the deleterious effects of modern life. According to Theda Skocpol, these groups "aimed to extend the domestic morality of the nineteenth century's 'separate sphere' for women into the nation's public life."[16] Their activities ranged from settlement houses to temperance laws to suffrage. In the crusade for pure food and drug laws, these new activists flexed their political muscles at the local, state, and national levels. Although many of the women's groups had achieved legislative success at the local and state levels, they increasingly turned their attention to national politics. The research and publicity activities of women's groups, the work of chemists and other scientists, and the muckraking articles of the new mass-market women's magazines convinced millions of ordinary women that only national action could save their families from dangerous and possibly deadly additives and from unsanitary processes in food production that were supposedly the usual business practice of national firms.

In addition to groups organized for purposes of societal or political reform, other groups were formed on the basis of professional, business, or functional interests. What united these somewhat disparate groups was the growing realization that during the early 1900s government and society were being transformed by forces both exogenous and endogenous. The new functional and trade organizations aimed to shape government activity not only out of strategic self-interest but also for defensive reasons. Of course, businesses organizing to extract favorable protection from the government was not a new phenomenon in American politics. Lobbying by the railroads is one example; rivers and harbors legislation was another achievement by pork barrel interests.[17]

What was new in the context of the first New Federalism was the appearance of groups that represented economic interests against the demands of other groups. Groups that emerged during this time included the National Association of Manufacturers (1895) and the Chamber of Commerce (1912). Whether this activity was a "triumph of conservatism" that effectively determined the form and content of Progressive legislation, as Gabriel Kolko has argued, or whether the response to government activity was much less organized, as Robert Wiebe contends, is still debated.[18] What is interesting about this organizational thrust is that government was seen as the playing field upon which business would have to compete, willing or not. In short, "the businessman would rather 'help shape the right kind of regulation' than have 'the wrong kind forced upon him.' "[19] Thus in the case of pure food and drug regulation, business interests largely opposed any kind of regulation, whether at the state or national level. However, as reformers and interest groups successfully pushed pure food and drug laws in several states, some large firms recognized that it was far preferable to meet one national standard than to comply with dozens of conflicting state standards.

Alongside reformers and economic interests were professional groups, which made up another source of group activity. They were constituted around both the creation and defense of new forms of professional identity and status.[20] Indeed, it was during the Progressive Era that the cult of the expert, and the hope of providing expert, technocratic solutions to society's problems, first appeared. The "gospel of efficiency" and the cult of the "efficiency" expert emerged first in business and then spread to other areas, most notably the new field of public administration.[21] The celebration of "scientific research and management" extended to areas not previously thought to need scientific techniques of control.[22] In the field of education, the movement helped shape the reorganization of public schools and led to the establishment of vocational education.[23] Science management played a key role in the shaping of the conservation movement, in the establishing of educational programs for farmers and for mothers, and in the development of "good roads" and the national highway system.[24]

Within the constellation of actors that made up the new organizational society of the first New Federalism, there was considerable debate in determining the means and the extent of national intervention in society and the economy. In some cases, reformers looked to civil society or to the individual to achieve their goals. The means to attain their goals ranged from changes in social organization, for example through settlement houses or a renewed commitment to agrarian life, to changes in individual behavior, for example temperance or Americanization.

In other cases, reformers pressed for political responses to their causes. The tools ranged from legislation, sometimes linked to administrative enforcement mechanisms, for pure milk or an eight-hour day, to the reform of political institutions or processes, such as the direct election of senators and the establishment of a civil service. For these reformers, the complexity of the problems they presumed to address needed the authority and the resources of the national (or state) government in order for responses to be effective. This embrace of political solutions was not by any means characteristic of all reformers. John Buenker argues that some reformers did not automatically seek a government solution because politics was often seen as part of the problem. Their organizations and technocratic solutions were intended to counteract the party and the spoils system.[25]

Despite their avowals of technocratic, nonpartisan ethics, the reformers and experts, and the interest groups with which they were allied, engaged in, a remarkably similar pattern of behavior, regardless of the issue. It involved "organiz[ing] a voluntary association, investigat[ing] a problem, gather[ing] mounds of relevant social data, and analyz[ing] it according to the precepts of one of the newer social sciences. From such an analysis, a proposed solution would emerge, be popularized through campaigns of education and moral suasion, and—as often as not, if it seemed to work,—be taken over by some level of government as a permanent public function."[26]

Business groups, reformers, and experts were organized in similar ways to battle against each other in order to claim the mantle of advancing the public or the national interest. Many of these groups agitated for greater governmental support of their policy objectives. Thus, to create—or in some cases to block—change on a broader level, reformers and the groups that they were a part of developed organizational strategies to overcome or adapt to the federal system. The federal system encouraged the development of a federal polity in which such actors as reformers, interest groups, and bureaucrats could and would use powers at both state and national levels to advance their preferred policies. A variety of local, state, and national strategies were used. When one level—usually the state—failed to meet their goals, another level—usually the national government—would be engaged. Since these interest groups often stood outside of the political party system, by intention as well as by accident of membership, they looked directly to Congress to enact their policy agenda.

The Rise of the Intergovernmental Bureaucracy

Herbert Croly, a leading Progressive thinker, was one of the earliest endorsers of national grants-in-aid.[27] According to Croly, "by the use of the . . . device of grants-in-aid . . . [f]ederal financial assistance will be offered to the states under conditions which tend to level local services up to a desirable national standard." With the use of such grants a corps of "disinterested [national] administrators," who presumably would have the national interests at heart, could influence the policies of the states.

During the first New Federalism, a Croly-like corps of administrators would indeed emerge to bridge the concerns and needs of the reformers and the economic interests, and to strengthen the role of the professional and the expert. Intergovernmental policy gave rise to an intergovernmental bureaucracy. In the three policies traced in the book—national food and drug law, the building of a national highway system, and maternal and child health—networks of bureaucrats at the national, state, and local levels worked together to create the first New Federalism state. However, despite Croly's hopes, the intergovernmental bureaucracy was not a corps of disinterested administrators. They too were interested in achieving their policy and professional goals, which were often intimately intertwined. Not only did many of them passionately believe in the policies they advocated, they saw themselves as the sole source of expertise capable of implementing these policies. These bureaucrats exercised their claim of expertise at both the state and the national levels. In the case of maternal and child health, that expertise was initially based on activities in nongovernmental organizations such as settlement houses and academic institutions, as well as in state and local governments. In the case of pure food and drug regulation and highways, expertise was lodged relatively quickly at the national level within the United States Department of Agriculture (USDA).

TABLE 1.1
Establishment of National Associations of Public Officials

Time Period	Number of Organizations	Examples
Prior to 1900	14	1884: Association of Official Agricultural Chemists 1886: Association of Land Grant Colleges and Universities
1901–1910	13	1902: Conference of State and Territorial Health Officers 1908: Governor's Conference
1911–1920	21	1914: American Association of State Highway Officials 1920: Association of State Foresters
1921–1931	12	1924: American Municipal Association 1931: American Public Welfare Association

Source: Leonard D. White, *Trends in Public Administration* (New York: McGraw-Hill, 1933), 290, 298.

Of the few bureaucratic structures extant in the late nineteenth century, the USDA stands out as one of a handful that would deploy state capacity. The USDA, home of two of the case study policies in this book, is the preeminent example of the emergence of the ethos of the "expert," the creation of new organizational norms, and the studied entrepreneurialism of agency leadership. As a result of these three developments, the USDA emerged as an "island of [national] state capacity" in the premodern American state.[28] Other bureaucrats and their allies would emulate the missionary work of the USDA, with varied degrees of success, creating in turn other islands of state capacity across policy areas, and across national- and state-level governments.

In keeping with the fragmented nature of the American federal polity, the intergovernmental public servants, along with experts and reformers with whom they often overlapped, began to organize themselves. Between 1901 and 1931, over forty-six new associations of public officials would be created (see table 1.1).

They ranged from the Association of Official Agricultural Chemists (1884) to the American Association of State Highway Officials (1914) to the American Public Welfare Association (1931). States and local governments also began to organize themselves. For example, the Governor's Conference was organized in 1908, while the International City Manager Association was created in 1914. Many of these groups were founded on the premise that they were part of a much larger, complex polity that involved both the states and the national government.[29]

The bureaucrats involved in shaping the policies of the first New Federalism engaged in remarkably similar behavior. Like the interest groups they emulated and cooperated with, these new bureaucrats defined new issues. They investigated and publicized these new issues and problems. They engaged in widespread public relations activities in order to broaden public support and to educate politicians about the valuable services the bureaucrats were supplying.

These entrepreneurial activities took place within organizational structures that were remarkably similar. The Bureau of Chemistry, advocating for food and drug rules, the Bureau of Public Roads, overseeing highway policy, and the Children's Bureau, advocating for health care, all developed an organizational ethos that emphasized professionalism and loyalty to the agency's goals. Through the creation of training programs, the establishment of industry or professional standards, and the creation and nurturing of national associations of relevant public officials, these national bureaucrats developed networks of support that would advance their professional and organizational preferences.

Bureaucrats attempting to create and implement policy in a fairly weak central state pursued strategies that would maximize the impact of their limited personnel and fiscal resources. These entrepreneurial bureaucrats labored to knit a new federalist state by allying themselves with national, state, and local interest groups, and by cultivating congressional sponsors and supporters.

Thus, the growth of the new federalist state made sense on the level of the individual policy. The delegation of power proposed by these bureaucrats and their allies would have to satisfy the suspicions of a Congress that was used to patronage-based bureaucracy, and hesitated to expand national power in the face of the perceived constraints of federalism. Overcoming these limitations required an enormous focusing of energy that united local, state, and national interests in a way that could plausibly sidestep the constraints of congressional governance and the federal system. Ironically, on an aggregate level, the efforts of these bureaucrats would lead to the development of what would later be called, critically, "picket-fence federalism."[30] Strong networks across national, state, and local levels emerged in specific policy areas. Only rarely were these lines of professional and administrative expertise deployed in other areas. In the first New Federalism, the roots of modern policy incoherence and fragmentation are readily visible.

The American States: Competition, Innovation, and Stasis

The states reflected the political, economic, and social complexity of the first New Federalism. The American system of what Henry Scheiber calls "rivalristic state mercantilism," or the competition between states for economic and political resources, had as many, if not more, supporters than a new system based on a strong, centralized national state.[31] Supporters of state competition derived important and powerful benefits, such as the protection of local markets or the advantages of weak state regulatory and tax structures.[32] To protect these benefits, supporters had access to a number of government institutions, the most important of these being the courts. Whether viewed as a source of competition and innovation, or as a source of a ruinous "race to the bottom," the existence of American states as distinct political economies would shape the political and organizational strategies of the state builders during the course of the first New Federalism.[33]

Supporters of weak state governments, or of state competition, did not dominate everywhere and at all times. In many states, reformers allied with new interest groups and experts struggled to reshape state and local governments in order to meet the new challenges of urbanization and industrialization. Many of the intergovernmental policies that would be enacted at the national level, such as pure food and drug laws or aid for building highways, were first enacted at the state level. However, other policies, such as workmen's compensation or child labor restrictions, met with mixed success in migrating across states or to the national level. While some states enacted such regulations, others, fearful of the economic impact on existing industries, or engaged in economic competition, resisted or rejected them. For every state like Wisconsin, whose progressive reputation gained its own label ("the Wisconsin idea"), there were numerous states and regions that resisted the expansion or strengthening of state governments.

The uniform state law movement was one response to unevenness in the states' embrace of the reformers' agenda.[34] The goal of the uniform law movement was to spread innovations in policy that advocates believed would generally benefit society, to other states and eventually to the national level, through the near simultaneous adoption of laws by all the states.[35] This approach was favored because it addressed the fears of individual states that they would lose competitive position to other states because of the higher costs of regulations or expenditures on social welfare.

The uniform law movement was also popular because it suited, to some extent, the pragmatic, limited goals of associations of state officials and other national groups of administrators and policy activists. These groups focused on limited goals because they believed that the Supreme Court was unwilling to endorse a greater role for national action, and that the Court would resist action on the part of the national government to impede intrastate commerce. Finally, the spread of policy innovations from one state to the next reflected the reigning ideology of states as "laboratories of democracy."[36]

Nonetheless, as a means of creating a strong, active role for government, the uniform law movement was weakened by its inability to overcome the pressure of interstate competition, the time-consuming and costly mechanics of passing the same law in every state, and varying conceptions about what the proper role of government ought to be. Aggravating these problems of coordination was the issue of administrative capacity. While states were often the providers of public services, their administrative and political capacity to do so was as varied as the number of states.[37] Thus while New York State by 1910 had initiated and oversaw a strong system of state-controlled highway building, other states gave minimal to no oversight and allocated little to no funds to road building.

States and Sectionalism

The political and economic influence of the American states was magnified by the sectionalism in national politics. Sectionalism, the political and economic competition between regions—between North and South, or Midwest and West against the "eastern monied interests"—was a particularly important force in American politics during the Gilded Age and Progressive Era.[38] Because of the geographic basis of congressional representation, the effects of sectionalism were magnified in national legislative institutions.

Sectionalism at times weakened party loyalty within Congress. During the first New Federalism, each party experienced sectionally based insurgencies. For the Democrats, the gains made under Cleveland collapsed with the rise of Populism and "Bryanism" and the party's decisive defeat in the 1896 presidential election. The party would be split until 1910 between urban Democrats (largely from the North) and southern Democrats.[39] Between 1908 and Wilson's election in 1912, the party reorganized and refocused its strategy while at the same time becoming more cohesive. Within the Republican Party, intraparty divisions stemmed from the emergence of the mostly Midwestern Insurgents.[40] By 1907, there was an identifiable faction of Insurgents in both the House and the Senate.[41] Their most visible institutional impact arose from their temporary alliance with the Democrats, which ultimately led to the overthrow of Speaker Joseph Cannon, the end of "czar" rule, and the beginning of the modernization in the House.[42]

Sectionalism thus pushed the limits of the party system and its role as the glue that held the American federal system together. When the parties were unable to contain intraparty or interparty divisions caused by sectionalism, and neither party held a decisive balance of power, policy stalemate was often the result.[43] On the other hand, sectionalism pushed party leaders to look for policies that would accommodate the often divergent preferences of each sectional faction within the party.

The presence of sectionalism and a political economy of core and periphery made the expansion of national power a contested process. From tariff policy to civil rights, through much of the late nineteenth and early twentieth centuries the assertion of national power was seen as a cloak for sectional interests. Within Congress, political stalemate often resulted, as each section attempted to limit the gains any other section might make. Outside of Congress, reformers and interest groups employed a number of tactics to weaken the divisive effects of sectionalism. The good roads movement combined the interests of northern urban cyclists and auto owners, southern progressives, and the country life movement to press for a national road-building program. Advocates for a nationally funded system of vocational education were able to make common cause with supporters of agricultural experiment stations and urban educators.

In other cases, sectionalism was not so easily transcended. Despite the mobilization of reformers, national civic and fraternal groups such as the Masons, and professional associations such as the National Education Association, a decades-long attempt to create national involvement in primary education was repeatedly defeated by a coalition of mostly northern urban ethnic groups and southerners, who feared greater governmental control over public education.[44]

During the first New Federalism, intergovernmental policy offered a way to ease sectional division and stalemate in Congress. Reformers and interest groups could use intergovernmental policy to build bridges across section, across class, and across identities.[45] However, to enact policy, politicians and interest groups had to confront dual federalism's chief supporter: the judiciary.

Judicial Constraints on Government Power

The courts, especially the Supreme Court, provided little consistent guidance to those interested in expanding the scope of government, whether at the state or national level. There was a series of conflicting judicial decisions arising out of the Supreme Court's shifting positions on the power of state governments to regulate. The Supreme Court did not block states from asserting limited regulatory powers.[46] One precedent was set in *Munn v. United States* (1877), in which the Court upheld a state's right to regulate intrastate commerce.

However, in later decisions the Court seemed to limit any state role in economic regulation.[47] An example was *Lochner v. New York*, 198 U.S. 45 (1905), which invalidated New York State law that set maximum hours for bakery workers. In the late nineteenth century, where the regulation of intrastate commerce ended and the regulation of interstate commerce began was unclear. The Court seemed less ambiguous in regards to expansions in the powers of the national government. Court decisions in cases such as *Pollock v. Farmer's Loan & Trust Co.*, 157 U.S. 429 (1895), invalidating the national income tax, and *United States v. E.C. Knight*, 156 U.S. 1 (1895), which ruled that mining or manufacturing, even when the product would move in interstate commerce, was not covered under the commerce clause, seemed to limit any governmental role, especially at the national level, in areas perceived as economic regulation.[48]

Yet this judicial hostility was not absolute, especially in the case of intergovernmental policy. While the Supreme Court did overturn a number of intergovernmental regulations on the ground that they overstepped the limits of national power, the vast majority of intergovernmental regulations went unchallenged.[49] The Court did not actually rule on the constitutionality of grants-in-aid, as such, until 1923 in *Massachusetts v. Mellon* (1923), decades after the first grant-in-aid made its appearance.

The degree to which the courts were hostile to the expansion of governmental power is an important issue for this discussion, given that the perception of that hostility affected the rhetoric and strategies undertaken by the nascent national state builders. Indeed the hold that *Lochner* and a few other decisions on the thinking and strategizing of reformers and interest groups was remarkable. In contemporary work ranging from Charles Beard's *An Economic Interpretation of the Constitution* to Frank Goodnow's *Social Reform and the Constitution*, echoed in more recent scholarship on American political development, the courts were seen as one of the key impediments in the creation of a new state.[50] The perception of the courts' attitudes, whether transmitted by the press, interest groups, or simply constituents, had an effect on congressional policymaking. Legislators would make strategic decisions on the type of legislation that could be enacted and not be overridden by the courts.[51]

The Case for Centralization

Among reformers, there was a growing criticism of the condition and quality of America's state and local governments. According to this critique, advances in communication and transportation had made existing state boundaries (and possibly states) less than satisfactory divisions by which to arrange expert responses to the complex challenges of the modern era.[52] Indeed, it was argued that the weaknesses of states, due to both administrative failings and the pressure of interstate competition, hindered effective local government. These weaknesses, therefore, had the unintended consequence of increasing public impatience and dissatisfaction and thus strengthening the trend towards greater centralization.[53]

For example, Theodore Roosevelt not only spoke about the "New Nationalism" but also the "New Federalism," in which there existed both "a strong central government and strong States, so geared together that there would be no hazy areas or governmental no man's land."[54] Echoing Roosevelt were other influential voices such as Herbert Croly, an advocate of centralization in the name of efficiency.[55] In his classic statement of Progressivism, *The Promise of American Life* (1912), Croly's support for centralization was based on his belief that state governments, no matter how well run, could not adequately or efficiently carry out duties such as the regulation of railroads that were beyond their technical scope.

> The best friends of local government in this country are those who seek to have its activity confined to the limits of possible efficiency, because only in case its activity is so confined can the States continue to remain an essential part of a really efficient and well coordinated national organization.[56]

Though at times Croly seemed to be calling for a strong national state, he like many of his contemporaries maintained a healthy respect for the role and power of the states: "Progressive Democracy will need and will value the state governments; but they will be needed and valued . . . as parts of an essentially national system."[57] Indeed Croly argued that the "nationalization of American democracy does not mean the abandonment of the federal principle, and the substitution for it of a lifeless centralization. Nationalization is not equivalent to centralization. It has frequently required administrative and legislative decentralization."[58]

Other members of the elite, such as Woodrow Wilson, were not eager to give in to what political scientist John Burgess called "creeping centralization."[59] Throughout his career and especially during his "New Freedom" program, Wilson attempted to straddle the crosscutting pressures of greater nationalization and greater protection of state independence.[60] Despite these political adaptations, his background, both personally and philosophically, was reflected in his commitment to states' rights. Wilson argued that "it would be fatal to our political vitality . . . to strip the States of their powers and transfer them to the Federal government."[61] Wilson, despite his Progressive rhetoric, was initially cool to the various interest groups "seeking to use federal authority to accomplish economic goals or social purposes."[62] Ironically, Wilson would preside over a surge in enactment of intergovernmental policy during the first New Federalism.

There seemed to be a slowly growing consensus that while discerning the national interest was possible, ensuring direct national action was difficult. Most southern politicians remained suspicious of any attempt to increase national power, fearing that it would interfere with the recently solidified racial state. In fact, the southern response to Roosevelt's New Nationalism speech summed up the anticentralization attitude: southerners deplored Roosevelt's agenda as an "exaltation of Federal centralization power . . . the destruction of home rule [and] an advance toward socialism."[63] The opposition of southerners was not always consistent. While southerners would vociferously oppose the enactment of the Pure Food and Drug Act in 1906, which they saw as an attack on the region's economic interests and cultural mores, southerners would also enthusiastically support the enactment of the Federal Highway Act and the economic development that came with it.

Constitutional Influences on Congress

The case for centralization and the transformation of Congress would also be supported by two important constitutional changes: the national income tax (Sixteenth Amendment) and the direct election of senators (Seventeenth Amendment). Reformers, interest groups, and politicians approached the income tax and direct election from an astonishing variety of viewpoints. For some, both signified a victory for the people over the "interests." For others, these two policies epitomized Madison's warnings about the "mischiefs of faction." No good would or could come from allowing any government an automatic source of revenue, or by allowing all of the national government's political institutions to be controlled by popular passions.

The introduction of a national income tax was an important institutional and state-building change for the national state.[64] With its own independent and nondiminishing source of revenue, the national government was now relatively independent of state-level interests. That is the national government no longer relied on awkward and inflexible sources of, revenue such as land sales and the tariff, each with its own attendant politics.

A centrally administered tax that was national in scope gave national legislators an independent source of revenue from which to advance their preferences and that of their constituents. Enabling the growth of a larger centralized state, the income tax can be seen as the "entering wedge" for a much stronger and centralized national state.[65] Ultimately, the permanent income tax shifted the incentives for Congress. A secure and permanent revenue source provided to members of Congress and their constituents the ability to shield their own particularistic interests under the cloak of the national interest.[66]

The movement for the direct election of senators echoed many of the other political and moral crusades of the era of the first New Federalism.[67] Direct election was a goal of the Populists and the Progressives. The Progressives in particular believed that the direct election of senators and other electoral reforms would make politicians and the political system more accountable to the people and thus more democratic. Muckraking journalists such as George Haynes, in articles and later in his book *The Election of Senators* (1906), blasted the Senate as a bastion of corruption and anti-democratic privilege. In addition, other claims were made about the negative effects of indirect elections. For example, the distraction of Senate elections were widely seen as blocking state legislatures from spending more time and energy on the problems of their respective states.[68] According to reformers, at the national level the direct election of senators would "free the institution from the control of political machines and the trusts."[69]

Like the other crusades, the push for reform first came from the states. Prior to 1905, state activity on behalf of direct elections was largely limited to the submission of state petitions to Congress, calls for a constitutional convention of states, or resolutions requesting Congress call a constitutional convention to consider direct election. With the publication of exposés such as Haynes's the political tenor and tactics of reformers shifted. South Carolina had started a formal process of reform in 1888 with the introduction of the direct primary that officially nominated candidates for senator. Other states, especially after 1905, would also embrace the direct primary. This technique spread through the Populist South and the Progressive Midwest and West. In 1909 Oregon took the process of direct primary a step further, amending its state constitution to require that the legislature elect "the people's choice."[70] By the time the Senate assented to the passage of a bill allowing for a constitutional amendment, thirty-seven states had indicated their support for direct election of senators, either through petitions or through the establishment of direct primaries. Indeed, a majority of the forty-eight states had enacted some form of direct primary by 1915.[71]

The immediate practical effect of direct election on the Senate was negligible, as none of the senators up for reelection following the ratification of the Seventeenth Amendment was defeated. There were, however, important long-term effects of this constitutional change. For example, the amendment produced a shift in the Senate that overwhelmingly favored the Democratic Party during the 1920s and 1930s. Indeed, by delinking senators from state legislatures, the Democratic Party was able to protect some its gains at the Senate level during the hostile Republican twenties.[72] This would prove vitally important in the struggle to enact and later save the Sheppard-Towner maternal and child health program, one of the case study policies in this book.

This constitutional change also had a number of long-term effects on the American federal system and on congressional representation. One effect was the gradual lessening of the importance of states. In retrospect, part of this decline can be attributed to the focus on the national government in the post–New Deal era. Part of the decline, however, also came from what some have argued was the political stagnation of the governor's office.[73] Senators no longer automatically came from the governor's house and were not necessarily the leaders of a strong state party organization.[74] As a result, state party politics became less important in national politics. In sum, senators more often were electoral outsiders and products of direct appeals to the electorate rather than products of the state political system. Researchers have speculated that, as a long-term effect of this constitutional change, the Senate, traditionally a bastion of states' rights, gradually became more supportive of an even stronger national government, eventually surpassing the House.[75]

In short, although neither of these constitutional amendments had an immediate, direct, and measurable effect on the preferences and actions of political actors, the fact that the amendments were proposed and ratified during the first New Federalism shows the impact of its ideas, interests, and institutions on the constitutional basis of the American federal system. The political incentives to create and expand the first New Federalism were shaped by and for members of Congress.

The Transformation of Congress

The sharply divergent positions of southerners over the enactment of the pure food laws and highway policy underscored the fragile basis upon which a new American state would be constructed. These sectional, partisan, and ideological divisions would be played out within Congress. In the late nineteenth and early twentieth centuries, Con-

gress was far from a static institution; it was undergoing significant
structural change. This structural change—modernization—was not
necessarily purposive. That is, it did not occur because members of
Congress decided to "modernize." Rather, as Eric Schickler argues,
members of Congress "adopt changes based on untidy compromises
among multiple interests, members build institutions that are full of
tensions and contradictions."[76] One result of this modernization was a
change in the calculus of political incentives for members of Congress.
The political incentives that increasingly motivated members were intertwined quests for reelection, for power, and for the ability to enact
policy.[77] Having achieved these goals, Congress was able to overcome
its status as the "weakened spring of government," that is, a body unwilling and, in many instances, unable to enact policy that asserted
national power.

The modernization of Congress during this period can be seen in a
number of pratices, among them specific rules changes, such as the
imposition (and later repeal) of the Reed rules in the early 1890s;
broader changes in congressional leadership, especially the decline of
the strong Speaker; and the rise of the committee system and the alleged growth in policy expertise.[78] The rise in incumbency, a decline in
the practice of rotation in office, the growth in constituent service, and
the emergence of legislators primarily motivated by reelection can all
be seen as measures of legislative professionalization. How this legislative professionalization affected the policy process is discussed in the
following section.

The Political Incentives of Intergovernmental Policy

Congressional modernization—the growing capacity of the institution
itself, as well as the change in legislator behavior—had a long-term
impact on policymaking and administration. First, there was a growing willingness to enact legislation that expanded national power and
offered opportunities to derive electoral benefits. Second, there was a
rise in congressional capacity to oversee bureaucratic agents in the implementation of new policy. The growing willingness of Congress to
assert national power derived from a new calculus of political incentives as the partisan struggles of late-nineteenth-century politics and
the constraints of the federal system intersected with long-term
changes in congressional structure and practice.

One outward manifestation of this was the 51st Congress (1889–91),
the so-called "billion dollar Congress." For the first time in six years,
both chambers were under the control of the same party and the presi-

dency. The Republicans who had achieved this feat began the 51st Congress with an ambitious attempt not only to protect and expand the politically popular tariff, but also to spend down the budget surplus produced by the tariff with a generous and expansive pension system for Civil War veterans and their dependents, and new spending on internal improvements such as rivers and harbors and public buildings.

Legislators responded to these goals enthusiastically. The number of bills introduced, private and public, skyrocketed from approximately 16,000 in the 50th to over 19,000 during the 51st Congress. Nearly 2,200 were passed, compared to only 1,800 in the previous Congress.[79] Although the "billion dollar Congress" was partially the creature of the Republican leadership's party-building efforts, individual legislators enthusiastically grasped for an opportunity to meet the needs of specific constituents.

Yet despite these numbers and the criticisms, this was not a legislative free-for-all. All of these partisan goals were accomplished under the firm control of House Speaker Thomas Reed, whose "Reed rules" cemented Republic control over the House. Attempts by the Democrats to influence legislation were decisively shut down by the new rules imposed by the Speaker.[80] The Reed rules highlighted an important but slow transformation of Congress into an organization that

> tends to use universalistic rather than particularistic criteria, and automatic rather than discretionary methods for conducting its internal business. Precedents and rules are followed; merit systems replace favoritism and nepotism; and impersonal codes supplant personal preferences as prescriptions for behavior.[81]

There were other changes in Congress that signified an institution increasingly relatively "well bounded" . . . [and] "complex." One change was the slow rise in congressional incumbency. At the beginning of the first New Federalism in 1877, the average tenure of representatives was only 1.1 terms, and nearly 47% of all members were in their first term. One of the reasons for this abbreviated tenure was the role of state politics. As Samuel Kernell has suggested, many state parties practiced a tradition in which political offices were rotated in order to resolve intraparty conflict.[82] This practice meant that with the exception of those legislators who dominated committees such as Ways and Means, the institutional capacity of Congress, in terms of legislative memory and expertise, was quite limited. It was not until the 57th Congress (1901–3) that returning members comprised two-thirds of the House and the average tenure had nearly doubled, to 2.1 terms in office.[83]

A second change in Congress was the slight increase in legislative staff during this era. In 1891, there was an average of two staff members for every committee (House and Senate), and by 1914, the average Senate or House committee had five staff members. From 1899 to 1909, the number of legislative staff increased by nearly 25%.[84] Again, this increase in staff was not always purposive. Some members of Congress simply wanted more persons on staff because other members had them.[85] Nevertheless, the reason for this growth was primarily the need to handle legislators' constituent business, and second to handle the increasing workload of committees.[86]

The "billion dollar Congress" not only satisfied constituents and party leaders, it also stimulated a new type of congressman, one who could envision a greater scope for national (as well as personal) ambitions. Though these incipient plans would come crashing down in the next midterm elections when Democrats recaptured the House, the 51st Congress planted the notion of the national government as the means to secure a more certain electoral future for both the party and the incumbent.

In the political context of the late nineteenth century, sectional and regional coalitions and partisan forces were critical in shaping legislative action, placing issues on the agenda and generating policy alternatives.[87] The nature of congressional representation encouraged Congress to embrace certain kinds of policy instruments that allowed for outcomes to be aligned with local preferences. That is, as members of Congress were increasingly motivated by reelection, their policymaking focus turned towards legislation that would satisfy not only the needs of the party, but also the preferences of constituents.

While pressure for distributive benefits and good policy has always driven members of Congress, the rise in professionalism, as marked by increased levels of incumbency, higher levels of legislative expenditures, and growth of staff, led members to search for new ways to serve their constituents and, by extension, improve their own prospects for election. Intergovernmental policy allowed the targeting of government goods and services to local constituents, at the same time allowing local control over the impact of the goods and services on the local political economy.[88] Intergovernmental policy allowed Congress to respond to geographic and political interests at the beginning (policy enactment) and at the end (policy implementation) of the legislative-executive process. This in turn helped to strengthen legislator and party relationships with constituents (whether individual or groups).

In the face of the strong inter- and intraparty divisions that characterized late-nineteenth- and early-twentieth-century American politics, intergovernmental policy offered members of Congress a way to put together enacting coalitions to pass legislation, contest national electoral coalitions, and to bypass the roadblocks to legislation in a separation-of-powers system. For party leadership, good policy was that which overcame intraparty divisions, whether based on region or preferences for policy, and allowed the majority party to retain its status. In many respects intergovernmental policy was optimal because it allowed significant payoffs, in terms of local control or the influence of interest groups over policy, to reluctant coalition members, while cementing the electoral support needed to help retain majority status.

There were also broader incentives for Congress to enact intergovernmental policy. As part of a separation-of-powers system, Congress has to make strategic accommodations with other branches. Intergovernmental policy allowed sharing of political benefits with the executive. On the other hand, intergovernmental policy could be structured to give Congress rather than the executive the upper hand in shaping outcomes. Who would have power, and the nature of that power, was an important question for both Congress and the executive, since divided government occurred in approximately half of the Congresses during the first New Federalism.

Two important characteristics of intergovernmental policy, quasi-voluntarist provisions and carefully worded exemptions carving out areas of state control, allowed Congress to come to terms with the problem of courts and states. These characteristics, which will be explored in greater depth in the following chapter, allowed Congress to skirt judicial limits on national power. Intergovernmental policy neither forced the states to undertake an action nor impinged upon the intrastate domain of police powers. Quasi-voluntarism and intrastate exemptions allowed states to escape from a race to the bottom in the (non)provision of regulations or social policies. At the same time, the provision of a national floor did not penalize a state interested in maintaining itself as a laboratory of democracy.

The conjunction of Congress's own institutional evolution with broader statebuilding attempts produced a unique policy and administrative response, the first New Federalism and, in particular, intergovernmental policy instruments. These instruments wed national interests to local preferences. They offered a way for individual representatives to satisfy local policy preferences while responding to national forces; and they allowed for the assertion of national power within ideological and judicial contexts that favored either state and local control over policy outcomes or, in some cases, the absence of government itself. The next chapter traces these intergovernmental policies, in depth, across time and across policy areas.

Chapter Two _____

Intergovernmental Policy Instruments and the Development of the New Federalist State

> The American subsidy system has come into
> being so unobtrusively, and has assumed its
> present vast proportions so recently, that it has
> scarcely attracted the attention of practical
> statesmen and students of political science.
> Many there are who do not realize that the
> scattered grants of the federal government to
> the states have been welded into a fairly
> definite system, and that they are serving as the
> basis of a constructive program of national
> supervision over state activities.
>   Austin McDonald, 1923

THE CONGRESSIONAL legislators who enacted the first New Federalism faced a difficult problem. How could they balance the assertion of national power against the ideological, juridical, and institutional hurdles that maintained the power of the states? The key to this balancing act would be intergovernmental policy, the "vast subsidy system" identified by Austin McDonald in 1923.[1] From 1877 to 1929, intergovernmental policy would provide the means to satisfy the statebuilding goals of reformers and interest groups, while at the same time acknowledging and adapting to the ideological and constitutional constraints of the American federal structure. For some, intergovernmental policy was a necessary first step that allowed them to escape the constraints of state competition or the limitations of state administrative capacity. For others, intergovernmental policy was a necessary compromise that reflected not only their policy goals, but also the partisan and institutional environment under which a particular policy was considered.

Even more importantly, intergovernmental policy fit the structure of nineteenth-century congressional governance. The content of intergovernmental policy—the choice of administrative structures and procedures—was the fulcrum on which centralization and dualism rested. Legislators paid close attention to the statutory language of acts because they embodied a critical partisan and institutionally fueled trade-off between a new centralization and a continued dualism. How intergovernmental policy was structured reflected which interests won and which lost. Choices over the administrative structure of intergovernmental policy reflected the institutional and partisan constraints of Congress.

From 1877 to 1929, the legislative enactment of IPIs became increasingly intertwined with decisions about administrative structure and procedures. These administrative structures and procedures, encoded within the statutory language of intergovernmental policy, became the basis for a differently structured relationship between the national government and states. The episodic interrelationship between them that had existed before 1877 was gradually replaced by a continuous system of interaction involving the national government, the states, national and state bureaucracies, and national and state interest groups. While this altered relationship was at times merely symbolic, eventually it led to a precise, carefully constructed substantive relationship between the national government and the states.

This chapter will trace how intergovernmental policy became the instrument of American state development. I first discuss the administrative structures and procedures that were developed as part of the policy instruments of the first New Federalism. To demonstrate that these instruments were the basis for the development of stronger and more extensive bureaucratic organizations at both the national and the state levels, I show how these administrative structures were deployed across a wide policy spectrum ranging from agriculture to social welfare policy. Although the national government operated unevenly across these policy areas, this brief overview demonstrates an involvement in policy activities more widespread than portrayed in most accounts of nineteenth-century governance. This again leads toward a rethinking of how the modern federal state came into being.

The Volunteer State and the New Federalism

The voluntary participation of the states made the new administrative structures and procedures work, and gave the national government the ability to slowly increase its administrative capacity during the era of the first New Federalism. In most instances of intergovernmental policy, states were not compelled to accept national monies in exchange for creating these centrally directed programs, or for implementing a nationally conceived regulatory regime. States could choose whether to accept grant monies and the administrative strictures that accompanied them.[2] Indeed, while many states were quick to accept, many others were not so enthusiastic, fearing a loss of control over a particular policy area.[3] In the case of intergovernmental regulations, the national government almost always carved out an exception for continued intrastate regulation. This element of choice enabled, at times, a collaborative (or cooperative) relationship rather than an adversarial (or strict hierarchical) relationship to become the basis of policy implementation. Just as good fences make good neighbors, the administrative structures and procedures contained within IPIs enabled the development of a fellowship of common interests, in which roles and expectations were clearly specified.

These new administrative structures and procedures had other benefits as well. The usually narrow scope of IPIs made them attractive to legislators. The narrowness of IPIs could be used to create enacting coalitions, since these instruments could be (1) tailored to emphasize certain policy goals; (2) simply monitored by Congress and interest groups because of their small size and discreteness; and (3) easily evaluated by legislators with respect to the distributive benefits expected based on a grant's proposed formula or matching requirements, or a regulation's enforcement patterns.

Despite these benefits, IPIs carried some risks. For example, since grants come "as of right" (if states apply) and on a predictable basis, in the long run states have less incentive to be responsive to national administrators or even members of Congress.[4] For members of Congress, some techniques of oversight and control are risky since the ability to sanction an individual state is low given the federalist-influenced representation in Congress. However, as will be discussed later, other types of administrative procedures and structures can mitigate such problems.

There were other benefits that came from the volunteerist aspect of IPIs. The quasi-voluntary nature of intergovernmental policy enabled national legislators to sidestep judicial objections to expansion of national power into areas traditionally dominated by the states. Legislators achieved mixed success with IPIs and in particular intergovernmental regulations, since regulations often raised a red flag to a Supreme Court on the lookout for any untoward (in its eyes) assertion of national power. However, cases such as *Hammer v. Dagenheart* (1918), overturning the Interstate Child Labor Act, signaled the Court's willingness to stand fast against any unilateral assertion of national power.

Nonetheless, if legislators did not want to directly challenge the Court by asserting Congress's power under the commerce clause, legislators could attempt an end run around the judiciary either through statutory language that denied the national government any control over intrastate commerce or through inducements such as national monies in exchange for the setting of state laws that matched or exceeded national standards. An example of this latter strategy was the Endangered Species Act of 1900 (the Lacey Act), which created a quasi-voluntary law covering endangered species in interstate commerce; states were eligible for national monies if they enacted laws and administrative plans consistent with those of the national government.

Legislators could also choose administrative procedures that would allow other legislators and relevant interests to have a formal say in how regulations were written, interpreted, or enforced. For example, in the case of the Pure Food and Drug Act of 1906, regulation-setting power was fragmented between three agencies in order to reduce the power of the pro-farmer USDA. At the same time, the regulatory powers of the states were limited out of concerns that states would develop standards impossible or very expensive for manufacturers to meet.[5]

Thus, the national oversight and control of state activities was in many ways contingent: upon states first agreeing to participate, upon states fulfilling their obligations, and upon the national government being able to sufficiently monitor and correct the performance of the states. The national government lacked, both then and now, the ability to directly coerce the states; thus the national government had to devise alternate means to ensure that its goals were achieved.

The Enactment of IPIs over Time and Across Policy Areas

The intergovernmental policy of the first New Federalism primarily involved two types of instruments: grants-in-aid (McDonald's subsidy system) and intergovernmental regulations. A third alternative, although rarely chosen, was the use of taxation to regulate an activity.[6] Neither grants nor intergovernmental regulations were completely unknown before this time. The Northwest Ordinance (1787), one of Congress's first pieces of legislation, was a grant program in which national lands were given to the states to sell. The proceeds of these land sales were to encourage the building of public schools. Indeed until the 1870s, land grants (and the proceeds from their sales) were *the* dominant intergovernmental policy used by the national government, although other intergovernmental regulations, as well as other types of national and state interactions, were also enacted.[7] The legislative scope and the policy impact of these early national-level interventions tended to be limited.[8]

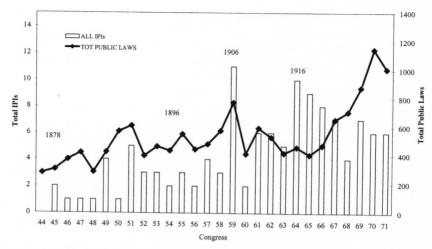

Figure 2.1. Enactment of IPIs, 44th to 71st Congresses (1875–1931) *Source*: U.S. Bureau of the Census, *Historical Statistics of the United States, Colonial Times to 1970*, Series Y 189–98: Congressional Bills, Acts, and Resolutions: 1789–1970.

During the era of the first New Federalism, 131 intergovernmental policy instruments were enacted (see appendix 1). These policies ranged from noteworthy pieces of legislation such as the Uniform Bankruptcy Act of 1898 and the Insecticide Act of 1910, to much smaller pieces of legislation such as an 1879 grant to aid states in the printing of books for the blind, or the Standard Barrel Act of 1912, defining standards for the interstate shipping of apples.

Approximately 4.5 IPIs were enacted per Congress. From the 44th to the 54th Congresses (1877–95), a period of heated partisan competition, Congress enacted an average of 2.1 IPIs (see figure 2.1). From the post-1896 realignment period to 1918 (55th to 65th Congresses), the mean number jumped to 5.5 IPIs per Congress. During the 1920s—the Republican Party's promised era of normalcy—the mean number of IPIs increased to 6.3 enacted per Congress. Compared to the trend line of bills enacted during the same period, the legislation of the first New Federalism seems to follow its own pattern of enactment.

There was also variation by policy areas in the enactment of IPIs. Using a classification scheme developed by Theodore Lowi, I divided IPIs into three broad categories: regulatory, distributive, and redistributive policies. Regulatory policy made up nearly half of the IPIs enacted (49%). The Pure Food and Drug Act of 1906, one of the case study policies, was a classic case of regulatory policy in that it affected only a few sectors, and implementation was made "by application of a general rule . . . [and] within the broader standards of law."[9] Other intergovernmental regulatory policies enacted during the first New Federalism included the Wilson Act of 1890, which confirmed the right of states to regulate liquor, and the Quarantine Act of 1906, which replaced individual state laws with a uniform system of regulations.

The next largest category was distributive policy, which made up 36% of all IPIs. The Federal Highway Act, the second of the case study policies, was undoubtedly of this type; distributive policies are characterized, as Theodore Lowi defines them, "by the ease with which they can be disaggregated and dispensed unit by small unit." In the case of highway and other intergovernmental policies, that unit of allocation is the state. Other examples of distributive policy included the Hatch Act of 1887, which established agricultural experiment stations, and the Dick Act of 1903, which created the modern National Guard.

Finally, the smallest category was redistributive policy, which comprised 15% of IPIs. Redistributive policy is similar to regulatory policy in that it involves "relations among broad categories of private individuals"; however, "The categories of impact are much broader, approaching social classes."[10] Redistributive policy includes the third case study policy, the Sheppard-Towner Act of 1921, which provided maternal and child health services. Under the act, local administrators—not the national-level bureaucracy—were instrumental in determining, first, whether citizens would gain access to a program and, second, which citizens to grant access to services. Other redistributive policies included the previously mentioned printed material for the blind in 1879 and the Vocational Rehabilitation Act of 1920.

Breaking down this policy categorization by eras of party dominance highlights some interesting variations over time (see figure 2.2). While regulatory policies dominated all the party eras, it is under the Republican-dominated years of 1921 to 1931 that regulatory policy drops to its lowest, only 40% of all IPIs enacted.

By contrast, while redistributive policy comprised about 2% of all IPIs enacted during the Republican years of 1897 to 1912, it increased to about 13% of all IPIs during the Republican-dominated 1920s. Distributive policy also increased markedly over time, from 14% during the Gilded Age to 47% during the 1920s. This brief comparison of party and policy suggests that the enactment of IPIs was linked not just to party politics, but to a particular kind of party politics, with Democrats favoring a larger national state and Republicans a smaller one. Finally, we see a gradual shift away from regulatory IPIs to distributive and redistributive policy.

Although this tripartite division gives a rough sense of the areas in which the national government was involved over time, it masks the

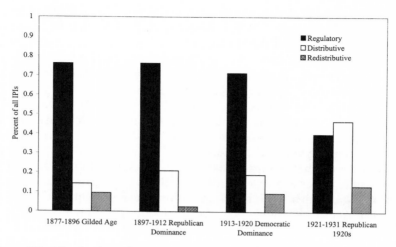

Figure 2.2. Distribution of IPIs by Policy Areas and Partisan Era

startling range of specific areas in which Congress would enact legislation during the era of the first New Federalism. To gain a better sense of this variation, intergovernmental policies were subdivided into the following six areas: agriculture, commerce, conservation, military, social welfare, and transportation.[11]

The largest policy area was commerce, which made up 35% of the IPIs enacted (see figure 2.3). This area was somewhat broad, primarily encompassing regulations that affected some aspect of general commercial life, such as the Interstate Commerce Act or the Interstate Commerce Act Amendments of 1906, both of which deal explicitly with the states. Also included are regulations covering the setting of national standards for banks, weights and measures, machinery, and working conditions.

Social welfare comprised 23% of all IPIs. The majority of legislation enacted in this area was for grants providing monies for education. Education covered programs ranging from printed materials for the blind to funds for state maritime schools. Three of the social welfare grant programs enacted from 1877 to 1931 dealt with veterans: nationally subsidized, state-operated homes for veterans; and for soldiers returning from World War I, a venereal health program and a vocational rehabilitation program.[12]

Agricultural legislation such as the Hatch Act, establishing agricultural experiment stations, and a number of regulatory programs such as the Cattle Contagious Diseases Act of 1905, involved 20% of the first New Federalism. Conservation was another significant area, compris-

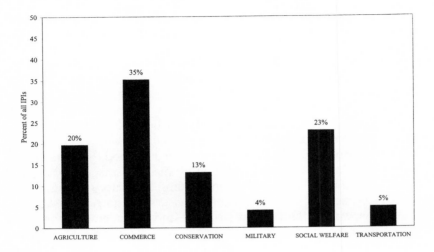

Figure 2.3. Distribution of IPIs across Policy Subareas

ing 11% of the instruments enacted during this period. Covered in this area were such issues as safety regulations for silver mines; legislation included a number of acts that protected fish and wildlife such as the Lacey (Endangered Species) Act of 1900 and the Migratory Bird Treaty Act of 1913. Rounding out the list are the policy areas of transportation (7%) and the military (4%). Transportation policy includes, of course, the Federal Highway Act of 1916 and smaller acts such as the establishment of the Waterways Commission in 1917.

A New Politics of Administrative Structure

The intergovernmental policy instruments of the first New Federalism were unique not only because they signified an often new national involvement in an area, but also because they involved joint action between states and the national government based on a clear narrowing of the "policy-making discretion enjoyed by the states."[13] Rather than simply giving the money away (or the cash value in land) and hoping for the best, the national government—specifically Congress—oversaw the spending of the money and the quality of the activity undertaken.

In order to grasp the importance of IPIs, we need a definition of administrative procedures and structures. The literature on the economics of organization has technical definitions of administrative structure and procedures; however, I will rely on a somewhat broader approach.

Generally speaking, administrative procedures, are "the structural and management arrangements used by Congress to structure its relationships with its agents."[14]

Structural arrangements are constraints built into legislation at the time of enactment, such as (1) the *scope* or purpose of the act; (2) the *instruments* or legal tools available to implement the act; and, (3) the *procedures* or rules by which the instruments will be used.[15]

Management arrangements, which may be built into legislation at time of enactment, include (1) *rewards* and *sanctions* such as appropriations and appointments; (2) *direct monitoring* methods such as legislative oversight; (3) *third-party monitoring* mechanisms such as public hearings or public comment on impending regulatory changes; and, (4) the selection of some aspects of *agency design* and *personnel*.

Another way to think about structure and management is in terms of *ex ante* and *ex post* controls. *Ex ante* constraints impose a "particular sequence on agency decision making . . . creat[ing] an 'early warning' system that alerts politicians (and their constituents) that an agency may attempt to change course . . . [and allows] politicians to adjust the set of pressures from the environment the agency faces, and in doing so, to stack the deck in favor of certain constituents."[16] Ongoing, or *ex post*, controls can include direct monitoring by congressional committee via public hearings and investigations.[17] Other oversight methods include the appointment process, by which legislators can ensure that at least the top level of the bureaucracy is sensitive to the policy preferences of the committee or of Congress as a whole.[18] Finally, Congress can use the appropriations process to reward or punish agencies. The use of this technique is problematic. As V. O. Key notes, a funding sanction is akin to "a shotgun behind the door. . . . [L]ike the shotgun, it possesses a mighty recoil: it is more potent when it remains only a threat; its actual use disrupts work."[19] By withholding funds Congress certainly can punish an agency, but in actual practice withholding funds ultimately harms legislators' own constituents.

Because grants and intergovernmental regulations made up the bulk of IPIs, the following sections focus on defining these instruments and the administrative procedures that were typically associated with each type of instrument.[20]

Grants-in-Aid

Modern grants-in-aid had their historical precedent in the Morrill Land Act (1862), which created land-grant colleges. Modern grants are defined as monies provided to a state government by the national government to support a nationally defined program that will be administered either wholly or partially by a state government or its administrative agents.[21] The relationship between the national government and states is structured by an ongoing and agreed-upon set of administrative structures and procedures. Thus the Hatch Act (1887), which created agricultural stations based in these land-grant colleges, marks the beginning of the modern grant period. For the first time, Congress gave money instead of land to the states *and* inserted a provision that required federal administrative approval of plans for state work.[22] With its relatively detailed (for its time) administrative structures and procedures, the Hatch Act would become the administrative foundation for later grants.

Grants comprised about 30% of all the federalist policies enacted from 1877 to 1929. Significant grants policies included the Hatch Experiment Station Act (1887) and the National Highway Act of 1916. Total spending on intergovernmental grants rose from $7 million in 1902 to $12 million in 1912, and to $123 million in 1927.[23]

Like the Hatch Act, early grants-in-aid tended to be distributed on the basis of population, although most programs distributed a minimum lump sum regardless of the amount determined by formula. By distributing funds based on formulas, legislators limited the discretion exercised by national bureaucrats; they could also create an enactment coalition by specifying the geographically targeted benefits ahead of time. Indeed, most grants-in-aid enacted during the first New Federalism exhibited a high degree of universalism in congressional support.[24] Many of the grants required full (100%) matching on the part of the states. This requirement gave states critical leverage, since they were putting up half of the cost of the program. A high matching ratio encouraged national administrators to see their role as technical advisors or facilitators, not implementers.[25]

In addition, some grants, such as those for highways, agricultural stations, vocational education, and maternal and child health, required the establishment of a state agency or some similar administrative arrangement. By the time the Federal Highway Act was passed in 1916, administrative requirements had become complex enough to include "advance examination of projects, detailed progress reports, audits of expenditures, careful examination of the finished work to ensure that plans had been followed and that there was proper maintenance."[26]

Intergovernmental Regulations

Emerging alongside grants were intergovernmental regulations, a specific subset of regulations in general.[27] An intergovernmental regulation is defined as (1) a national law that prohibits state governments from exercising particular powers (i.e., direct order or total preemption) or, (2) the national replacement of a state or local law or regulation with a minimum national standard for a function or service (i.e., partial preemption).[28] An example of the first type of intergovernmental regulation is the Interstate Commerce Act (1887), which asserted national control over interstate carriers, in essence precluding state regulation of them. During the era of the first New Federalism this type of regulation usually involved the prohibition of state or local regulation of an economic activity (de)regulated by Congress. In these cases, the national government assumed almost complete regulatory authority.[29] The basis for congressional assertion of power traditionally rested upon three areas: the commerce clause, the spending clause, and the "necessary and proper clause."[30] In most cases, however, Congress's assertion of power was tempered by a provision in the statutory language that denied the national government any control over intrastate commerce, or by offering inducements such as national monies in exchange for the setting of state laws that matched or exceeded national standards.

The number of intergovernmental regulations enacted from 1877 to 1929 grew from nineteen between 1877 and 1900, to twenty-two between 1901 and 1912, to forty-one between 1913 and 1929. Intergovernmental regulations ranged in impact from the Animal Industry Act of 1884 to the Federal Water Power Act of 1920.

Under the Animal Industry Act, state authorities were invited to cooperate in execution and enforcement of regulations. The secretary of agriculture was authorized to expend funds in states where USDA regulations were adopted. The Federal Water Power Act gave the national government control over waterways, while states retained control over a portion of the revenue, as well as the right to regulate (but not issue licenses for) power generators. More limited intergovernmental regulations included the Wilson Act of 1890 and the Standard Barrel Act of 1912. Other intergovernmental policy instruments were also enacted as part of this new system. The Oleomargarine Act of 1886 and the Esch Act of 1912 used the national taxing power to regulate margarine and phosphorous matches, respectively.

IPIs: Structures and Procedures

The new system of administrative structures and procedures developed to govern the relationship between the national government (and its agents) and the states (and their agents) during the first New Federalism was relatively straightforward (see table 2.1).

Some of the most common new methods of control for regulations were limitations of national preemption, such that it applied to interstate commerce alone. Approximately 52% of the regulatory IPIs included this limitation. Total national preemption of state regulations or standards was included in 26% of regulatory IPIs, while 25% allowed states to enforce national standards, and 19% allowed states to set standards themselves.

For grants, the most common methods of control required state legislative assent (37% of all grants). In 32% of grants the national level was allowed to withhold funds. A national oversight or advisory board was a requirement in 32% of all grants, while state plans were required in 29% of grants. Of all of the grants, three-fifths (61%) did not require matching funds from the states. These types of grants allow more national control than grants with high matching ratios.[31]

The majority of the administrative procedures and structures were binding only on state officials or agencies. However, a number of controls applied solely to national bureaucrats. Some required agencies to send reports back to a relevant congressional committee, or to hold hearings prior to rule promulgation, or to obtain the assent of a state governor or legislature prior to taking action. In the case of pure food and drug regulation, producers were able to use hearings to block or delay proposed rules, and to limit the effectiveness of the early Food and Drug Administration. In the case of the Sheppard-Towner program, the required assent of a state governor or legislature meant that a number of states either delayed participation or did not participate in the program, thus blocking the wishes of state-level interest groups.

Food, Highways, and Babies: A Sketch of Administrative Structures and Procedures

To this point, the discussion of administrative structures and procedures, and of discretionary power has been fairly abstract. To give a broader context and more meaningful detail, I turn to a brief examination of the three case study policies: the Pure Food and Drug Act of 1906, the Federal Highway Act of 1916, and the Sheppard-Towner Act of 1921.

The *Pure Food and Drug Act of 1906* gave the national government the right to prohibit the "manufacture, sale, or transportation of adulterated, or misbranded or poisonous or deleterious foods, drugs, medicines, and liquors." The development of uniform regulations was to take place through the cooperation of the secretaries of the Treasury, Commerce and Labor, and Agriculture. The actual administration of

TABLE 2.1
Administrative Structures and Procedures in IPIs

Regulations	Percentage Including Provision	Grants	Percentage Including Provision
Preemption for interstate commerce alone	52%	State legislative assent needed	37%
Total preemption/set uniform standard	26%	National can withhold funds	32%
State enforcement	25%	National board required	32%
States set standards	19%	State plan required	29%
National can act in absence	5%	State appeals	24%
Impose tax on states	4%	Agency requirement	21%
Allow identical state laws	4%	State governor defined role	21%
National required to hold hearing	4%	Other national requirements	21%
Grant attached	4%	National certifies state delivery	18%
Allow more stringent state	2%	Minimum lump sum	18%
National can withdraw certification/ funding	2%	Maximum amount	11%
Require state plan/certification	2%	State-determined delivery level	16%
Require state agency	2%	Maintenance of effort	1%
Exempt from state tax	1%	Determination of Amounts	
Preempt if state law conflict	1%	Categorical	53%
Allow nonconflicting state law	1%	Project	29%
Require state governor notification	1%	Formula	18%
Require state legislature notification	1%	Match ratio 0%	61%
Require formal state assent	1%	Match ratio 50%	3%
Exempt state/local government from regulations	1%	Match ratio 75%	5%
State can request waiver	1%	Match ratio 100%	24%
Congressional committee specified	1%	Match ratio determined by agency	5%

Note: Included are administrative structures or procedures that appear at least once in the legislative text of the intergovernmental grants or regulations enacted from 1877 to 1929.

the law would be carried out by the Bureau of Chemistry within the Department of Agriculture. The secretary of agriculture was limited in the application of food and drug regulations.

A specific sequence for enforcing the new regulations was laid out in the legislation. First, the secretary was required to give notice to a party if that party was found by the department to be adulterating or misbranding a product. Second, the accused party was granted the right to a hearing. If after a hearing the finding of the violation appeared to be correct, the secretary was authorized to refer the case to the district attorney. States were given the right to "exercise supreme authority" over manufacturing and intrastate commerce. States also could supplement congressional statutes as long as they did not interfere with interstate commerce.[32] States were also given the power to refer violations to the federal district attorneys. Finally, appeals by affected individuals were directed to the secretary of agriculture.

The *Federal Highway Act of 1916* appropriated $5 million a year annually in grants-in-aid to the states up to a total maximum of $25 million by 1921. The grant program was also lodged within the USDA, although under the Bureau of Public Roads. The grants-in-aid were offered based on a fifty-fifty matching ratio. However, each state's maximum allotment was determined by formula based on area, population, and miles of rural postal routes.[33] States were required to establish state highway departments or commissions by 1921.[34] The location of roads and the standards to be used were to be identified by the secretary of agriculture (i.e., the Bureau of Public Roads) in conjunction with the states. All other regulations needed for carrying out the provisions of the act were left to the Department of Agriculture (which in turn consulted with the states).

The *Sheppard-Towner Act of 1921* distributed funds to enable states to provide maternal and child health services. The program was overseen by the Children's Bureau, which was under the control of the Department of Labor. The act distributed grants on a fifty-fifty matching basis to the states. Every dollar spent by the states would be matched by a dollar from the national government, up to $5,000 for each state. In addition, a $5,000 lump sum was given to all states, and an additional amount was distributed to each state based on population.

The act required that states develop "detailed plans" for carrying out the program. Plans were to be approved by a three-member Federal Board of Maternity and Infant Hygiene and were binding on states accepting the monies. A state's failure to conform to an approved plan was cause for withholding funds. Each state had to establish or designate a state agency that would coordinate with the Children's Bureau. The federal board did not have the power to impose national standards, that is, merit requirements, on state personnel.[35] The act made the receiving of national funds contingent on the approval of the state legislature, or if the legislature was not in session, then on an interim basis by the state governor. No funds appropriated by any state could be used "for payment of benefits for maternity and infancy or for the purchase or repair of buildings or equipment."[36] States could use national funds to provide services such as health clinics. National funds could not be used to construct the buildings in which services were provided.

In each of these three policies, Congress used grants and intergovernmental regulations, as well as different types of administrative procedures, to shape the actions of both national- and state-level actors. In the case of food and drug regulation, in order for enforcement to occur, a particular sequence of administrative actions was laid out in the legislation. By contrast, highway building operated under relatively few constraints other than the targeting aspects of the legislation. For example, the 1916 legislation specifically prohibited spending in communities of more than 2,500 people. The Sheppard-Towner program reflected the somewhat hostile environment in which the legislation was enacted. Thus, while Congress laid out a detailed set of administrative structures and procedures for states to follow, Congress gave the Children's Bureau (the national-level bureaucracy) little power to enforce those standards. According to Jane Perry Clark, an early intergovernmental researcher, administrators in the Children's Bureau followed Congress's intention. Given the agency's weakness, it was more likely to encourage cooperation than attempt to "impose standards."[37]

The preceding brief excerpts from the case studies provide only a snapshot of the ways that Congress used administrative structures and procedures. The following section presents a more systematic examination of how Congress developed and employed IPIs to enact policy that could satisfy the preferences of multiple actors while overcoming the structural, ideological, and logistical hurdles of federalism. To trace this process over time and across policy areas, two measures were devised to measure the granting of discretionary power to the national bureaucrats, and the sharing of authority with the states.

Discretionary Power: Index Construction

Congress developed a wide range of rewards, sanctions, and monitoring methods to use in its oversight of national administrators, and to structure the national bureaucracy's interactions with its state counterparts. Two indices, national power and state power, were constructed to trace the administrative structures and procedures that evolved during the first New Federalism. These indices are used to determine the effect of congressional institutionalization and partisanship on the emergence of intergovernmental policy. To construct these measures I developed two submeasures: delegation of power, and constraints. Together these measures constitute what I call *discretionary power*. Discretionary power is defined as the actions taken by bureaucrats or agencies that are independent of, or different from, the wishes of legislative or executive principals.[38]

Delegation of power can occur at both the national and the state levels. On one end of the delegation-of-power spectrum is the varying ability of national legislators or their designated bureaucratic agents to act unilaterally—that is, without the consent of the states. For example, power granted to the national level could include the ability to act in absence of states taking action, or the ability to withhold money or plan approval from the states. In the case of contagious diseases of people, cattle, or plants, the national government was given the power to act (e.g., quarantine) if a particular state failed to take action (e.g., Contagious Disease Act of 1878 or the Cattle Contagious Diseases Act of 1903). In the area of commerce, some intergovernmental regulations preempted the power of states entirely, while other intergovernmental policies gave the national government the right to impose taxes on the states in order to regulate some aspect of commerce. Finally, some grants-in-aid gave an agency secretary the power to allocate funds among the states.

On the other end of the spectrum is the power given to (or rather reaffirmed in) the states. That is, Congress did not, and indeed could not, "give" power to the states; rather, intergovernmental policy during this period often reaffirmed state power.[39] For example, regulations involving interstate commerce usually also contained a provision that denied the national government any control over intrastate commerce. Indeed, despite the presumption that power ultimately rested with the states, Congress inserted explicit checks on the national government in some intergovernmental policies. These checks included the requirement that national agencies notify state governors or the state legislature of any grants that were applied for by state agencies, and of proposed changes in regulations. Some IPIs even went to the length of requiring that state legislatures formally give their assent to the receipt of a grant-in-aid.

Balanced against these delegations (or reaffirmations) of power were constraints. Examples of constraints Congress placed upon national bureaucrats included the requirement that national agencies hold hear-

TABLE 2.2
Discretionary Power in IPIs: National and State Power

	Mean	Standard Deviation	Median	Mode
NATIONAL DISCRETION	.13	.15	.01	0
Delegation	.19	.19	.29	0
Constraint	.30	.22	.20	.2
STATE DISCRETION	.18	.21	.17	0
Delegation	.25	.27	.25	0
Constraint	.21	.24	0	0

ings or obtain governors' or state legislative assent before taking any action. Other national management constraints or ongoing controls included the ability of states to set standards or deliver services without national input. In short, congressional decisions over agency design and structure also aided in the structuring and monitoring of national and state bureaucratic performance.

Finally, in a federal system, the range of discretion includes some combination of discretionary scope lodged with national agency, and discretionary scope lodged with states. Given that delegation in a federal system basically involves some level of shared authority, I assume that there is a nonnegative "floor" for agency discretion.[40]

The first index, NATIONAL DISCRETION, measures for each IPI the balance of power delegated to national bureaucrats and the constraints imposed upon those bureaucrats that limit their exercise of power (see table 2.2). For each scale, common characteristics between grants and intergovernmental regulations were identified based on a factor analysis.[41] The index runs from 0, meaning virtually no discretionary power granted to the national bureaucrats (that is, delegated power is perfectly balanced by constraints), to a score of 1, indicating that bureaucrats enjoy maximum discretionary power (in this instance, there is a maximum of delegated power but no constraints on their actions).

The second index, STATE DISCRETION, measures the discretionary power held by the states. Unlike the first index, the state discretion index is more complex. Constructing the index meant acknowledging key issues raised by the structural hurdles of federalism. The first issue is that for constitutional as well as political reasons Congress, especially during the era of the first New Federalism, was not in any position to explicitly constrain the activities of the states. For example, as

TABLE 2.3
Discretion and Policy Areas

Policy Area	Regulatory	Distributive	Redistributive
National Discretion	.16	.14	.10
Min, Max, SD	0, .46, .13	0, .46, .13	0, .43, .13
State Discretion	.16	.18	.23
Min, Max, SD	0, .5, .16	0, .5, .16	0, .75, .24

discussed earlier, Congress, in an attempt to ease its way past the Supreme Court, often inserted intrastate commerce exemption clauses into intergovernmental regulations. These exemptions allowed states to set standards (or not), or to enforce (or not) policy-specific regulations within a particular state. As a result, in these instances, while Congress did not explicitly constrain the states, it certainly limited the impact of a particular state on national policy.

Nonetheless, Congress, within the context of a specific intergovernmental policy, can give or at least offer additional administrative powers to the states. Therefore, while requiring national bureaucrats to obtain a governor's or a state legislature's approval prior to taking action is a constraint for the national bureaucracy, it is also a source of power for the states. In some cases, but not all, a constraint for the national level is a power that can be exercised by the states—again, though, within the narrow limits of a particular policy.[42]

Thus, like the national discretion index, the state discretionary power index, STATE DISCRETION, measures the balance of power between the power given or offered to the states or reaffirmed, and the constraints or controls on state activity (see table 2.2). A score of 0 indicates a virtual balance between power and constraints, while a score of 1 indicates that states' administrative or managerial power is not limited by administrative or managerial constraints or controls. With the development of these two indices we can take a new look at the enactment of intergovernmental policy across time and across policy areas during the first New Federalism.

In general, the degree of discretion granted by Congress to national administrators, and the amount of discretion that remained with the states, was limited. For both types of discretionary power (national and state), delegation of power was more or less matched by constraints on that power (see table 2.3).

The only difference in these scores was in the redistributive policy arena, where state discretionary power was over twice the level of dis-

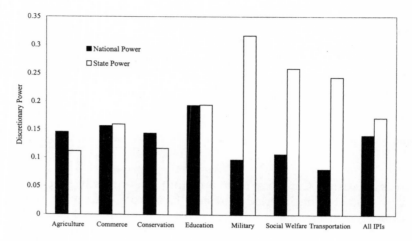

Figure 2.4. Discretionary Power across Policy Subareas

cretion granted to national administrators.[43] Further subdividing the
policy areas into smaller clusters reveals another interesting pattern
(see figure 2.4). In four of the policy areas—agriculture, commerce, education, and natural resources—the degree of national discretion
granted by Congress matched or exceeded the power of the states. In
the other three policy areas—military, social welfare, and transportation—state discretionary power exceeds national discretion. These
findings suggest that IPIs were quite sensitive to the politics that surrounded a given policy.

IPIs, Discretionary Power, and the Rise of the First New Federalism

Against the vast expansion of the American state in the post–New Deal
era, the first New Federalism and the IPIs that constituted a critical
ingredient in its formation appear to be a curious anachronism—a
small moment of strong "stateness" in an era often portrayed as a time
of national government weakness. From a typical developmental perspective, an explanation for the rise of IPIs is fairly straightforward.
Increases in IPIs and the policy areas that they represented resulted
from the emergence of new, highly organized interest groups such as
farmers, women, or consumer advocates.[44] Given the localistic orientation of Congress, it was inevitable that congressional representatives
would eventually take up the goals of these interests.

Despite the attractiveness of this narrative, two key assumptions about supply and demand of intergovernmental policy limit the fit of this developmental story. First, because of America's federal structure, interest groups are not monolithic in their concerns or goals; nor are they geographically balanced. For example, in the area of agricultural policy, small producers squared off against large producers, while regions and sectors of the agricultural economy were divided against each other. Competition and conflict among groups meant that new adoptions as well as stalemates over policy were just as likely to occur at the national level.

Though interest groups (and their bureaucratic partners) were rapidly growing in numbers and strength, it is doubtful that they alone could induce the sustained increase in intergovernmental policy, across time and across policy areas, during the first New Federalism that is posited in many demand-side theories of federalism. Demand for national activity was indeed created by politicians, reformers, bureaucrats, and interest groups working at the local, state, and national levels. However, the success of these actors varied. Response to their demands was not automatic; to paraphrase E. E. Schattschneider, with respect to the state, some interests are organized in, and some interests are organized out.[45]

While state and local governments may desire the benefits of national policy, they often want to minimize their disruptive effects on the local political economy. An adequate theory of federalism must explain how the federal structure and the separation-of-powers system shaped the strategies and actions taken (or not) by these disparate actors, and the varied levels of success they encountered in creating the demand and supply of intergovernmental policy.

The second, and in some ways more fundamental, assumption about intergovernmental policy is that Congress (and by extension the national government) can influence the activities of state and local governments.[46] By influence I mean not only the ability to act—in terms of gaining judicial approval (or simply not incurring disapproval) and bureaucratic implementation—but also the desire to act, that is, the legislative will. It is one thing for legislators to conceive of policy as "manipulable, discrete packets" of electoral benefits.[47] It is wholly another for legislators to see a possible policy enactment as explicitly creating and asserting a national prerogative. This ability to influence developed over several decades and involved, among other things, the emergence of a legislature that was not only capable of asserting a stronger national role, but also saw political incentives for the creation of a larger role that rested upon the needs of legislators first, and interests and other actors second.

During the first New Federalism, four processes converged that made possible the development and exercise of these new types of congressional controls. The first development was the strengthening of committee government as the locus of congressional policymaking. The second was the rise of the professional legislator and the concomitant rise in legislative expertise and policy entrepreneurship. Together these developments produced an institution in search of new ways to exert its powers on behalf of party and interests. The third was the development of greater oversight and management capacity within Congress, with the rise of legislative support staff and services. Finally, the fourth was the slow increase in administrative capacity within the national government itself as the patronage-based systems of administration slowly gave way to administration based on merit and apolitical, technical expertise.

These processes did not occur steadily across time or policies. In fact, the unevenness of these developments was reflected in the enactment of IPIs. As a result of this unevenness in legislative will and bureaucratic capacity, Congress developed a variety of ways to achieve its need to oversee and monitor intergovernmental policy. For example, in some cases the national government created new national-level agencies or other types of administrative structures like the Department of Agriculture's Bureau of Public Roads and Bureau of Chemistry, which were charged with continually overseeing and interacting with the state agencies or administrative structures that had agreed to carry out national policy. Still another equally important means to achieve national policy was the development of administrative procedures that would accompany the policy instruments, especially those instruments that involved the disbursement of funds. The next chapter probes the relationship between the internal dynamics of the national government, especially Congress, and the emergence and growth of IPIs over time and across policy areas.

Chapter Three _____

Congressional Politics, Structure, and the Enactment of IPIs

> The essence of a national objective is "the
> general welfare" and in that regard road
> making stands pre-eminent. The tax of bad
> roads is more evenly distributed than any
> other. It falls alike on producer and consumer,
> but with especial weight on the poor in towns
> and cities who depend so largely on farm
> products for their subsistence. Road
> improvement would bring relief to every class.
> Moreover, the mere expenditure of hundreds of
> millions annually for labor and materials in the
> rural districts would give years of prosperity to
> the whole country.
>   General Roy Stone, 1892

In 1893, Congress, at the behest of an unlikely coalition of urban bicyclists, automobile owners, farmers' groups, railroads, and national
merchants, displayed a formal interest in road building. Even that interest was small, with the creation of an Office of Road Inquiry within
the Department of Agriculture.[1] With an initial budget of $10,000 and
two employees, including its director, General Roy Stone, the office's
main duties were to provide road-building and maintenance advice to
state and local officials. For the next twenty-three years until the passage of the Federal Highway Act in 1916, Stone and his successors
would work tirelessly with allied interest groups to get funding for a
national highway system onto the legislative agenda.[2]

To get their broader vision onto the congressional agenda, these interests would have to find congressional supporters who were not only
willing, but had sufficient political clout and skill, to successfully advance a legislative proposal. Supporters would also have to depend to
some extent on political timing. Which party controlled Congress, the
cohesiveness of the majority party, and the presence of sectionalism or
divided government were all factors that shaped the legislative possibilities open to highway supporters. Finally, to create an enacting coali-

tion, supporters would have to structure their national highway plan
in a way that would minimize opposition and attract enough members
of Congress to pass the legislation. Although Stone and other highway
advocates were able to create a widespread support coalition under the
rubric of "relief [for] every class," it was the partisan and institutional
features of Congress that played a decisive role in determining when
highway policy made it onto the legislative agenda, and in shaping the
structure of the policy.

This chapter explores the partisan and institutional factors that
shaped Congress's enactment of IPIs, such as the federal highway bill
that was passed in 1916. The first section of this chapter uses a brief
overview of highway policy as a way of demonstrating how the inter-
related partisan and institutional features of Congress shaped the enactment of this policy. With that background in place, the primary variables used in this chapter's analyses can be better understood and
linked to the analyses that follow.

In the second section of this chapter, I analyze the enactment of IPIs
over time and across policy areas. The enactment of IPIs was decisively
shaped by partisan factors such as party strength, party cohesiveness,
sectionalism, and divided government. The emergence and growth of
IPIs was also shaped by the modernization of congressional institutions. The rise of professional legislators and the growth in legislative
staffs played key supporting roles in the enactment of IPIs. I find that
the impact of these partisan and institutional factors varied markedly
across policy areas. In particular, agriculture and commerce were areas
in which different patterns of enactment were found. Contrary to expectations, controlling for all else, Republicans were more likely to
enact agricultural IPIs and less likely to enact IPIs in the area of commerce policy. Why Republicans and not Democrats—the party histori-
cally identified as the representatives of agrarian interests during the
era of the first New Federalism—emerged as the enactors of IPIs is
explored in more depth in this section.

The third section of this chapter analyzes the two power indices, NA-
TIONAL DISCRETION and STATE DISCRETION, which were first introduced
in chapter 2. I show that these different types of discretionary power
changed across time and policy areas. Again, through statistical analysis I show that the partisan and institutional features of Congress that
shaped the enactment of IPIs also influenced the structure of IPIs, albeit in different ways. Congress's granting of power to national bureaucrats was shaped by the degree of sectionalism that faced legislators. National bureaucrats, were more likely to be granted greater
discretionary power during periods of increased sectionalism. On the
other hand, states were less likely to be given greater discretionary

power in the administration of IPIs when Republican Party strength increased. Why these differences occurred, as well as important differences that occur across policy areas, is further discussed in this section.

The final section of this chapter situates the findings from the analyses within the context of the book's broader claims about the first New Federalism and the development of the American state.

Highway Policy: Ideas, Interests, and Institutional Development

Convincing Congress and a skeptical public that highway spending was in the national interest meant overcoming beliefs about the role of the national government and its relationship with the states. Converting the external support created by the entrepreneurial activities of Stone and his successors and their interest group allies into actual legislation also meant the development of a nucleus of long-term support within Congress. Finally, the creation of an enacting coalition within Congress rested on structuring highway policy in a way that would appease its critics and not alienate its core supporters.

Resistance to national building or funding of highways came on a variety of fronts. First, should the national government be involved in the building of roads at all? Since Jackson's veto of the Maysville Turnpike in 1830, roads were seen as falling under state police power. Beyond these constitutional issues, did the national government have the administrative and fiscal capacity to engage in such a project? These questions had largely remained dormant since Jackson's administration. Second, if state governments had to be involved in building roads for constitutional, political, economic, and administrative reasons, did they have the capacity to undertake such a project? Some members of Congress believed that state governments—*as a whole*—simply did not have the administrative capacity or professionalism to undertake what would essentially be a *national* project involving large sums of money. At the state level, while some states successfully created and implemented ambitious road-building programs, others did not. In states that did implement road-building programs, the means by which they did so wildly varied. Some only provided technical advice, while some engaged in direct construction. Some states used convict labor; others contracted with county governments. Given these varied types of performance, how could Congress ensure the minimization of the political risks and the maximization of political benefits?

Adding to Congress's doubt over policy implementation was the belief that highway policy was pure and simple pork barrel politics. Indeed, congressional Republicans believed that the enactment of any highway legislation was an irresponsible attempt by the Democrats to establish a large and costly pork barrel program. Although Congress had long enjoyed a predilection for pork barrel legislation such as rivers and harbors projects, highway spending as conceived by its advocates opened up the possibility of a long-term commitment of government resources. The ratification of the Sixteenth Amendment in 1913, creating a national income tax, provided an added source of temptation to expand the commitments of the national government.

Thus, lurking within the charges of pork barrel politics was not only the question of whether the United States could *afford* to engage in a particular policy area, but also whether it *should* expand the scope of national government. For supporters of highway building, the benefits of such a program seemed manifest—roads would connect isolated farmers to markets, schools, and cultural life. Urban consumers and travelers could reap the benefits of an expanded transportation network. Yet there were equally fervent arguments that portrayed national highway building as another step in a trend of greater nationalization and a loss of local control of policy.[3]

The solutions to these questions and other issues were largely worked out within the institutional structure of Congress. The core of support for highway legislation within Congress was found in two places: individual legislators and specific committees. Two legislators, Representative Dorsey Shackleford (D-MO) and Senator John Bankhead (D-AL), became the champions for a national highway bill. Shackleford and Bankhead were typical members of the modernizing Congress in that both had spent numerous terms in office, had served on a variety of committees, and were closely linked to new interest groups on whose behalf they sponsored legislation.

Both Shackleford's and Bankhead's careers can be linked to emerging characteristics of the modern Congress: the growing attractiveness of a congressional career; the decreasing importance of the practice of political rotation; and, the decreasing competitiveness of congressional elections after 1896.[4] Shackleford served nine terms in the House from 1899 to 1917. In the 63rd Congress (1913–15), he resigned from the Ways and Means Committee and became chair of the newly constituted Committee on Roads.[5] Bankhead also had a long congressional career, first serving in the House from 1886 to 1906 (ten terms), and then in the Senate from 1906 to 1920.[6] In the House, Bankhead was a member of Committee on Public Buildings and Grounds, and in 1898 became a member of Rivers and Harbors Committee. In the Senate, Bankhead served on a number of committees including the Post Office and Post Roads Committee.

The longer rates of incumbency enjoyed by Shackleford and Bankhead enabled them to become advocates for the good roads movement.

As members—and in the case of Shackleford, as the chair—of committees that had jurisdiction over road building, they were able to work closely with bureaucrats from the Office of Road Inquiry and to develop relationships with the constellation of groups that supported a national role in highway building.[7] By 1910, both Shackleford and Bankhead had introduced a highway-funding bill to expand this initial exploratory program.

While neither Shackleford's Committee on Roads nor Bankhead's Post Office and Post Roads Committee was a high-prestige assignment, it served an important purpose for highway advocates.[8] Unlike other Gilded Age and Progressive Era legislation that died quietly in hostile committees, highway legislation found a friendly home because of efforts by Shackleford and Bankhead and their committees. Not only were these committees friendly, they also had some degree of institutionalization. For example, the Post Office and Post Roads Committee was one of the first to be assigned permanent staff.[9] The effect of these institutional changes was magnified with end of "czar" rule in the House after 1910, and the reorganization of the committee system when Democrats finally regained power in Congress after sixteen years as a minority party.

In the meantime, various bills introduced by Shackleford and Bankhead attempted to address the concerns of critics and lessen the opposition, especially among Republicans, to highway spending. While some early bills proposed a simple transfer of funds from the national government to the states, some advocates proposed transferring the entire project to the nationally directed and staffed Army Corps of Engineers. In the end, involving the states was a necessity in order to assure reluctant national representatives—again especially from the opposition party—and especially the Supreme Court, that the national government was simply a partner in a voluntary arrangement, rather than the leader in the project of building good roads. In addition, to lessen the risks of malfeasance and poor performance on the part of the states, new legislation would have to require some measure of state-level fiscal and administrative responsibility from the states.

As highway legislation wound its way through the congressional labyrinth, there were battles over which interests (urban versus rural, northern versus southern) within the party would be treated more favorably than others in the legislation. The administrative structures and procedures written into the 1916 highway legislation helped to resolve these disputes. For example, changes in the funding formula satisfied the sparsely populated western states and the poorer southern states, while the requirement that the bulk of funding be directed for rural post roads satisfied representatives with rural constituents. Although cities were explosively growing during this era, since state legislatures were largely dominated by rural interests who drew district lines that favored rural areas, state congressional delegations reflected this rural skew.[10]

Ultimately, despite sustained interest group and bureaucratic mobilization and the legislative advocacy of Shackleford and Bankhead, it took two critical partisan and institutional shifts in Congress for highway legislation to be enacted. The first was the midterm elections of 1912, in which Democrats gained control of the Senate but lost many of the seats they had won in the House. With control of both chambers, but running scared, Democrats gave highway legislation sustained and serious attention in the 63rd Congress. The second partisan shift was President Woodrow Wilson's reelection struggle of 1916, during the 64th Congress. Wilson embraced new legislation in an attempt to keep together his electoral coalition against the now reunified Republican Party. Faced with the need to keep themselves and Wilson in power, Democrats during the 64th Congress passed highway legislation and a host of other IPIs in an effort to shore up their disparate electoral coalition.

In the end, the Federal Highway Act was passed in 1916 by overwhelming bipartisan majorities in both Senate and House. With a structure that minimized political risk and maximized the political benefits for individual legislators, highway policy found many friends and few enemies.

This short example suggests that the enactment of intergovernmental policy, even one such as highway building that would allow substantial distributive benefits, was no easy task. In the case of highway policy, concerns about implementation and future outcomes commingled with concerns over the fiscal and ideological impacts of legislative enactment. Gaining a place for a policy on the legislative agenda, and retaining it, required the presence of a new type of legislator, one who saw policy expertise and advocacy directly linked to future electoral success at home and to increased power and prestige within Congress. In addition to these institutional factors, highway legislation passed in the particular way that it did because of a host of partisan factors. Not only were Democrats the majority party, they were also unified internally, faced little sectional stress, and controlled both Congress and the executive. The next section explains how these factors shaped the enactment of not just highway policy but IPIs as a whole.

Partisan Influences on the Enactment of IPIs

From 1877 to 1929, two parties, the Republicans and the Democrats, dominated national politics. Both parties were, on the whole, sympathetic, and responsive, to the goals of the new large corporate and industrial interests, the banks, and the railroads. Despite this similarity, there were exceptions. The Republican Party particularly saw itself as the partner of business and the protector of the American economy. Thus Republicans in the late nineteenth century were pro-tariff, anti-silver, pro-pension, and pro–imperial expansion. While the Democratic Party leadership was also pro-industrialization, its core constituents of the late nineteenth century—southerners and disaffected midwestern-ers—ensured that the concerns of rural America would somehow re-main on the party's agenda even after the waning of Populism and the realignment of 1896. The concerns of the agrarian periphery were persistent and significant enough that the two parties had recognizable and fairly distinctive party programs during this period.[11]

What are the implications of these party positions on the enactment of IPIs? First, we can assume that in most respects Republicans stood against any direct expansion of the national government. The Republi-can Party and, by extension, the national government facilitated busi-ness. Thus regulation, whether over the railroads or pure food, was to be resisted at all costs until constituency pressures offered no other alternatives. By contrast, Democrats, especially at the height of the Populist movement, advanced a program of agrarian legislation that would in essence harness national power to support rural and agricul-tural interests. In short, we can assume that Republicans were, on the whole, *against* intergovernmental policy, while Democrats were, on the whole, *in favor* of intergovernmental policy.

These divergent party positions were mediated by other factors, namely party strength, the ebb and flow of sectionalism, and the possi-bility of divided government. These factors posed formidable, but not insurmountable challenges to governing a new kind of American state. A brief explanation of the impact of each factor on the enactment of IPIs follows. I will also discuss how these factors will be operation-alized into variables that will be used in the analyses in the second and third sections of this chapter. A summary table of the variables used in the analyses is included in table 3.1.

PARTY STRENGTH AND COHESION

As seen in the case of the highway legislation, party strength—in terms of seats held by the majority party—and voting cohesion were two of the key factors in explaining the enactment (or not) of the legislation. By 1913 (the 63rd Congress), Democrats had gained control of the Sen-ate by a seven-seat majority. With a majority in both chambers, and the presidency, the party itself was more unified than ever. Party strength, in numbers and in voting cohesion, were critical factors as the party

TABLE 3.1
Partisan and Institutional Variables

Variable	Definition	Mean	SD	Min	Max
Republican Party %	Republican seats in House/total seats[a]	52	.09	.32	.68
Party Cohesion	% party vote per Congress[b]	.64	.13	.43	.90
Turnover %	% members replaced[a]	.32	.12	.13	.58
Divided Government Type I	President and Congress same party = 0; otherwise = 1[a]	.50	.51	0	1
Divided Government Type II	Split party control of Congress Same party = 0; Split control = 1[a]	.21	.34	0	1
Sectionalism	Average sectional deviation in presidential vote[c]	2.57	1.61	.46	7.38
Legislative Staff	Number of legislative branch employees/total number of members of Congress[d]	.37	.46	.75	1.61
Deficit Year	Increase in congressional deficit Positive change = 1, no change = 0[e]	.36	.44	0	1
Business Cycle Trough	Trough in business cycle = 1, otherwise = 0[f].	.54	.43	0	1

Sources: Notes below show sources of data.

[a] Norman J. Ornstein, Thomas E. Mann, and Michael Malbin, *Vital Statistics on Congress, 1997–1998* (Washington, DC: American Enterprise Institute, 1998).

[b] Jerome M. Clubb, William H. Flanigan, Nancy H. Zingale, *Analyzing Electoral History: A Guide to the Study or Voting Behavior* (Beverly Hills: Sage, 1980)

[c] Harvel L. Schantz, *American Presidential Elections: Progress, Policy, and Political Change* (Albany: State University of New York Press, 1996)

[d] U.S. Census, *Historical Statistics of the United States, Colonial Times to 1970*, Series Y 308–317 (Washington, DC: GPO, 1975).

[e] U.S. Census, *Historical Statistics of the United States, 1789–1945*, Series P 89–98 (Washington, DC: GPO, 1975)

[f] NBER, Survey of Current Business, October 1994, table C-51

faced the political risks and uncertainty that resulted from their nearly sixteen years in the congressional and presidential political wilderness.

Democrats were acutely aware of the tenuousness of their position. If they enacted policy that lodged power at the national level, and they then subsequently lost control of national government, they would be faced with the possibility of policies being enacted without their preferences being taken into account. If, however, national policy also formally shared policy enforcement or implementation power with the states, the Democrats could be assured that no matter what their electoral fortunes at the national level, they could still exert some control over policy outcomes at the state level. For Democrats, with a solid base of power in state governments in the South, the risk of sharing authority with the states was low, while the resting of power at the national level was risky given their tenuous hold on national power.

On the other hand, for Republicans, who were loath to expand government in the first place, with a broad national base but little or no presence in the South, it was far more preferable to lodge power at the national level than at the state level. The expansion of government and the possibility of out-of-control bureaucrats could be minimized if control was kept under the direct gaze of congressional Republicans.

Thus for Democrats the choice was clear in the case of highway policy. More benefits could be gained by continuing to work with state-level partners. Second, given the party's tenuous hold on power, vesting the power of implementation at the state level, where Democrats had a solid base of friends and allies, seemed a more advantageous strategy than a strictly national program that could come under the control of, or become dismantled by, a Republican majority.

Thus, in the analyses that follow I test the proposition that the stronger the party is in terms of seat strength and party cohesion in voting, the more likely that the party will be able to act on its collective policy preferences. For Republicans, when strength in terms of seats held and party cohesion is high, this means a preference for the enactment of less IPIs. If the enactment of IPIs is unavoidable, the Republican preference will be for policy that vests control at the national level, where the party was the strongest. For Democrats, being the majority party and having strong intraparty cohesion should correlate with a preference for the enactment of more IPIs. Second, given the regional base of the party, Democrats should exhibit a preference for greater sharing of power with the states.

Since Republicans were the dominant party during the first New Federalism, Republican Party seat strength is used as one of the explanatory variables (see table 3.1). Party cohesion is measured using a standard scale of party voting that measures the degree to which Republicans and Democrats voted against each other. A low score indicates that parties are not voting cohesively, while a high score means the opposite. Low levels of cohesive party voting reflect high levels of intraparty division.

SECTIONALISM

Legislators during the first New Federalism represented both party and district. However, sectionalism also affected policy preferences—legislators could find themselves as part of a group that felt itself besieged by the "eastern monied interests," corrupt urban machines, or the antidemocratic tendencies of the "Solid South."[12] At times sectional interests, whether economic or political, trumped the interests of the party. Sectionalism mattered to legislators. For some legislators it was inconceivable to contemplate any policy that would spread the nation's money and authority into possibly politically unfriendly, undoubtedly incompetent, and probably corrupt hands at the state and local levels. For other legislators, devolving funds and authority to the states addressed what they perceived as the national government's neglect and exploitation of the periphery.

To complicate matters, the opposite of these beliefs also resonated within legislators. What better way to blunt the demands of sectionalism than by blocking and fragmenting representatives' attempts to capture national government authority? What better way to escape the negative side effects of state and sectional competition than by establishing a nationally mandated level playing field?

In short, to congressional legislators facing continued sectionalism during the first New Federalism, the benefits of IPIs were numerous. To increase the likelihood of creating an enacting coalition and overcoming the sectional divisions, legislators crafted policy around an IPI framework. This framework could offer disparate regional interests the ability to share authority over a policy area if that was to their advantage. If yielding policy authority to the national government was to their section's advantage, IPIs could do that as well. Thus the analysis tests whether the increased presence of sectionalism in the political system led to a greater congressional preference for the enactment of IPIs. I then test the effect sectionalism has on the decision to give more power to the national government, or to share greater power with the states. Since an equally compelling argument for both cases can be made, no a priori claims about the influence of sectionalism can be made.

To measure the presence of sectionalism, I use the average sectional deviation in the Republican vote for president from 1876 to 1928 (see table 3.1). The strength of a region's vote for a presidential candidate can indicate the extent to which there was political agreement within the party and *across regions* in terms of the policy preferences embodied in the presidential candidate. Again in practical terms, regional disunity in the party vote for president is one indication that sectional interests could not be overcome by partisan loyalty. The extent of these deviations may, thus, better show the degree of regional enthusiasm for and connection with a party's position than might be revealed in aggregating elections at the state level.[13]

DIVIDED GOVERNMENT

Divided government is the last of the partisan variables that is used in the analysis. Even as members of Congress dealt with divisions caused by intraparty or sectional disputes, congressional policymaking was also a part of a separation-of-powers system. Divided government was a fairly frequent occurrence during the era of the first New Federalism. Between 1877 and 1893, no party controlled the House for more than one congressional term at a time. Power sharing between the national government and the states was difficult enough task. Power sharing between the executive and Congress presented its own benefits and risks.

In an era when, despite the ongoing efforts of civil service reformers, partisan politics and administration were virtually one and the same at both national and state levels, the problem of controlling the implementation of national policy was of particular concern to members of Congress. Was the national bureaucracy able, and could it be trusted, to carry out the goals of another branch, especially if the opposite party controlled it? Conversely, would states aligned with the congressional majority party really be responsive to the preferences of an executive in the hands of the opposite party?

Given these political risks, the enactment of IPIs should be highly sensitive and negatively associated with the presence of divided government. On the whole, neither party would prefer to enact IPIs under the condition of divided government. In fact, the number of IPIs enacted decreased in Wilson's second term when Republicans regained control in the 65th Congress (1919–21).

Nonetheless, if IPIs are enacted during periods of divided government, we should see different preferences over whether power should be granted to the national bureaucrats, or shared with the states. Like sectionalism, the arguments for granting more or less power to the national government or the states might be more tightly linked to particular circumstances or policy areas than the other partisan variables.

Institutional Influences on the Enactment of IPIs

The institutional positions of Shackleford and Bankhead allowed them and their interest group and bureaucratic allies to respond quickly to objections raised by congressional colleagues about the scope and cost of proposed road-building legislation. The ability to nurture a policy goal and also adjust to changing circumstances rested on two characteristics of the modern Congress: incumbency, or rather the ability to get reelected, and legislative staffing. Longer terms in office not only encouraged the growth of policy specialization, but also the strengthening of committee government, as committees increasingly became the focus of member's policymaking efforts. To support their committee policymaking, legislators increasingly turned to a new kind of government functionary, the committee staff. The institutional variables used in the analysis are measures of incumbency and legislative staffing.

INCUMBENCY

Shackleford's and Bankhead's highway advocacy was in many ways symbolic of an important but slow-moving transformation of Congress, into an organization that rewarded seniority and expertise. As Samuel Kernell argues, a new breed of congressman was ever more vigilant in the search for ways to reward supporters and in general remind constituents of their representative's ability to look after the district's needs.[14] Highway policy, as critics argued, was the ultimate in pork barrel projects.

To gain the benefits that came from seniority, members of Congress would have to be reelected. While members before this period had pursued long-term careers in Congress, many more had served very short periods before leaving, out of interest in pursuing other opportunities or because of the practice of "rotation." This pattern of behavior had changed by 1916 when highway legislation came under consideration. By this time, the average representative had spent about 3.4 terms (almost seven years) in office. The increase of incumbency in the Senate is even more striking. During the late nineteenth and early twentieth centuries, David Rothman argues, the Senate was at its height of power, with senators increasingly acting as careerists, and the entire body increasingly adhering to and privileging "seniority norms."[15] For southern politicians such as Bankhead who were beneficiaries of the Solid South, the incumbency rate was even greater. The benefits of incumbency became even more important for senators with the ratification of the Seventeenth Amendment in 1913, which provided for the direct election of senators.

Yet the achievement of seniority (outside of the South) was not an easy task. Although the sectional polarization of the parties endured, within each party electoral reforms and the slow weakening of the patronage system created a newly challenging political landscape. Despite the gradual increase in incumbency, getting elected and keeping one's seat was easier said than done.[16] To capture the uncertainty of reelection and its impact on policymaking, I use the percentage of member turnover in the House from one Congress to the next, rather than the average number of terms in office. Members of Congress, especially representatives, both then and now were probably far more aware and sensitive to the short-term shocks of witnessing colleagues who lost their seats, than to the long-term benefits that accrued from keeping one's seat.[17] The relationship between member turnover and enactment of IPIs should be positive, as members could view IPIs as an important tool in keeping one's seat.

LEGISLATIVE STAFFING: THE PROMISE OF OVERSIGHT

Despite the distributive benefits of highway spending, there were pockets of resistance to the highway legislation. This resistance was multifaceted. While issues of cost and constitutional authority certainly motivated the opposition of a number of members, there was another significant impediment to the legislation's enactment: unease over administrative capacity—whether the implementation was at the national or the state level.

Congressional opposition based on issues of administrative capacity, or the lack thereof, was not absolute. As Elizabeth Sanders, Daniel Carpenter, and others argue, Congress in its oversight of large sprawling bureaucracies such as the United States Post Office or the Department of Agriculture was increasingly "trained in regulation."[18] Legislative oversight was carried out by an increasing number of congressional staff members, who either worked for the committees or for an individual member of Congress.

Thus, depending on existing staff and resources, Congress could experiment with its assertion of power. Congress could decide to "make" policy itself using national agents to implement policy; it could have implementation of policy be a joint national-state endeavor; or it could decide not to enact policy. Alternatively, Congress could enact so-called self-executing legislation, which required little or no delegation of power to the executive or any other entity and contained extremely detailed legislative specification. Indeed, this latter example fits what Richard Bensel has argued was a congressional "predisposition . . . toward statutory articulation" both prior to and during the Progressive Era.[19]

In general the enactment of IPIs should be positively associated with the growth in legislative staff. As the growth in legislative staff increases, Congress's preference should be for the granting of more power to national bureaucrats, since Congress has more ways to directly oversee and control the actions of national bureaucrats, than of the states.

The Enactment of IPIs across Time and Policy Area

This section presents an analysis of congressional enactment of IPIs. To determine the ways in which partisanship (party control, party unity, sectionalism, divided government) and institutional change (member turnover and growth in legislative staff) together shaped the enactment of intergovernmental policy, weighted least squares (WLS) statistical models were estimated for the enactment of all IPIs and for each policy area. I control for the possible effect of possible exogenous demand for intergovernmental policy with the inclusion of two economic dummy variables: one that captures periods of national economic distress (the trough year of the business cycle); and another that indicates the presence of a legislative deficit. The variables used in the equation are presented in table 3.1.

The partisan variables are percentage of total seats held by the Republican Party in the House; party unity voting score in the House; sectional deviation of the most recent presidential vote; and the presence of divided government. Institutional variables are percentage of member turnover in House in the most recent election and the log of legislative staff. The time period of the analysis is 1877 to 1931, the 45th to the 71st Congresses.

Key Findings

The enactment of IPIs was analyzed in three ways: the enactment of IPIs as a whole; the enactment of IPIs within each of the three divisions, regulatory, distributive, and redistributive policy; and the enactment of policy within each of six policy subdivisions. In each analysis, the dependent variable is the number of IPIs enacted per Congress. The major findings of each type of analysis are briefly summarized.

TABLE 3.2
Enactment of IPIs per Congress across Policy Areas

	All IPIs	Distributive	Redistributive	Regulatory
Republican % Seats	10.25*	4.78**	2.82**	−1.14
	(1.89)	(2.12)	(2.67)	(−.324)
Party Cohesion	−9.31**	−5.11**	−3.07***	.485
	(−2.18)	(−2.84)	(−3.68)	(.173)
Sectionalism	−.453*	−.179	−.067	−.088
	(−1.73)	(−1.71)	(−1.32)	(−.532)
Divided Government	−2.95*	−1.05*	−.237	−2.43**
	(−1.79)	(−1.74)	(−.738)	(−2.34)
Member Turnover	2.49	−7.96*	−.723	−.376
	(.453)	(−2.00)	(−.151)	(−.178)
Legislative Staff	−4.30	1.27*	1.18	4.95
	(−.408)	(2.42)	(.577)	(.766)
Deficit Year	.729	−.418	.193	.805
	(.615)	(−.892)	(.836)	(1.12)
Trough	−.741	−.569	.279	−.644
	(.781)	(−1.20)	(1.51)	(−1.52)
Constant	10.14	4.69***	1.25*	3.55*
	(2.98)	(2.99)	(1.88)	(1.88)
Log likelihood	−55.24	−32.47	−11.75	46.09
Adj R^2	.45	.47	.35	.35

Note: $N = 28$; t values in parentheses. WLS estimates.
*$p \leq .10$ **$p \leq .05$ ***$p \leq .01$; one–tailed test.

ENACTMENT OF ALL IPIs

Overall the enactment of IPIs was influenced (in a statistically sig-nificant way) by all of the partisan variables. The percentage of seats held by the Republican Party had a positive effect on the enactment of IPIs (see table 3.2). On the other hand, an increase in intraparty disunity, an increase in sectionalism, and the presence of divided gov-ernment had a negative effect on the enactment of IPIs. In the pres-ence of these three variables, the number of IPIs enacted decreased. Contrary to expectations, the two institutional variables, member turnover and legislative staff, had no statistically significant effect on the enactment of IPIs.

Neither sectionalism nor divided government led members of Congress to enact more IPIs. One reason for this result is that the distributive nature of IPIs made them central to a legislator's relationship to his or her constituents (however that constituency was defined). Thus it is not surprising that with the strong connection between politics and administration, in the presence of high sectionalism or divided government, members of the majority party in Congress would be reluctant to enact policy in which the administration, or members of an opposing section, could share in any possible political benefits.

ENACTMENT BY POLICY AREA

The impact of partisan and institutional variables changes when policy area is examined. For both the distributive and redistributive policy areas, two of the partisan variables, Republican seats and intraparty unity, significantly affected the enactment of IPIs (see table 3.2). As the percentage of Republican seats increased, the likelihood of enacting distributive and redistributive IPIs also increased. As intraparty unity decreased, the likelihood of Congress enacting IPIs decreased. The enactment of regulatory policy displayed a different, almost contradictory pattern in response to these two variables. As Republican seat strength increased, the enactment of regulatory IPIs decreased, while increases in intraparty unity led to an increase in the likelihood of regulatory IPIs being enacted.

In other ways the enactment of regulatory, distributive and redistributive policy was similar. Sectionalism, divided government, and member turnover had negative effects on enactment in these policy areas, while growth in legislative staff had a positive effect. The effect of divided government was statistically significant in the case of distributive and regulatory policy. The two institutional variables, member turnover and growth in legislative staff, were statistically significant only in the case of distributive policy.

When looked at by broad policy areas, the enactment of distributive policy seems, not surprisingly, the most responsive to many of the political and institutional variables. Regulatory policy, on the other hand, was most influenced by the presence (or not) of divided government, the most obvious manifestation of the separations-of-powers system and the uneasy balance of power that existed between Congress and the executive. Redistributive policy was most affected by the broader impact of party seat strength and party unity. This latter result supports an initial conclusion that in the context of the limited national state of the first New Federalism, finding the consensus

TABLE 3.3
Enactment of IPIs per Congress across Policy Subareas

	All IPIs	Agriculture	Social Welfare	Commerce	Conservation
Republican % Seats	10.25*	3.89**	2.34	.518	.967
	(1.89)	(2.19)	(1.47)	(.253)	(1.07)
Party Cohesion	−9.31**	−2.60*	−2.40*	−.124	−.962
	(−2.18)	(−1.84)	(−1.89)	(−.076)	(−1.33)
Sectionalism	−.453*	−.165*	−.133*	−.127	.141**
	(−1.73)	(−1.98)	(−1.77)	(−1.32)	(3.31)
Divided Government	−2.95*	−1.12*	−.835*	−1.87**	−.208
	(−1.79)	(−2.13)	(−1.77)	(−3.08)	(−.778)
Member Turnover	2.49	−4.07***	1.12	−.566	−.273
	(.453)	(−3.81)	(1.17)	(−.459)	(−.502)
Legislative Staff	−4.30	3.22	8.57**	−.119	.607
	(−.408)	(.990)	(2.93)	(−.032)	(.366)
Deficit Year	.729	−.054	.392	.417	.072
	(.615)	(−.149)	(1.20)	(.997)	(.387)
Trough	−.741	−.868***	.413**	−.168	−.061
	(.781)	(−4.06)	(2.15)	(−.684)	(−.565)
Constant	10.14	2.22**	1.41	2.58*	−.459
	(2.98)	(2.32)	(1.64)	(2.34)	(−.941)
Log likelihood	−55.24	−27.64	−24.74	−31.48	−9.44
Adj R²	.45	.46	.19	.24	.11

Note: N = 28; *t* values in parentheses. WLS estimates.
*p≤.10   **p≤.05   ***p≤.01; one-tailed test.

for the enactment of redistributive IPIs would depend upon the existence of broad levels of party support. The next section discusses the impact of political and institutional factors on subsets of these three broad policy areas.

ENACTMENT OF IPIs BY POLICY SUBAREAS

In many ways, the enactment of IPIs in the four policy subareas of agriculture, commerce, conservation, and social welfare reflected the three broader policy areas of distributive, redistributive, and regulatory policy (see table 3.3).[20] Agricultural policy most closely reflected distributive policy in that the partisan variables of Republican Party seats, party voting, sectionalism, and divided government all had a significant impact on the enactment of agricultural policy. While increases in Republican Party seat strength had a positive impact, the rise in intraparty disunity, the presence of increased sectionalism, and the presence of divided government had negative effects. Unlike the broader category of distributive policy, the statistically significant institutional variable was staff turnover, which had a negative effect on the enactment of agricultural policy. However, unlike the broader distributive policy category, the presence of economic hard times had a negative effect on the enactment of agricultural policy. This is surprising, since agricultural policy was viewed by its supporters as way to alleviate the sufferings of the agricultural sector.

Like the broader redistributive policy category, the enactment of social welfare policy was affected by partisan variables. Both party disunity and sectionalism decreased the likelihood of enacting social welfare IPIs, while strength of the Republican Party had no effect. Unlike the broader redistributive policy area, economic hard times made Congress more likely to enact social welfare IPIs. On the other hand, unlike all the other policy and policy subareas, growth in legislative staff had a statistically significant and positive effect on the enactment of social welfare IPIs. The growth in legislative staff was accompanied by the enactment of IPIs that went beyond the broad categories of district and section, or even economically defined interests such as whisky distillers. Thus it is interesting that of all of the policy areas, social welfare policy, which most directly challenged reigning assumptions about the relationship between state and society, was the one most closely liked to legislative oversight.

Finally, the enactment of IPIs in the two areas of commerce and conservation were affected by limited variables. In the case of commerce, like the broader regulatory category, the enactment of IPIs in this area was negatively affected by the presence of divided government. For conservation, the presence of increased sectionalism had a positive effect on the enactment of IPIs. Although Congress was less likely to enact IPIs as whole in the presence of sectionalism, this stance was reversed when sectionally specific legislation such as the Forest Reserve Funds or the Weeks (Irrigation) Act was considered.

The Politics of Discretionary Power

As the highway legislation made its way through Congress, it became clear to many members that building a national administrative apparatus that was dependent upon state and local partners was a highly charged decision that would have to balance the benefits of enacting policy against the risks of bureaucratic drift. Bureaucratic drift—the possibility that bureaucrats will not act in the interests of their legislative principals—would be a particularly acute problem in the American federal system, where a weak national government was counterbalanced by numerous states of varying political preferences and levels of administrative capacity.[21] Thus, bound up in the decision to enact (or not) highway legislation was a key political issue: How could members of Congress ensure that policy outcomes would reflect their current as well as their future political and institutional interests?

In short, making the decision to enact an IPI was only part of Congress's decision calculus. Inextricably bound up in its decisions were the choices of administrative structures and procedures that would determine which interests (whether partisan, group, or bureaucratic) won and which ones lost. At best, an optimal choice of administrative structure and procedures could accomplish the following: ensure that certain interests were favored at the outset; guarantee that a certain level of congressional control was established in the implementation of policy; and alert Congress to undesired changes in bureaucratic behavior. As an added bonus, these administrative structures and procedures would allow Congress to overcome some of the constitutional and administrative hurdles imposed by the American federal system.

Given the varied effects of partisan and institutional developments on the enactment of IPIs, what effects of these variables could we expect to see on the assertion of national power or on Congress's balance of power with the states? To measure these effects, we must first clarify the choices Congress makes in enacting intergovernmental policy.

Congress when enacting intergovernmental policy makes two choices: (1) how much discretionary power to give to the national bureaucracy; and (2) how much discretionary power to give to (or share with) the states. That is, Congress when considering a particular intergovernmental policy determines the allotment of discretionary power it will give to its agents under the national bureaucracy. At the same time, Congress also determines the amount of power it will share with the states. Thus, to estimate changes in national discretion, we must also control for state discretion, and vice versa.[22] We do this with the understanding that while the decision to grant each type of discretionary power is simultaneous, different underlying processes determine the decisions.

For example, one of the elements that comprises the state discretion variable is whether the policy has an intrastate commerce exemption clause. These clauses allowed Congress to enact national laws while skirting the edge of unconstitutionality. Congress's use of this administrative element was the result of its relationship with the courts rather than the result of any internal congressional dynamics.

Thus, based on the intrinsic differences between each dependent variable, NATIONAL DISCRETION and STATE DISCRETION, separate models for each type of discretionary power are estimated.[23] Again, economic hard times, as captured by the economic dummy variables (business cycle trough year and legislative deficit), was included to control for possible exogenous demand for IPIs that increased national or state discretionary power.

Table 3.4 presents Tobit and ordinary least squares estimates of the effect of partisan and institutional developments on Congress's granting of national and state discretionary power for IPIs enacted during the first New Federalism.[24] Since results were similar for both OLS and Tobit equations, I discuss the Tobit results, which presented a better fit.

At the aggregate level, of the partisan and institutional variables estimated only sectionalism played a clear, statistically significant role in the granting of national discretionary power across all IPIs. Higher levels of sectionalism led to more discretionary power being vested at the national level, and less discretionary power given to the states (although the latter was not statistically significant). With higher levels of sectional stress, sharing power with the states could be risky to national legislators, thus leading to a lower amount of discretion given to the states and a greater discretion given to the national level.

State discretionary power was much more sensitive to partisan variables. As the percentage of seats held by Republicans increased, Congress decreased the amount of power that the national government would share with the states. This again supports the claim that because Republicans tended to dominate national politics during the first New Federalism, they would prefer policies that concentrated power in the hands of the national government (given, of course, their overall reluctance to enact IPIs).

Finally, considering the enactment of IPIs as a whole, for both national and state discretionary power there was an overall trade-off. Increases in either type of discretionary power inevitably led to a decrease in the other. That is, a decrease in national discretionary power was almost always matched by an increase in state power. Although Congress considered both sides of the discretionary continuum, it was usually a zero-sum game. The first New Federalism was thus a federalism that was bounded; increases in national authority did not come freely.

TABLE 3.4
National and State Discretionary Power, Tobit and OLS Estimates

	National Discretion		State Discretion	
	OLS	Tobit	OLS	Tobit
Republican % Seats	−.213	−.355	−.584**	−1.18***
	(1.29)	(1.13)	(2.33)	(2.59)
Party Cohesion	.146	.192	−.107	−.278
	(1.31)	(.907)	(.619)	(.905)
Sectionalism	1.29*	1.99*	−.381	−1.01
	(1.79)	(1.43)	(.335)	(.506)
Divided Government I	−.002	.008	.011	.044
	(.056)	(.137)	(.220)	(.502)
Divided Government II	.01	−.023	−.099*	−.201**
	(.268)	(.307)	(1.68)	(1.85)
Member Turnover	−.046	−.082	−.099	−.481
	(.225)	(.206)	(.317)	(.813)
Staff Growth	−.028	−.074	.006	−.007
	(.329)	(.444)	(.045)	(.034)
Deficit Year	−.011	−.033	−.125***	−.267***
	(.361)	(.558)	(2.79)	(3.19)
Trough	.029	.04	.015	−.021
	(1.03)	(.755)	(.344)	(.281)
State Discretion	−.242***	−.334***		
	(3.67)	(2.79)		
National Discretion			−.423***	−.729***
			(3.39)	(3.09)
Constant	.177	.248	.703*	1.28**
	(.652)	(.464)	(1.68)	(1.76)
χ^2/R^2	.16	−189.1***	.20	−143.6***
DW	2.0		2.1	

Note: t values in parentheses.
*$p \leq .10$ **$p \leq .05$ ***$p \leq .01$; one–tailed test.

Policy Areas and the Politics of Discretion

Within the policy specific areas of agriculture, commerce, and social welfare, partisanship and institutional development also played an important role in the granting of discretionary power to the national bureaucracy and the sharing of power over policy outcomes with the states.[25] Again, increasing Republican seat strength was negatively (and at times statistically significant) associated with the granting of greater national discretionary power across all policy areas, with the exception of natural resources, where the effect was positive but statistically insignificant (see table 3.5).

In two policy areas, agriculture and commerce, Republicans were also less willing to grant states greater discretionary power in the IPIs enacted. For social welfare policy the Republicans were less likely to give national discretionary power, and doubly less likely to grant discretionary power to the states. Greater party disunity, however, led to the granting of greater national discretion in the areas of agriculture, commerce, and social welfare, but less in natural resources and transportation. Interestingly, intraparty conflict had no statistically significant effect on the granting off discretionary power to the states.

The effect of sectionalism on the granting of national and state discretionary power in the area of commerce was particularly notable. Under greater conditions of sectionalism, there was a higher degree of discretion granted to the national government, and almost two times less sharing of authority with the states.

However, for the two other key policy areas, agriculture and social welfare policy, increases in sectionalism were met with both a decrease in national discretion and a decrease in state discretion. The decrease in state discretion, like that in the arena of commerce policy arena, was nearly two times less than the degree of discretion granted to the national government.

Agricultural policy was the area where the greatest insight from institutional variables can be drawn. An increase in legislative staff was positively associated not only with the granting of greater national discretion, but also with the granting of greater state discretionary authority. This finding is important because it goes to the heart of arguments that have been put forth, both here and elsewhere, about the growth of the national government. Agricultural policy was one of the key policy areas that drove Gilded Age and, to some extent, Progressive Era politics. The growth—both in size and capacity—of the Department of Agriculture reflected not only that organization's key location between organized groups and the national state, but also the national state's own developing capacity.[26]

The positive relationship between growth in staff and national discretionary power supports the notion that as Congress's own oversight abilities increased, its willingness to grant discretion to national administrators increased as well. However, like other policy areas during the first New Federalism, the granting of greater discretionary power to one side of the federal power continuum was not matched by an

TABLE 3.5
National and State Discretionary Power by Policy Subarea

	Agriculture		Commerce		Social Welfare[a]		Natural Resources and Transportation	
	National	State	National	State	National	State	National	State
Republican % Seats	-.378	-1.63**	-.923**	-1.79**	-.479	-8.63***	.386	.815
	(.536)	(2.02)	(2.07)	(2.27)	(.740)	(-.72)	(.581)	(.605)
Party Cohesion	.997*	.331	.545*	-.226	.279*	1.21	-.538*	-.164
	(1.73)	(.601)	(1.65)	(.366)	(1.36)	(1.30)	(1.42)	(.241)
Sectionalism	-4.49	-10.79***	3.34*	-7.48*	-3.55**	10.34***	11.84***	13.69**
	(1.277)	(2.16)	(1.49)	(1.46)	(2.24)	(2.67)	(3.77)	(2.02)
Divided Gov't I	.059	-.036	-.133*	.048	-.012	.505	.183*	.457**
	(.264)	(1.18)	(1.45)	(.294)	(.143)	(.936)	(1.52)	(1.84)
Divided Gov't II	-1.17	1.29	.206**	-.300*	.065	-1.73*	-.234	-.262
	(.023)	(.023)	(1.83)	(1.43)	(.330)	(1.49)	(1.04)	(.766)
Member Turnover	1.07	.069	.502	-1.02	-.053	5.12	-2.28***	-1.21
	(.634)	(.040)	(.798)	(.847)	(.066)	(.889)	(2.88)	(.736)
LegislativeStaff	1.12*	1.23**	.217	.557	.058	2.74*	-1.32**	-.986
	(.598)	(2.51)	(.656)	(1.05)	(.202)	(1.37)	(2.63)	(1.14)
Deficit Year	-.049	-.389*	-.058	-.245***	-.184*	-1.61**	-.076	-.426*
	(.280)	(1.59)	(.752)	(1.91)	(1.66)	(2.54)	(.703)	(1.74)
Trough	.213**	.123	.01	-.037	-.116	-.684*	.216**	-.082
	(1.82)	(.866)	(.124)	(.275)	(1.25)	(1.36)	(2.24)	(.354)
National Discretion		-.729***		-.456		-.171		1.97**
		(3.09)		(1.24)		(.320)		(2.39)
State Discretion	-.583*		-.162		-.174		-.467*	
	(1.64)		(.906)		(1.19)		(2.05)	
Constant	-3.31*	-1.69	1.72**	.607	.453	-2.59	3.38**	1.85
	(1.44)	(.912)	(2.66)	(.401)	(.599)	(.524)	(2.32)	(.831)
X^2/R^2	-30.6***	-24.9***	-64.1***	-64.3***	.40	-6.4	-24.9**	-24.1**
N	23	23	52	52	22	22	13	13

Note: t values in parentheses.
*$p \leq .10$ **$p \leq .05$ ***$p \leq .01$; one–tailed test.
[a] OLS estimates. DW = 2.4

attenuation of power on the other states' side. Indeed the opposite occurred, with the granting (or again affirming) of greater state power
when Congress enacted an agricultural IPI.

Congress and IPIs: Common Interest, Politics, and Structures

Far from an overwhelming national state, the first New Federalism
was a state based on partnership of common interests, common politics, and common structures. The granting of greater national discretion along with the sharing of power with the states was linked to the
growing network of state partners—whether interest group or bureaucratic—that were created or sustained by IPIs.

Indeed, the Hatch Act stands as the perfect example of this new
governing arrangement. As one of the first IPIs, the Hatch Act created
a system of state-based agricultural experiment stations that worked
in partnership with the USDA, with reformers and experts, with rural
and agrarian interest groups, and in close contact with their local
members of Congress. When enacting IPIs, members of Congress
could be reassured on two fronts. First, that the policy outcomes from
these state partners would be in accordance with their wishes, not
only because of the tight linkages between the states and the USDA,
but also because of the greater oversight Congress itself exhibited over
the USDA and the IPIs through the growth in legislative staff (and,
by extension, capacity).

The enactment of IPIs was also reassuring for members of Congress
because, through these tight linkages between interests, politics, and
structure, more power could be granted to the states, thus satisfying
the needs of key constituencies. This does not mean that this situation
was necessarily optimal. As Grant McConnell would argue in his devastating critique of agricultural policy, quite often these tight linkages
would result in an "exercise of public authority by ... private
groups."[27]

The opposite of this type of private politics were the IPIs enacted
during deficit years. For these IPIs, Congress granted both less national
and state discretionary power. And in the case of social welfare policy,
even less discretionary power was shared with the states. We can speculate that Congress wanted no misunderstandings as to who was the
provider of any possible benefits that derived from a given intergovernmental policy, and wanted no bureaucratic interference with members' relationships to their constituencies.

Conclusion

The administrative procedures and structures of intergovernmental policy were the foci of partisan battles. While Republicans struggled to limit the spread of discretionary power (either to the national level or with the states), party competition within Congress and across regional sections, ensured that these changes would be reflected in the granting or sharing of power.

Across time and across policy areas, Congress repeatedly made decisions about how to structure its relationship with the national bureaucracy and with the state. Members of Congress cared intensely about this relationship because of the political and institutional risks and incentives that surrounded them. For example, for some members of Congress supplying particularistic goods such as grants for highways or agricultural education became increasingly tied to their own electoral fortunes. However, as Republicans secured larger seat margins, this need for particularism did not translate into a desire for granting greater discretionary power. Instead, in alignment with their party beliefs, under Republicans the statutory scope of intergovernmental policy was constrained; even the prospect of sharing power did not appeal to them.

For other members of Congress, although also motivated by electoral concerns, the shaping of intergovernmental policy to balance the concerns of national and state or local interests was also motivated by ideology. Decreases in intraparty unity tended to increase both national and state discretion in the distributive policy arenas of agriculture and social welfare. By contrast, heightened intraparty unity led to a decrease in the amount of power shared with the states in commerce and the dual areas of natural resources and transportation. The latter finding is not unsurprising; as we saw in the case of highway policy, the states both gained and "lost" regulatory power under these types of intergovernmental policies.

The American state development literature posits that institutional development or modernization is almost synchronous with the rise of the administrative state and its tool, delegation. This analysis found that institutional development played a relatively insignificant role in the granting or sharing of discretionary power. In terms of intergovernmental policy, even disaggregating by policy area, the impact of institutional development was decidedly mixed. Indeed, the effect for the most part was weak, with the exception of agricultural policy and social welfare policy.

This analysis highlights the uneven effect of party and institutional factors on the development of public policy. The development of American state capacity did not occur steadily or evenly across time or (policy) space. Congress was one of the primary actors in this un-evenness because of its own electoral, partisan, and institutional features. Although members of Congress examined the benefits and risks of each intergovernmental policy through a prism shaped by party and institution, the intergovernmental policies they considered were shaped by the direct and indirect effects of federalism.

The next section of the book explores how the constraints and opportunities of the first New Federalism contributed to the emergence of a congressionally enacted policy system in which distinctive policy spaces and politics grew up around clusters of intergovernmental policies. This in turn has led to our present system of fragmented and disjointed creation and implementation of policy.

Chapter Four _____

Nationalizing Regulation: The Pure Food and Drug Act of 1906

> The absence of national food laws hitherto in
> the United States may not well be understood
> in other countries, but is plain to all who
> understand the limitations of our federal
> government. Municipal and State laws, in some
> cases models of their kind, we have; but the
> necessity of a national law, covering the whole
> question in its relation to manufacture and
> commerce . . . is becoming apparent to all
> thinking men. By no other means can we hope
> to secure laws uniform in their scope,
> requirement and penalties among ourselves,
> and for foreign commerce nothing less
> can avail.
>   W. D. Bigelow, 1898

MODERN AMERICAN consumers often take safety for granted. The food
and beverages consumed, the drugs prescribed or recommended by
health care providers, and the cosmetics and personal care items used
on faces and bodies have already been vetted for safety and purity.
When these assumptions are not met—when children die from tainted
hamburgers, or when drugs are found to have harmful, potentially
deadly effects—a regulatory mechanism, largely in the hands of the
Food and Drug Administration and the Federal Trade Commission, is
ready to address safety. Although the effectiveness of this mechanism
is hotly debated, the fact of its existence is remarkable given the decades-long struggle it to took to first enact a national regulatory system, and then to give it enough power to make a substantive change
in the lives of individual Americans. In the end, this contested step
towards the assertion of national power would fundamentally shape
large segments of the American economy.
    The first step on this path to national regulation was the enactment
of the Pure Food and Drug Act of 1906. Traditionally, the story of the
enactment of food and drug regulation has been told as a battle be-

tween the interests.[1] For example, farmers and ranchers sought the protection of their markets against the meatpackers and food manufacturers seeking to rationalize their business activities. Meanwhile, women's groups and temperance crusaders inveighed against the physical and moral dangers of patent medicine and the dishonesty and greed of its makers. Aiding these various groups was yet another set of interests—bureaucrats, physicians, scientists, and other experts, all eager to assert their newfound professional identity and carve out their own sphere of autonomy. According to this conventional story, most of these interests sought to cloak their goals under an ill-fitting and slightly hypocritical mantle of the public interest. Establishing the public interest was the purview of newly assertive and constituted women's groups such as the General Federation of Women's Clubs and the Women's Christian Temperance Union, as well as groups such as the National Consumer's League, which claimed to speak for a wide cross-section of the people. These public interest groups were aided in their struggle to put pure food legislation on the political agenda by new forms of political pressure emanating from the national press, in particular, the so-called muckraking journalists.

Lost from this story, and key to understanding the nature of the first New Federalism, was the influence of the American federal polity on the enactment of national regulation. The issue of pure food did not simply materialize out of thin air.[2] It was not solely the result of interest group bargaining presided over by a president who would later become the standard-bearer for Progressivism. Rather, the pure food legislation that would be considered by Congress from 1904 to 1906 was fundamentally shaped by the federal political economy of the late nineteenth century. The first effect of federalism was the existing dual nature of government in the late nineteenth century, in which each level of government—national and state (and local) had a widely agreed upon set of powers. These multiple power centers encouraged the development of different kinds of political activity aimed at influencing and using them. The second effect of federalism, related to the first, was the development of regulatory efforts at the state and local levels prior to the enactment of national regulation. The successes and failures of this subnational regulatory regime would have important effects on framing the regulatory alternatives considered at the national level. Finally, the third effect of the federal political economy was the impact of state-level economic competition on political representation. Like all regulations, any proposed national food and drug regulation would have concentrated costs and diffuse benefits. The costs would prove to be sectional (as well as industry-specific) in nature, and would thus shape the actions taken by state and national political actors.

A second crucial element lost from the traditional story was the role of Congress. While Theodore Roosevelt did play a role in encouraging the final enactment of the pure food bill, the wording of this legislation, its structure (in terms of administrative structures and procedures), even the timing of its consideration and its final passage reflected the emergence of a Congress whose members were caught between its rising electoral imperatives and the strong centralized (and deeply conservative) party leadership of the nineteenth century.

The end result of the Pure Food and Drug Act of 1906 was the establishment, for the first time in the United States, of widespread means for creating national standards and regulations for the food, drink, and drug industries. To implement and enforce these standards, the national government relied on a small central staff that worked in cooperation with a network of state and local partners. Yet this regulatory system was far from effective; critical concessions to sectional and business interests had limited the ambitious goals of pure food advocates, including their state and local allies. Ten years after its enactment, and in the face of congressional indifference if not hostility, regulators believed that they lacked the enforcement power necessary to safeguard the public.

By the 1920s, the most fervent supporters of the act were not optimistic about that legislation's ability to grapple with current issues facing American consumers. Changes in technology and marketing practices, as well as the vast increase in the American consumer market, exposed the limitations of the 1906 law. The weakness of the old law was made glaringly apparent in the Elixir of Sulfanilamide tragedy in 1937, when over one hundred children and adults were killed by a patent medicine that had been legally sold. Although the 1906 law had put some teeth into consumer protection, the sulfanilamide tragedy demonstrated to reformers and FDA bureaucrats that still more needed to be done.

Spurred by the sulfanilamide tragedy, the Food, Drug, and Cosmetic Act (FDCA) of 1938 embodied the ethos of the old, Progressive crusade of moral reform and the new, New Deal ethos of faith in centralized power. Indeed, despite the dissatisfaction with the 1906 legislation, opponents of attempts to reform that law did not want to revert to the dualist federalist system that existed before 1906. The scope of the argument rested on how much power would be vested in the national government in the guise of protecting the general public interest, and how that power could be constrained so as to protect private interests from government overreaching.

What did occur in the passage of the FDCA was a grafting of New Deal regulatory forms and expectations upon a still remarkably resilient older federalist administrative structure. While the 1938 legislation would ultimately put substantial new powers into the hands of the FDA (and the Federal Trade Commission), at the same time, the administrative mechanisms of the FDCA would continue to rely on decentralized national administration coupled with joint oversight and coordination with the states. As a result of this conflict between judicial goals and administrative structure, the issue of federal preemption, which had been lurking in the footnotes of the debate on the first New Federalism, would begin to take center seat in the preoccupations of those interested in modern welfare state federalism.

The Path to Pure Food: State and Local Regulation

In the small villages and towns of the United States, merchants who were caught selling spoiled, adulterated, or misbranded goods saw the loss of customers through communal sanctions, or were (in egregious cases) fined by local authorities under a wide array of local ordinances. The power of local and state authorities lay in the common-law principle of *salus populi*, or the public welfare (or health), in which it was recognized that the public—meaning civil authority—held sway over matters that affected the public as a whole.[3]

After the Civil War, this dual pattern of enforcement changed. Citizens who lived in the rapidly growing cities were increasingly immersed in a different kind of consumer economy where food came from a variety of sources, both local and national. Merchants and consumers gradually faced less and less control over the quality and purity of the goods that entered the urban market. Indeed, the pressures of competition induced some merchants to alter the composition of their goods in order to extract more profits. Due to the vast numbers of merchants in the urban economy, citizens thus faced a "lemons" problem, an inability to gain enough information to discern the quality of the goods being sold to them.[4]

Local and state government regulation of food and drugs grew increasingly strained with the advent of the modern, urban economy. Reformers and regulators attempted to address these issues though a variety of different means, such as enacting laws addressing specific goods such as milk. For example, at the local level, reformers in Chicago, Milwaukee, and New York were successful in creating effective regulatory agencies to regulate the purity of each city's milk supply.[5] At the state level, new products such as oleomargarine, a butter substitute comprised of animal fats or vegetable oils and flavorings, posed multiple threats to public health and economic well-being.[6] By 1886, seven states had prohibited the manufacture and sale of oleomargarine, while an additional fifteen states had enacted some form of oleomargarine laws, with varying degrees of comprehensiveness over labeling or packaging. Despite this initial success, the fact that states could not control the movement of oleomargarine in interstate commerce would lead to calls for a national regulation to limit the spread of oleomargarine. Sectional divisions within Congress notwithstanding, the pressures from state-level interest groups were too great. The national government enacted the Oleomargarine Act in 1886, which imposed a tax on the sale of oleomargarine itself, and separately on its producers, wholesalers, and retailers.[7]

The struggle over oleomargarine was just one aspect of the larger struggle to solve the "lemons problem" that afflicted consumers (and retailers) in the modern national economy. This struggle would become a decades-long project involving the identification of the problem as one that required articulating the public's interest, analyzing and publicizing the issue, and creating a solution, which would almost certainly employ government power.

The Creation of a State-Level Regulatory Framework

Fundamental to the emergence of a broad-based state regulatory framework for food, drinks, and drugs was the fact that unlike other areas of regulation, under the common-law principle of *salus populi*, state and local governments had a clear basis for enacting increasingly restrictive regulations to protect public health. *Salus populi* was also buttressed by the police powers of the states. This power was affirmed in a range of cases such as *Powell v. Pennsylvania*, 127 U.S. 678 (1888); *Plumley v. Massachusetts*, 155 U.S. 461 (1894); and *Crossman v. Lurman*, 192 U.S. 472 (1904). In the *Powell* decision, the Court commented,

> If there be any subject over which it would seem the states ought to have plenary control, and the power to legislate in respect to which it ought not to be supposed was intended to be surrendered to the general government, it is the protection of the people against fraud and deception in the sale of food products. Such legislation may, indeed, indirectly or incidentally, affect trade in such products transported from one state to another state. But that circumstance does not show that laws of the character alluded to are inconsistent with the power of Congress to regulate commerce among the states."[8]

While states had the legal right to create and enforce regulation, it was not quite as clear whether they wanted to assert those rights through the enactment of regulation, and whether the states could effectively enforce regulations, once enacted.

By 1890, twenty-five states had some form of pure food law, and by 1900, almost every state had enacted some version of a pure food or drug law, or both. The beginning of a regulatory framework was beginning to emerge.

Yet the ability of states to enforce laws against adulteration or misbranding varied. States such as New York and Massachusetts were early enactors of food or dairy laws, and reportedly had strong and effective state food and dairy commissions. Other states such as Illinois or Michigan had food and dairy commissions that existed more in name than in fact.[9] For example, one study found that by 1898, while Michigan's state commission had developed 53 cases, it only managed to obtain eight convictions (see table 4.1).[10] A later study, reported in the 1904 *Congressional Record*, reported wildly varying levels of prosecutions and convictions (see table 4.1). While the Massachusetts State Board of Health brought prosecutions in more than 211 cases and Pennsylvania's Department of Agriculture brought 1,085 cases, Michigan prosecuted only 17 cases, Washington only 4 cases, and in most states no cases were ever prosecuted.

In addition to the unevenness in effectiveness and coverage, the regulatory power of the states was not unassailable. The courts increasingly determined that "regulat[ion] . . . could not be justified under the state's police power to protect its citizen's health unless the state legislature made an actual finding that a particular product harmed the public health."[11] For example, while a case could be made that oleomargarine (and other new products) was a threat to public health, a case could be made (and indeed in the previously cited cases, had been made) that oleomargarine regulations were based on issues of commerce, not health. Thus, states would have to create and support a means of providing clear evidence that a product was in fact harmful.

In addition to this looming evidentiary problem, states faced a complex logistical and legal problem. The rise of national firms that shipped goods across state lines, such as H. J. Heinz or the National Biscuit Company, proved to be a significant challenge for state and local regulators. One of the ways that manufacturers could evade state laws was through the shipment of goods in "unbroken and original packages," thereby retaining the goods' interstate character.[12] Thus, for state regulators, "once an inferior product reached the labyrinth of interstate commerce, it was difficult if not impossible to control."[13] Although the courts would allow some measure of regulation, local reformers and officials found it difficult to regulate national firms in

TABLE 4.1
Pure Food and Drug Laws, 1877–1907

State	Pure Food Law (as of June 1906)	Regulatory Agency	State Level Prosecutions/ Convictions (as of 1905)	Enact 1907 Statute?
Alabama	1896			
Arizona				
Arkansas	1893			yes
California	1895			yes
Colorado	1893			yes
Connecticut	1895	yes	216/216	yes
Delaware				yes
District of Columbia	1895		448/437	
Florida	1897			yes
Georgia	1895			
Idaho	1887			yes
Illinois	1899	yes	268/162	yes
Indiana	1899	yes		yes
Iowa	1896	yes		yes
Kansas	1897			yes
Kentucky	1900	yes		
Louisiana	1882	yes		
Maine	1896	yes		
Maryland	1890	yes	0	
Massachusetts	1882	yes	211/208	
Michigan	1893	yes	17/16	
Minnesota	1889	yes	664/664	
Mississippi	1892			
Missouri	1899		0/0	yes
Montana	1899			
Nebraska	1899	yes	0/0	yes
Nevada	1897	yes		
New Hampshire	1891	yes		yes
New Jersey	1881	yes	231/0	yes
New Mexico	1897	yes		
New York	1899	yes		
North Carolina	1899	yes		yes

TABLE 4.1 *(cont'd)*
Pure Food and Drug Laws, 1877–1907

State	Pure Food Law (as of June 1906)	Regulatory Agency	State Level Prosecutions/ Convictions (as of 1905)	Enact 1907 Statute?
North Dakota	1899	yes	7/7	
Ohio	1886	yes	243/213	
Oklahoma				
Oregon	1899	yes		
Pennsylvania	1893	yes	1,085/58	
Rhode Island	1896			
South Carolina	1898	yes		yes
South Dakota	1899		0/0	yes
Tennessee	1897	yes		yes
Texas				
Utah	1898	yes	/2	yes
Vermont	1894			
Virginia	1880			
Washington	1899	yes	4/3	yes
West Virginia	1899	yes		yes
Wisconsin	1899	yes	/124	yes
Wyoming	1899		3/3	yes

Source: U.S. Senate (1901), "Adulterations of Food Products," Document No. 141, vol. 4039, 56th Cong. 2nd sess., February 6th, 1901, pp. 144–45; and *Congressional Record* 59th Cong. 1st sess, 8901–02.

ways that would not overstep the boundaries of state police powers and into the realm of interstate commerce.

The impact of interstate economic competition also made an appearance. Some states like North Dakota and Wisconsin, home of significant dairy industries or farming industries, enthusiastically supported the work of state and local regulators. For these states, the regulation of artificial products was an important way of leveling the economic playing field between the small farmer and the business interests. Other states, fearing economic competition or economic losses from imposing regulation, limited some reformers from pushing for pure food or drug regulation that would harm local industries.

Finally, in some cases, there was a complete absence of popular or official agitation for pure food legislation, beyond a token pure food law. In some states there was active hostility. This was particularly the case in the South, where whisky and other liquor distillers, as well as the proprietary medicine manufacturers and distributors, were located. This hostility went beyond idle threats. In the course of his investigations, one muckraking journalist discovered the existence of "red clauses," by which manufacturers would cancel all advertising in newspapers of a state that enacted a law restricting the sale or manufacture of proprietary medicines.[14] Since revenues from advertisements for patent medicines comprised a significant portion of newspapers' revenues, this threat proved an important tool in muzzling journalists. This sectional division would be replayed in Congress, with legislators from midwestern farm states generally supporting pure food legislation, and southern states almost solidly opposed to it.

States thus faced complex issues at the crux of the American federal system. Crusaders and regulators in states where they had enjoyed considerable success were wary of losing hard-earned higher standards with a possibly diluted national standard. In the context of this limited success, advocates were concerned that goods coming from states with weaker standards would undermine regulation. Some states with weak rules or none at all worried that tougher national standards would make local producers uncompetitive. Some regulators feared that national regulation would mean a diminution of their own status within their states. Other crusaders and bureaucrats stymied by lack of interest on the part of state governments welcomed the power that national regulation could confer upon their work.

Although under the doctrine of dual federalism, the responsibility for regulating the manufacture and distribution of food and drugs seemingly lay securely in the hands of the states, among reformers and interest groups there was not a clear consensus over whether state governments could effectively regulate food and drugs. In the case of pure food, as in other policy areas, the slow and uneven pace of enactment and enforcement at the state level and the political, economic, and institutional differences between states left reformers grasping for another alternative—national action.[15] This alternative was not implausible as by the late 1880s some national legislators begin to agree.

> In ordinary cases the consumer may be left to his own intelligence to protect himself against impositions. By the exercise of a reasonable degree of caution, he can protect himself from frauds in underweight and in under-measure. If he cannot detect a paper-soled

shoe on inspection he detects it in the wearing of it, and in one way
or another he can impose a penalty upon the fraudulent vendor. As
a general rule the doctrine of laissez faire can be applied. Not so
with many of the adulterations of food. Scientific inspection is
needed to detect the fraud, and scientific inspection is beyond the
reach of the ordinary consumer. In such cases, the Government
should intervene.[16]

With proliferating and confusing range of state standards and regulations, the need for a coordinated national approach was increasingly
apparent.

The Move toward Centralization

From 1898 to 1900, reformers and interest groups met on an annual
basis at the National Pure Food Congress.[17] The attendees included delegates appointed by state governors; representatives of relevant national, state, and local departments and bureaus such as public health
and food and drug agencies; representatives from national professional
societies and associations; and representatives from individual food
and drug manufacturers, distributors, and retailers.

In 1899, the National Pure Food Congress endorsed uniform legislation, arguing that "since each state must legislate independently, the
only hope in securing uniformity lies in persuading the states to legislate in unison."[18] For national manufacturers the debate turned on
whether consistent, possibly higher national standards outweighed the
costs (as well as benefits) of multiple (and in some cases less strict or
nonexistent) state standards. For these national industries, the inefficiency and cost of complying with numerous conflicting state laws was
burdensome. A national standard would not only reduce these ineffi-
ciencies, but might also regulate market entry.[19] International competition also provided a spur to develop a coherent and standard set of
regulations. From 1879 to 1891, because of safety concerns (as well as
attempts to protect domestic markets), a number of European countries had banned American pork products.[20]

By 1900, the call for national action was even more insistent and specific. The National Pure Food Congress once again endorsed a bill that
had been introduced by Pennsylvania senator Marriott Brosius.[21]
Among the bill's provisions were the regulation of goods bound for
interstate commerce as well as export; the raising of the Division of
Chemistry "to the dignity of a bureau"; and the appointment of a review board made up of representatives from various national agencies,

experts appointed by the USDA secretary, and a representative of the Association of Official Agricultural Chemists. The USDA and specifically the Bureau of Chemistry would administer the law, "mak[ing] use of the chemists and appliances of the various States engaged in food inspection, in order to render the service local, where the infringement of the law may have taken place."[22]

The measures endorsed by the National Pure Food Congress bore the imprint of an group that would shape the structure of pure food legislation: the national and state bureaucrats who would use their claims of scientific expertise to support the pure food advocates and disarm the "interests."

Linking State and Nation: State Chemists, the USDA, and Harvey Wiley

The regulation of food or drugs was not simply the enacting of law; it also meant the creation of standards on which to base enforcement. The creation of these standards and the development of a professional field would take place together. In general the creation of the scientific establishment that would give the pure food movement its legitimacy was the work of chemists and other staff employed directly by the new state and local boards of health, but also chemists that were employed by the state experiment stations created by the Hatch Act of 1887.

State chemists were in many ways emblematic of the first New Federalism. The creation of their position (and in many ways their field) was the result of intergovernmental policy. The intergovernmental policy that created them displayed the contradictions of IPIs. On a day-to-day level, they were the agents of state governments. At the same time, the chemists' fiscal, political, and professional interests were strongly shaped by their national principals.

In sometimes uneasy cooperation with these state-level scientists and officials was the USDA's Bureau of Chemistry. Created in 1862 as the Division of Chemistry, the bureau conducted its first investigation into adulteration in 1867. By the 1870s, with a growing body of evidence being produced by state chemists, as well as by the bureau, the USDA's chief chemist, Peter Collier, recommended the enactment of a national food and drug law. Although Collier would later lose his position, his call for national regulation set the precedent for the Bureau of Chemistry. In 1883, Harvey Washington Wiley succeeded Collier as its head. Wiley would stay on in the position of chief chemist and head of the bureau until his retirement in 1912.

The formal basis of the relationship between the state chemists and the USDA was the establishment of the Office of Experiment Stations (OES) within the USDA, which used the powers granted in the Hatch Act amendments of the 1890s to protect state scientists against attempts by state college administrators and legislators or the chemist themselves to divert resources from their research duties. According to one account, in its oversight role the OES was able to "make tactful suggestions to the well-meaning, find jobs for the innocent victims of local power conflicts, and better places for the competent."[23]

These experiment station scientists were themselves searching for ways to promote and strengthen their status as a legitimate part of the scientific establishment, and were struggling to insulate themselves from the attacks of state legislatures who were not sympathetic to the idea of "book-farming."[24] Thus, some chemists in western states created a niche for themselves through their knowledge of food chemistry, and their willingness to share with legislators their findings that their states were "dumping grounds" for adulterated foods. State legislators used the findings as a source of political agitation against "eastern interests."[25]

For some of these chemists, the detection of adulterated and even possibly poisonous foods or drugs was part of their civic and professional responsibility and identity. Working to advance the cause of the pure food crusade was consistent with previously held sympathies with the small farmers that the chemist and the experiment station professed to help.[26] While these activities helped the profession as a whole, they also had individual benefits, as Senator Edwin Ladd's career would demonstrate. Ladd began as a chemist at North Dakota's agricultural experiment station and gained fame through his extensive purity tests of foods. Ladd was named state food commissioner in 1902; he later became president of the state agricultural college in 1916, and was ultimately elected a U.S. senator in 1920.[27] As state food commissioner, Ladd was responsible for the enactment of a pure food and drug measure "so severe that proprietary manufactures set out to boycott the whole state."[28]

Although the state chemists were increasingly acting in their own interests, many of them (especially those at Hatch-funded experiment stations) maintained close ties with their patrons within the USDA, the national agency charged with their oversight. A formal and mutually beneficial relationship existed between these experiment station chemists and the USDA. To advance their multiple goals, state chemists, with the active assistance of the USDA, first organized themselves in 1884 as the Association of Official Agricultural Chemists (AOAC). The organization and the USDA then worked together to develop standards in food purity, fertilizers, and other aspects of the agriculture industry.[29] In fact the relationship was so close that Harvey Wiley, the USDA Bureau of Chemistry's chief, served as secretary of the organization. In 1885, at the AOAC's second annual meeting, the commissioner of agriculture called for the association to focus on food purity standards, an objective that the AOAC formally adopted the following year.

As a result of this close collaboration with the Bureau of Chemistry, the state chemists achieved significant success in creating standards for detecting dangerous additives or fraudulent adulterations.[30] In some states, these standards became part of the state regulatory code, while other states preferred to leave the question of standards largely unanswered in the face of strong opposition.

This is not to say that the AOAC was the sole state-level scientific group in its area. The close relationship between the AOAC and the USDA was a source of tension for officials who worked for state and local regulatory agencies. To these officials, the AOAC was simply an extension of the USDA, and as such reflected the USDA's priorities, as opposed to their own. In 1896, in response to this relationship, two new groups appeared. The National Association of State Dairy and Food Departments (NASDF) and the Association of American Dairy, Food and Drug Officials were created to influence the parameters of food and drug policy by establishing an alternative source of technical knowledge.[31] Indeed, in 1901, the NASDF created its own standards committee to compete with the state chemists and later proposed that a new separate bureau have the power to enforce any new pure food law.[32]

Wiley, Bureaucratic Entrepreneurialism, and the Coalescence of the Movement

At the national level, leadership of the pure food movement in the two decades prior to the 1906 law has been attributed to Harvey Wiley, the chief of the USDA's Bureau of Chemistry (BOC).[33] The emergence of Wiley as a key figure in the pure food movement has been attributed to a variety of factors. One reason given for Wiley's leadership role was his entrepreneurship on behalf of the organizational survival of the Bureau of Chemistry.[34]

During the 1890s, the bureau occupied an uncertain place in the USDA. Under a reorganization plan pushed by Secretary James Wilson, other units in the USDA would absorb many of Chemistry's original duties.[35] In order to shore up his position, as well as the bureau's,

Wiley cast about for a mission and for allies. According to this interpretation, the mission Wiley found was the pure food crusade, or,
more narrowly, securing the consumers' right to know what was in
the foods they ate. The allies Wiley found were numerous and strategically placed. Wiley found allies not only in the state chemists employed by the agricultural experiment stations created by the Hatch
Act of 1887, but also in the growing nationwide network of pure food
advocates, including the influential women's clubs that were in close
communication with state and national political figures. Surprisingly
enough, Wiley also found some allies among manufacturers and
packers, who increasing tried to influence the shape of any potential
national legislation.

Yet this view of Wiley's entrepreneurialism downplays his long-
standing professional links to field of chemistry, to state and university
chemists, and to the pure food movement.[36] Although his allies would
disagree over the issues he emphasized, his credibility in the field was
unimpeachable. Thus the second factor explaining Wiley's emergence
as one of the leaders in the pure food movement is that his personal
and professional interests coincided with, and indeed were an organic
part of, a broader interest in pure food and drug regulation.

Wiley increased the credibility and domination of the Bureau of
Chemistry through the development of standards for analyzing the purity of foods and drugs, the publication of numerous reports, and the
development of successful and publicity-generating partnerships with
pure food groups. So successful was the bureau in establishing itself
as the preeminent authority in standard setting for food additives and
drugs that "[b]y 1903, there was no longer any substantial debate
among bureaucratic interests regarding who should enforce the federal
pure food law. By this time, the AOAC and the interest groups repre-
senting state regulators, were all in more or less unanimous agreement
that enforcement of a federal pure food and drug law should be placed
in the USDA's Bureau of Chemistry."[37]

This claim to scientific dominance was the result of the acquisition
of technical expertise as well as savvy publicizing of this often tedious,
and not easily accessible (for the nonscientist) work. Over a course of
fifteen years (1887 to 1902), working with the AOAC and other groups,
the bureau produced a ten-part research bulletin, *Food and Food Adulterants*, which reported the results of tests on foods from dairy products to alcoholic beverages, canned vegetables, and preserved meats.[38]
Although these reports produced a wealth of information, they were
largely ignored outside of the pure food movement.[39]

To raise the stakes, educate the public, and increase the bureau's visi-
bility, in 1902 Wiley pursued a much more flamboyant tactic to publi-

cize his cause: the creation of a volunteer "Poison Squad" that would personally test the effects of additives and preservatives on humans. In doing so, Wiley publicly addressed a key criticism of the pure food movement, that its call for regulation was based largely on shaky scientific grounds, anecdotal evidence, and hearsay.[40] On a broader level, the "Poison Squad" was a resounding success for the relatively small bureau. Numerous mass-market periodicals such as *Collier's* and the *Ladies Home Journal* published the bureau's findings under sensational titles such as "The Patent Medicine Curse," "The Great American Fraud," or "The Subtle Poisons." The allegations in the newspaper articles and the results from Wiley's experiments were given an additional airing in congressional hearings held in 1904.

Wiley did not stop the process of standard setting while working within the broader pure food movement. In 1903, the Agricultural Appropriations Act authorized the Bureau of Chemistry to "investigate preservatives and colors to determine their relation to digestion and health" and to "set standards of purity for foods and to define adulterations 'for the guidance of officials of the various States and of courts of justice.' " Given this power, Wiley and his allies—the agricultural chemists of the AOAC—developed and issued a set of initial standards.[41] With the science of pure food established, and the standards for states and the courts developed as almost as a fait accompli, all that was needed (but difficult to secure) was political action.

Pure Food and Drug Legislation at the National Level

The appearance of national pure food and drug legislation was preceded by a series of laws enacted by the national government to primarily control the importation (or export) of specific types of drugs or foods. The first such law was the Drug Importation Act (1848), enacted to curb the import of adulterated medicines.[42] It was followed by the Tea Importation Act (1883), which mandated U.S. Customs inspection of imported tea.[43] The Oleomargarine Act (1886) not only controlled the interstate commerce of the substance, but also its importation. The Meat Inspection Act of 1890 authorized the inspection of cattle (both live and slaughtered) that were part of the export market.[44] The last specific law was the Biologics Control Act (1902), in which Congress asserted the right to regulate the safety of human vaccinations and serums.[45]

In addition to these specific laws, over 190 bills for broader regulation of food and drugs had been introduced in Congress between 1879 and 1906.[46] Among these were the Brosius bills that were endorsed by the National Pure Food congresses of 1898, 1899, and 1900. Despite the rising interest in some form of national action, and periodic and brief victories, enactment of a general pure food bill seemed frustratingly out of reach. For example, of the 190 bills that had been introduced, 6 bills had passed in the House (but not the Senate), and 3 had passed in the Senate (but not the House).

Most contemporary accounts of the pure food debate attribute Congress's, and especially the Senate's, resistance to the legislation to its capture by the "special interests."[47] According to these accounts, Senate opponents such as Nelson Aldrich, Republican senator from Rhode Island, were supporters of big business or beholden to the producer interests in their states.[48] Ideology also played a role in explaining the fitful legislative action on pure food and drug legislation. Accounts of congressional policymaking during the Gilded Age and Progressive Era highlight the ideological concerns among members of Congress. The notion that the national government should play a role in regulating the economic and social aspects of American life was highly controversial. A coterie of legislators in the Senate and the House, especially Aldrich and the Republican "old guard," saw themselves as the bulwarks against undue, unjustified, and, in their opinion, unconstitutional expansion of the scope of the national government.

Key to maintaining this inaction on pure food legislation was the partisan environment and institutional structure of Congress before 1901, which determined the chances for legislative enactment. The Congress of the 1870s and 1880s was an institution noted for its amateurism. Individual legislators, who did not yet see service in Congress as a career, were loath to offend powerful interests or their state parties. Turnover was high, with approximately 43% of representatives leaving after each term. The mean term reflected this turnover, hovering at 2.3 terms in office. Yet there was also a positive aspect to this fluidity. In the 44th Congress (1877), for example, over half (53%) of the House Representatives had previously sat in state legislatures.[49] It stands to reason, then, that quite a few representatives were exposed to the economic and health issues that surrounded pure food legislation, and the appeals of groups such as reformers, farmers, and labor.[50]

Exposure to the issue, however, was not enough. Longevity and power also counted. The leadership of both chambers used the power of seniority and control over assignment to consign pure food legislation to committees, such as the Committee on Manufactures, that had little or no power.[51] Indeed, Wiley bitterly complained in his autobiography that this legislation was "regularly committed to the Committee on Manufactures, much as an infant would be left to starve in a barren room."[52] When the leadership did allow one chamber to pass a bill, they were sure to block the other chamber from letting it come up for a vote.[53] With Congress traditionally meeting in short sessions of six to eight months, this was an effective tactic to block unwanted legislation.

By the time Congress passed the Pure Food and Drug Act in 1906, some of these conditions had begun to change. Turnover had decreased to an average of 33% of representatives leaving office, while the mean term of service rose to 2.9 terms (nearly six years) in office.[54] In addition, the committee system slowly reconstituted itself, from a system dominated by the Speaker and party leadership towards a system dominated by the norms of seniority and hierarchy. Finally, the political context had also changed. Pure food legislation was being considered in the post-1896 realignment, which firmly cemented control of the national government in Republican hands until 1911. With safer seats, individual representatives were becoming concerned about their individual fortunes as separate from the party's.

Nonetheless, the growing assertiveness of individual members of Congress was more than matched by the continued presence of strong Speakers in the House, and the conservative "old guard" leadership in the Senate. The tension between the needs of the members and the desires of the leadership would come to a head by 1906, and ultimately lead to the enactment of pure food legislation. Three members of Congress emerged who would critically jump-start the legislative process and rebel against the leadership: Representative William Hepburn (R-IA), and Senators Porter J. McCumber (R-ND) and William Heyburn (R-MT).[55]

The careers of these congressional sponsors of pure food and drug regulation reflected the newly institutionalizing Congress. Representative Hepburn was elected to the House in 1881 and served until 1887, when he joined the Harrison administration. Hepburn was elected again in 1893 and served for eight consecutive terms until 1909. In the 54th Congress (1895–97), he became the chair of the powerful Interstate and Foreign Commerce Committee. McCumber was elected to the Senate in 1899, serving until 1923. Along with other committee assignments, McCumber was chair of a revamped Committee on Manufactures, which had conducted publicity-generating hearings on pure food issues in 1900. Heyburn, who would replace McCumber as the Senate's main sponsor of pure food legislation, was elected to the Senate in 1903. Heyburn's Senate career was predated by long service in both the Montana state and national Republican Party.[56]

Pure Food: A Legislative History

The first legislative breakthroughs occurred in the 56th (1899–1901) and 57th Congresses (1901–1903). In 1899, the Senate Committee on

Manufactures, chaired by Sen. William E. Mason (R-IL), appointed the United States Pure Food Investigating Committee, which met from 1899 to 1900. The committee held hearings across the country, which publicized the issue of pure food.[57] The congressional hearing along with the concurrent pure food congresses demonstrated that a widespread coalition could be formed that could garner significant legislation support.

In the 57th Congress, in March 1902, hearings were also held, one set chaired by Senator McCumber, who had replaced Mason as chair of the Committee on Manufactures.[58] William Hepburn chaired a second set of hearings as head of the House Interstate and Foreign Commerce Committee.[59] Building on the success of the hearings, both Hepburn and McCumber introduced pure food bills in the next (58th) Congress. On January 10, 1904, Hepburn's bill (H.R. 6295) was passed in the House on a voice vote of 201 to 48.[60] In the Senate, despite a motion for consideration that passed 40 to 18, foes of the bill attempted to block consideration of the Hepburn bill.[61] When Senator McCumber (R-ND), the bill's sponsor, asked for another vote for consideration, the measure failed 28 to 32. Attempting to get around the opposition to the Hepburn bill, Senator Heyburn in March introduced a substitute.[62] This bill was also blocked until the specter of the fall presidential elections made consideration of any serious legislation difficult. According to Rep. James Mann, one of the pure food supporters, "While there ought to be no politics in a bill of this character," there was, as neither party wanted to offend potential business interests.[63] By December (the start of the third session), with the election over and his bill still blocked, Heyburn called up the stalled Hepburn bill. Again opponents mobilized to stall any consideration of it. Despite newspaper editorials condemning the delay, time ran out without further action being taken, and the 58th Congress came to an end on March 3, 1905.[64]

Pure food advocates, including Wiley, continued their mobilization during the long hiatus between the end of the 58th Congress and the beginning of the 59th in December 1905. On the legislative front Heyburn and McCumber introduced a new bill that they hoped would pick up more supporters. The new bill, S. 88, introduced on December 6, 1905, and reported out of committee on December 14, loosened some of the provisions contained in the earlier Hepburn bill. The new bill gave significant concessions to the food and drug interests. The most important concession was that the authority over standard setting would rest in the courts. In particular, the new bill provided additional protection to retailers who inadvertently sold adulterated, misbranded, or dangerous goods. The bill got a slight push later that month from President Roosevelt. In his annual message, the president stated,

I recommend that a law be enacted to regulate interstate commerce in misbranded and adulterated food, drinks, and drugs. Traffic in foodstuffs which have been debased or adulterated so as to injure health or to deceive purchasers should be forbidden.[65]

Despite this presidential support, it looked likely that Heyburn and McCumber's attempt would fall short once again.

In the House, Representative Hepburn was unable to get action on the new bill. The Senate debated the bill on January 10 and 18; the bill was dropped both times without consideration.[66] Once again, it seemed that the Senate leadership would prevail. However, in February a curious event happened. Senator Aldrich sent word to Senator Albert Beveridge that if Heyburn "asks for consideration for the Pure Food Bill there will be no objection."[67] There are a number of theories as to why Aldrich suddenly reversed years-long opposition. Some, like Senator Albert Beveridge, suggested that Aldrich and others had given up opposition to the pure food bill "to save something else they thought more important," and that the House would in the usual pattern kill the bill at a later date. Given that Aldrich himself is silent on this reversal, it remains an open matter. However, it is important to note that Aldrich was himself the subject of a series of muckraking articles. On February 16, *Cosmopolitan* magazine began a series of articles collectively titled "The Treason of the Senate." Written by David Graham Phillips, the articles accused Aldrich and other senators of receiving large payments from corporations to advance their interests in the Senate. On the heels of a larger corruption scandal involving two senators, this may have induced Aldrich to avoid being seen as a "tool" of the food interests, a claim about him that was consistently made by pure food advocates.[68]

The second key factor that may explain Aldrich's reversal and that changed the tone of the legislative struggle was the publication, and immediate success, of Upton Sinclair's *The Jungle*. Intended to show the plight of the immigrant working class, it shocked readers with its graphic portrayal of dangerous and unsanitary conditions in the Chicago meatpacking houses, and its allegation of bribery of federal meat inspectors.

Given this background, with the bill finally before the full Senate, both supporters and opponents pressed their case. Southerners in particular (and not surprisingly) pressed the constitutional issue, arguing that national regulation would inevitably lead to centralization of power and a diminution of state power.[69] Senator Hernando DeSoto Money (D-MS) did not settle for constitutional argument, introducing a substitute bill, primarily supported by trade groups, that he claimed would protect the states against federal intervention.[70] It excluded patent medicines, and enforcement would not lie in the Department of Agriculture (and specifically the Bureau of Chemistry), but under the business-friendly Department of Commerce and Labor. Second, goods in their "original unbroken packages" could be sold irrespective of the laws of the states to which the goods were shipped. Manufacturers were not punished for the making of harmful goods, but for the shipping of harmful goods. The analysis of suspect goods was to be done by the Public Health Service (which had no experience in the area), with the setting of standards in the hands of Congress rather than the Bureau of Chemistry.

McCumber countered Money's claims, arguing that his bill in fact weakened the ability of states to regulate goods entering their respective domains, since the Money bill would take away the ability of the national government to set a uniform, minimum standard. Other amendments, made on behalf of affected industries such as the whisky distillers and the patent medicine makers, were introduced and voted down. Although the Money bill eventually lost on a voice vote, its presence pressured the supporters of the Heyburn bill into compromises over specific issues such as purity and labeling standards, as well as the liability of manufacturers and distributors.[71]

On February 21, the Senate passed the Heyburn-McCumber bill (S. 88) by a sixty-three to four vote, with Aldrich and the "old guard" senators among those not voting.[72] The House leadership did everything in its power to delay consideration of the Senate measure, as perhaps Aldrich had calculated (and Wiley alleged).

Despite this attempt to block consideration of the bill, pressure from outside of Congress was mounting. First, the meat inspection scandal was steadily unfolding, with newspapers such as the *New York Times* calling for action; state and local officials, especially in Illinois and Chicago, initiating investigations; and, consumer demand for meat and canned goods slumping by anywhere from one-third to one-half.[73] Roosevelt, stung by the bribery allegations, ordered the establishment of a commission to study the meat safety and recommend solutions. Pure food advocates seized on this crisis and renewed their calls for the pure food bill to be passed by the House. Congressional representatives, especially the Republican Insurgents, fearful that voters would punish them in the upcoming election, joined the advocates in calling for the House leadership to allow the pure food bill to come up for a vote.[74]

At the same time that S. 88 was being considered in the Senate, Representative Hepburn reintroduced a different pure food bill (H.R. 4527) in the House, which was sent to the Commerce Committee. This bill contained none of the compromises that were in S. 88, the senate bill. Standard-setting, rule-making, and enforcement powers were all given to the secretary of agriculture, who would work with the state chemists association (AOAC) as well as with other experts of his own choosing. After several weeks of hearings and work in subcommittee and full committee, the bill was reported out of the Commerce Committee on March 7, 1906.

The bill as reported reflected some of the provisions in the recently passed Senate bill. First, it reduced the power of the secretary of agriculture. Regulatory power was to be shared by Agriculture with the departments of Commerce and Labor and the Treasury. In addition to the AOAC, the National Association of State Dairy and Food Departments (NASDF), friendly to the food industry, was also given a role as another source of expert knowledge, along with the appointment of an additional expert board. Finally, the revised bill set forth administrative procedures for the secretary of agriculture to follow in the enforcement of the law. Despite these revisions, the bill remained in limbo for the next few months because Speaker Cannon was reluctant to allow the bill to come up for debate and vote.[75]

On June 6, 1906, the *New York Times* began the first of a series of editorials attacking the House leadership, and specifically Speaker Joseph Cannon, for blocking the bill.[76] Cannon unconvincingly replied that it was the House, not he, that was unwilling to consider the bill. The *Times* rebutted Cannon's claim with its own assertion that he was a "pawn of the powerful industrial interests." The momentum for pure food legislation grew when on June 19, the House (and later the Senate) approved a meat inspection amendment to the agricultural appropriation bill.

As they had done the previous summer, pure food advocates continued to press the issue through rallies, exhibits, and the media. At their annual meeting held in St. Paul, Minnesota, in early June, the General Federation of Women's Clubs showcased the issue of pure food and the lack of movement in the House.[77] Nonetheless, with the ferociousness of public outrage still unabated (and still being stoked by the press), and with members of Congress alternately cowed by or exuberant over the swift passage of the meat inspection amendment, Cannon reluctantly acceded and allowed the pure food bill to come up for debate and vote. On June 20, the House voted on a motion to resolve into the Committee of the Whole to debate and vote on the bill. The motion was agreed to 143 to 72.[78]

On June 21, Representative Mann began the debate with a lengthy discussion and presentation of adulterated and dangerous goods. The debate unfolded much like the earlier Senate debate, with opponents invoking states' rights or the ruinous effect on honest business, and supporters citing the pernicious effects of "the interests" on the health and safety of American consumers.[79] The House bill contained significant differences from the Senate version. One of these was that the secretary of agriculture was authorized to "determine standards and wholesomeness of food products." The secretary was also authorized to call on the standards committees of the Association of Official Agricultural Chemists (the state chemist group) and the National Association of State Dairy and Food Departments, "and other such experts as [the secretary] deemed necessary."[80]

By June 23 it was over. The House passed the pure food bill, 241 to 17, with 112 representatives abstaining. Sixteen of the negative votes were southern Democrats[81] A conference committee was called to resolve differences between the House and the Senate bills. Mann, Hepburn, and William Ryan (D-NY) represented the House, while Heyburn, McCumber and Asbury Latimer (D-SC) represented the Senate. Differences between the two bills still remained. At the insistence of the Senate, the USDA was not given sole authority to determine standards.[82] The Senate preferred and got a provision that essentially left the setting of standards up to the courts, which in turn increased the burden of proof for state or national regulators. Differences between the two versions were resolved and the conference report submitted and formally adopted on June 28. On June 30, 1906, the president signed the Pure Food and Drug Act into law.

Pure Food: Administrative Structure and Implementation

The Pure Food and Law Act (34 Stat. 768) gave the national government the power to prohibit the "manufacture, sale, or transportation of adulterated, or misbranded or poisonous or deleterious foods, drugs, medicines, and liquors." The new powers given to the Department of Agriculture's Bureau of Chemistry (headed by pure food advocate Harvey Wiley) and its administrative structure clearly bore the imprint of the first New Federalism. The administrative structure of the law reflected the contending forces between large and small industries, and the need to balance the centralization of power at the national level with the centrifugal forces of the states.[83]

Although the actual administration of the law would be carried out by the Department of Agriculture, the secretary of agriculture was limited in the application of food and drug regulations. First, the development of uniform regulations was to take place through the cooperation of the secretaries of the Treasury, Commerce and Labor, and Agriculture. As a result of this fragmented power structure, the pro-farmer and pro–pure food advocacy influence of the USAD was decreased. Second, the secretary of agriculture was required to give notice to a party if it was found by the department to be adulterating or misbranding a product. The accused party was granted the right to a subsequent hearing. If, after a hearing, it appeared that the finding of the violation was correct, the secretary was authorized to refer the case to the district attorney. This provision, requiring the holding of hearings, was specified in a number of other IPIs as well.

The statute also reflected the struggles between and among the national and state governments. The key feature of the 1906 legislation that would come back to haunt reformers was the distinction between intra- and interstate commerce. Under the Pure Food and Drug Act, states were given the right to "exercise supreme authority" over manufacturing and intrastate commerce. States also could supplement congressional statutes as long as they did not interfere with interstate commerce. Indeed, in 1919 the Supreme Court affirmed that states had the right to enact standards that were higher than national standards, as long as the standards did not interfere with federal standards.[84] States were also given the power to refer violations to the federal district attorneys. Part of this diminution of state power was due to concerns that Wiley, along with his allies at the state level, would develop standards that would prove to be impossible or very expensive for manufacturers to meet.

As soon as the legislation was passed, there was intense desire among advocates that the "interests" not capture the regulatory process. At the state level, the advocates used the momentum from their fight to press for the enactment of more comprehensive state laws that would complement the national law, since the "federal measure obviously cannot protect consumers from evils existing within a state."[85] At a convention of the National Association of Dairy and Food Departments, delegates stated, "Until uniform state laws are secured with provisions corresponding to the national law the battle for pure foods in the United States will not have been won."[86] The women's clubs and other advocates continued to pressure members of Congress to live up to the spirit of the law and the movement that had pushed for its enactment. In this desire they would ultimately be disappointed. By 1909, the Consumer's League would charge that a "concerted effort has been made to defeat [the law's] purpose and to concede to special interests privileges that meant the final destruction of the integrity of the law."[87]

What the advocates were referring to was a perception that the Bureau of Chemistry had lost significant power within the USDA. In 1907, the secretary of agriculture, James Wilson, created a three-person Board of Food and Drug Inspection with Wiley as chair, with the department's solicitor general, and with a chemist appointed from outside of the Bureau of Chemistry. The board was given the right to conduct its own hearings on alleged violations and to report directly to the secretary. Wiley and his supporters correctly saw the board as an attempt to limit his power. In the years to come, Wiley was out-voted in two-thirds of the cases that came before the board.[88] One of the reasons for this new administrative arrangement was that Wiley, though at the forefront of the pure food movement, was still a USDA employee who had managed to offend not only members of Congress but also his superior, Secretary James Wilson, and most importantly, President Roosevelt.

By 1908, relations between the USDA and Wiley and his allies in the states had deteriorated. One of the issues that split Wiley and his group from the USDA was how to determine the standards for additives used in products for human consumption. To resolve this public squabble, Roosevelt created a five-member board, the Reference Board of Consulting Scientific Experts, or the "Remsen Board," to oversee the setting of standards. The president of the National Association of State Food and Dairy Departments protested to Wilson not only the USDA's unwillingness to "cooperate in food standards work" but also the creation of the Reference Board as a weakening of their authority. In 1912 Wiley resigned from his position, convinced that the special interests had eviscerated the pure food law.

In response to state officials and the departure of Wiley, in 1913, an Office of Cooperation was created in the Bureau of Chemistry. Nonetheless, despite the protests of state officials, control over standard setting had migrated to and seemed securely in the hands of the USDA, which was itself constrained in its rule-making abilities. By 1917, facing this loss in national influence, the Association of American Dairy, Food and Drug Officials recommended that the association decentralize itself and focus instead on local issues.[89]

The Enforcement Issue

A critical enforcement issue that faced the Bureau of Chemistry from the very beginning was how to define misbranding and adulteration. The 1906 act prohibited the addition of any ingredients that would sub-stitute for the food, conceal damage, pose a health hazard, or constitute a filthy or decomposed substance. Despite this language, judges could find no specific authority in the law for the standards of purity and content the bureau had been set up to oversee. The agency was only successful in establishing informal standards for food, while drug standards (for strength, quality, and purity) were set in the *United States Pharmacopoeia* and the *National Formulary.*

The Supreme Court gave conflicting opinions on misbranding culminating in a decision in 1911 (*U.S. v. Johnson*), in which it ruled that the Food and Drug Act of 1906 did not prohibit false therapeutic claims, but only false and misleading statements about the ingredients or identity of a drug. Congress responded to this ruling relatively swiftly with the Sherley Amendment in 1912, which prohibited labeling medicines with false therapeutic claims intended to defraud the purchaser. Nonetheless, the amendment still required the government to prove that the claims were made maliciously. That is, if manufacturers or promoters personally believed in claims, then they could escape prosecution. This was followed in 1913 with the Gould Amendment, which required that food package contents be "plainly and conspicuously marked on the outside of the package in terms of weight, measure, or numerical count." The enactment of the McNary-Mapes Amendment in 1930 strengthened the Bureau by authorizing the agency to determine standards of quality and fill-of-container for canned food, excluding, however, meat and milk products.

Theoretically, enforcement power shifted to the national government once those goods crossed states lines into the realm of interstate commerce. Enforcement was achieved with what the commissioner called a "cooperative rather than punitive" approach that emphasized "cooperation rather than conflict with industry."[90] By 1930, enforcement issues were growing serious. First, more categories of goods were placed under the agency's oversight. Indeed in 1930 in keeping with its growing regulatory scope, the name of the agency was changed to the Food and Drug Administration (FDA) to reflect its responsibility for goods such as caustic poisons, insecticides, milk, naval stores, and tea.[91] The second problem for the agency was the logistical hurdles it had to overcome to establish that a particular good was part of interstate commerce and thus subject to the agency's jurisdiction. For example, in order to begin an enforcement procedure, samples had to be taken in such a way as to demonstrate "the interstate character of the samples." This meant that multiple samples had to be obtained along with supporting documentation before an investigation, let alone enforcement, could begin.[92]

To lessen the burden of its growing regulatory scope and to aid the agency in overcoming its enforcement hurdles, and in keeping with the cooperation that had predated the pure food law, the agency formally established an Office of State Control to coordinate its activities with the states.[93] This coordination was critical given the awkward, multilayered nature of enforcement. In addition to the Office of State Control, there also existed the Food Standards Committee, appointed in 1914. Appointed by the secretary of agriculture, the committee was staffed by three representatives from the FDA, three from the Association of American Dairy, Food and Drug Officials, and three from the Association of Agricultural Chemists. The purpose of the committee was to formulate standards that would be adopted by the national government and the states after comment and review by manufacturers and other interested parties. Once standards were formulated, they would be submitted to the states for adoption. After adoption by the states, the FDA would then issue the standards as a "regulatory announcement."[94] The regulatory process of the FDA was thus both top-down and bottom-up.

This fluidity was reflected in the FDA's decentralized administrative structure. The head office, located in Washington, D.C., was small in terms of number of personnel. The bulk of the agency's personnel was located in field offices, inspection stations, and laboratories grouped into one of three districts: eastern, central, and western. Working with state chemists and inspectors, the field offices collected and analyzed samples of articles that were covered under the agency's interstate jurisdiction. Selection of FDA personnel still followed the norms established under Wiley: appointments (and removals) were made under the authority of the secretary of agriculture. The small size of the agency, according to one contemporary account, "made careful selection [of personnel] possible and contributed to the development of an admirable *esprit de corps*."[95] With a tight organizational focus and relatively strong bonds with state and local counterparts, the FDA managed to function within a challenging environment of limited statutory power and increasing number of goods available to the market.

The Legislative Struggle for the Food Drug and Cosmetic Act of 1938

The push for a new law began in earnest with the start of the Franklin Roosevelt administration.[96] The earliest supporter for a new food and drug bill was Assistant Secretary of Agriculture Rexford Tugwell, one of the key architects of the New Deal.[97] In Tugwell, the FDA found an unexpected warm source of support. In addition, Tugwell provided the FDA a personal connection to Roosevelt, who was generally uninterested in pursuing reform of the agency. Tugwell's support, however, was a two-sided sword. The food, drug, and cosmetic industries adamantly opposed what they perceived as Tugwell's radicalism, especially his endorsement of strong government regulation of their industries.

Gaining a congressional sponsor initially proved to be difficult, although eventually one was found: Senator Royal Copeland (D-NY), after whom the proposed legislation was named. Copeland was a physician as well as a former New York City health commissioner who was elected to the Senate with the support of Tammany Hall. Copeland's support, however, was problematic, as he was a "New Dealer by party affiliation rather than philosophical inclination."[98] Copeland's relationship with Roosevelt, his fellow New Yorker, was never warm, and by 1937 he was in open revolt against the party. Thus, Copeland's sponsorship, especially after the departure of Tugwell from the Roosevelt administration, proved to be a hindrance in terms of motivating presidential support in favor of a new food bill. On the other hand, Copeland's ties with the food industry and his willingness to compromise enabled the fight for a revised law to stay on the legislative agenda for the five years it took for passage. Even more important in terms of support was the fact that in the aftermath of the 1934 elections, he became chair of the Senate Commerce Committee.[99] Finally, we can speculate that in addition to his institutional position, Copeland's membership in the Conservative Coalition that would strongly influence the 75th and 76th Congresses also aided in bringing about the enactment of the FCDA.[100]

Although those within the FDA had been growing steadily more frustrated with the limitations of the old law, getting public support for change and thus congressional support for legislative change seemed impossible. According to one commentator, the main barrier to effective reform was a "killing disinterest" on the part of the public.[101]

To change the unreceptive political environment, the FDA returned to its early roots in creating a public relations campaign to convince Congress to support a new law. First, the FDA created a public information campaign, writing articles, giving newspaper and radio interviews, and supplying speakers for groups. In addition, the agency created a poster exhibit later dubbed the "Chamber of Horrors" that showed how inadequate the 1906 law was in protecting the public.[102] Much like Wiley's Poison Squad at the turn of the century, the goal of this campaign was to dramatize the stakes of the upcoming legislative battle to the average American citizen.

The agency was aided in its tasks by a number of exposés in the popular press such as *100,000,000 Guinea Pigs*, which detailed the dangers of the largely unregulated cosmetics industry, and, Ruth Deforest Lamb's book *The American Chamber of Horrors*, detailing the hazards of food preservatives.[103] In addition to these works, Harvey Wiley, the "father" of the FDA, became increasingly critical of the effectiveness of the pure food law and of the agency's performance.[104] These works as well as other articles and books, combined with the FDA's own campaign, demonstrated to the American consumer the dangers of the current weak law.

Nonetheless, the FDA of 1933 faced a different institutional environment than the Poison Squad of 1904. During the first New Federalism, bureaucratic entrepreneurs became adroit at creating and using agency-sponsored events, activities, and publications to secure funding for highways, agricultural research stations, child health, and pure food. This publicity-seeking strategy was forestalled, however, with the passage of the Deficiency Appropriations Act of 1919, which prohibited national agencies from spending money on lobbying. As a result of the FDA's success with its "chamber of horrors" exhibit, the food and drug industry was able to use the Deficiency Act to muzzle the agency. For the next years the FDA was forced to become more circumspect in its effort to drum up public interest in the topic of food and drug law reform, and in aiding its interest group supporters.[105]

The third source of support for the agency was national interest groups. As in the case of the 1906 legislation, these groups included federated women's groups such as the National League of Women Voters and new consumer-oriented groups such as Consumers' Research and the Consumers Union. Organized much in the same way they were for the enactment of the 1906 law and for the passage of the Sheppard-Towner program in the 1920s, the women's groups turned their considerable energy and influence on the issue of regulation of food, drugs, and cosmetics.[106] As federated organizations, these groups were able to exert critical pressure at the state as well as national level. As a result, they were able to sustain the cause through the long five years it took until a new law was enacted in 1938.[107] Although the consumer groups were more recently established, they trod much of the same path as their progressive muckraking ancestors.[108] Consumer groups focused largely on publishing exposés of gruesome antics or greedy tactics engaged in by the industries, testifying before government bodies, and expanding their membership base.

Despite this push for new legislation, two Tugwell-supported Copeland bills (S. 1944, and later S. 5) did not pass in the first Roosevelt administration. In fact, the first bill (S. 1944) was greeted with hostility and doubt from the food, drug, and cosmetics industry. According to industry critics (as well as some members of Congress) the proposed legislation vested too much discretionary power in the hands of the secretary of agriculture.[109] For example, under the proposed legislation, the FDA would have the power to set standards for ingredients and for labels for the food and drug industry. The legislation would also bring the cosmetics industry under the control of the FDA for the first time.[110]

Nonetheless, as the battle for new legislation dragged on, other sources of pressure for enacting some kind of legislation mounted. One important source of pressure for passage of a new law was the growing fear among producers that states would step into the breach and enact conflicting laws as the legislative battle for a new law spanned from one administration into the next.[111]

By 1936, the concerns of the national manufacturers were being confirmed. In light of the legislative impasse in Congress, a number of states began to enact or propose significantly strengthened food, drug, and cosmetic laws. By 1936, thirty-nine states had enacted ninety-two drug-related laws. States that enacted significant laws included Pennsylvania, North Dakota, and Virginia, while Louisiana enacted a sweeping statute (similar to the proposed bill in Congress) in 1936.[112] A key element of Louisiana's legislation was a provision for registration fees for all "processed foods, proprietary medicines, cosmetics, and prophylactic devices."[113] The registration fees would finally provide a significant and independent source of funding for the enforcement of the law. Women's groups wielded this state option even more effectively. They threatened to introduce model food legislation in every state legislature that would be meeting in January 1937.[114]

Despite the concerted efforts of interest groups, the (intermittent and somewhat low-key) public relations campaign of the FDA, and the growing consensus among the national manufacturers and producers about the need for uniform standards, the proposed bill still remained stuck in Congress. The policy terrain would decisively shift when the Elixir of Sulfanilamide tragedy occurred.

Elixir of Sulfanilamide was manufactured by the Samuel E. Massengill Company of Bristol, Tennessee. As a result of manufacturer negligence, a poisonous solvent—diethylene glycol (a type of antifreeze)—was included as an ingredient in an over-the-counter antibiotic-like medicine. Distribution of the product began on September 4, 1937. The first death was reported on October 11 in the Tulsa, Oklahoma, area. The drug ultimately killed 107 people, including many children, before the FDA was able to warn the public about the dangers.[115] Despite the deaths, the FDA could only prosecute Massengill on the relative minor violation of misbranding. Under the 1906 law the manufacturer was not required to list the composition of the elixir on the label. Further, under the 1906 law, the FDA had neither the authority to require pre-market testing nor the authority to seize drugs. Only because the drug was misbranded could the FDA take action.

This event, which unfolded across the nation (but primarily in the South and Midwest) helped to dramatize the need to establish new drug safety laws. Like Upton Sinclair's *The Jungle*, published during the debate over the Pure Food and Drug Act of 1906, a timely public event helped to push Congress into finally taking action.[116]

The Federal Food, Drug, and Cosmetic Act of 1938 (52 Stat. 1040) was passed on June 25, 1938.[117] The act contained seven new provisions: it (1) extended FDA control to cosmetics and therapeutic devices; (2) required new drugs to be shown safe before marketing; (3) eliminated the Sherley Amendment requirement that the FDA prove intent to defraud in drug-misbranding cases; (4) provided that safe tolerances be set for unavoidable poisonous substances; (5) authorized standards of identity, quality, and fill-of-container for foods; (6) authorized factory inspections; and (7) added the remedy of court injunctions to the previous penalties of seizures and prosecutions. In addition, to satisfy manufacturers' concerns that the FDA was granted too much power, the Wheeler-Lea Act was passed in March 1938.[118] Under this latter act, the Federal Trade Commission was given the power to oversee advertising associated with products that were otherwise regulated by FDA. The exception to this was in the area of prescription drugs.

The Administrative Structure of the FDCA

What is remarkable about the FDCA is that despite the new powers given to the FDA, organizationally it retained the same decentralized structure. Of the 950 people employed by the agency in 1946, 575 were classified as scientific workers.[119] Two-thirds of all workers were located in district offices (including station, substation, and inspection posts) outside of Washington, DC. The majority of the personnel assigned to the Washington office were assigned to technical divisions.

The agency's relationship with the states became even closer as states enacted their own complementary versions of the FDCA. By 1949 twenty-one states would enact "little" food and drug acts; while ten states, including Texas and New Mexico, had no "adequate" state law.[120] This federalist structure was buttressed by the inter- and intrastate commerce distinction that was written into the 1938 legislation. Despite the expansion of regulatory power during the New Deal, this specific piece of legislation retained language more reminiscent of the first New Federalism than of the current New Deal federalism.

Ironically, the vast expansion in national power of the FDA came from the courts, the very institution that the food, drug, and cosmetic industry had turned to in order to protect themselves from the power of the USDA. Ten years after the FDCA was enacted, the Supreme Court handed down its decision in *United States v. Sullivan*.

The *Sullivan* decision was the first of many cases that effectively ended the legislative fig of the interstate commerce clause that Congress had inserted into IPIs in order to make them judicially and politically palatable. Now, according to the Court in the *Sullivan* case, the provisions of the FDCA held for the sale of a good even after it had been shipped via interstate commerce, whether or not it was the first sale. One interpretation of this ruling is that it added an additional basis to national power. That is, once any commodity moves in interstate commerce, the national government has the power to regulate that good until it reaches the ultimate consumer.[121]

Ultimately, despite the best intentions of its opponents, and beyond the wildest imagining of its supporters, the modern-day FDA is remarkably centralized and powerful within its policy domain. This power, though, is constrained. Through its rule-making abilities the FDA can set the research and marketing agendas of thousands of companies and shape consumer markets for thousands of goods. However, in its enforcement of its rules and regulations, the FDA is still reliant on a constellation of watchdog interest groups, the courts, and its own formal and informal network of cooperative state and local officials.

Chapter Five _____

Goods Roads to Fiscal Stimulus: Highway Policy from 1900 to the New Deal

> I believe that there is a positive need for a
> centralized control and a highly skilled
> supervision on the part of [a road] agency of
> the state, particularly with reference to the
> design and inspection of highway bridges, the
> expenditure of large local bond issues, the
> handling of local funds for highway work as to
> systems of accounting and cost keeping, and
> finally as to the qualifications of the men
> locally suited to carry on road work.
>   Logan Waller Page, 1915

PRESIDENT JACKSON'S Maysville Turnpike veto in 1830 fatally weakened the case for national involvement in road building for much of
the nineteenth century. However, by the end of the century new interests would begin to make the case for a national policy. This renewed
interest led to the establishment within the USDA of an Office of Road
Inquiry in 1891, an important focal point for groups, bureaucrats, and
politicians interested in creating national highway policy.[1] This office,
later renamed the Bureau of Public Roads (BPR), would play a key role
in developing a network of allies and supporters, at both the national
and state levels, in order to advance the highway-building agenda. The
end result was the Federal Highway Act of 1916, which created a massive (for the time) infusion of national funding into state governments,
and stimulated the development of state administrative structures to
oversee this building project.

The decade following the creation of the highway program, the
1920s, was a period in which the policy goals of the program were
turned upside down. With millions of cars and trucks suddenly on the
roads, what had begun as a small and fairly limited program to serve
rural interests became one the first national programs that would ap-
proximate the internal improvement schemes proposed by Alexander

Hamilton and Henry Clay nearly a century earlier.[2] Yet despite this shift in policy goals towards national direction, the intergovernmental administrative structure of national and state partnership, with national dominance, remained intact.[3]

The BPR (and the national highway engineers who ran it) was the dominant partner until 1956 and the passage of the interstate highway program. Part of this dominance was due to the effectiveness of its leadership in the field (both professionally and politically). The BPR and its engineers developed and set construction and materials standards that were adopted by almost all of the states. The BPR played a formative role in the development of professional standards, training, and norms for highway engineering. Coupled with this technical expertise was a cultivated image of apolitical administration that enabled the BPR to create coalitions across regions and across the political spectrum, from southerners and westerners, to farmers and reformers, to railroads and national merchants. The BPR's ability to form, lead, and maintain a constantly evolving coalition of interests was critical in enabling it to maintain its influence over highway policy until 1956. Nevertheless, the administrative structure set up in this era, including decentralized planning and decision making, had complex effects on society, politics, and the economy.

Altruism, Economic Development, and Recreation: Interest Group Activity

As in the case of food and drug regulation, interest groups were important in finding and creating an issue that the public and key politicians could understand and support. Under the rhetorical and organizing umbrella of "good roads," a variety of disparate interest groups ranging from urban recreational enthusiasts (bicycles and then early automobiles), to agricultural reform movements such as the country life movement, to more prosaic railroad and commercial firms, were unified and mobilized.

For example, supporters of the country life movement, looking for ways to improve rural life and to stem what was seen as the widespread abandonment of rural America, turned towards the notion that rural life could be improved by building good roads and getting farmers "out of the mud."[4] Good roads would not only decrease the economic and social isolation of farmers, they would also help the farmer to get produce to local markets. The latter effect would also reduce the dependence of farmers on what were seen as predatory railroads. Rural interest groups such as the National Grange and the Country

Life Committee of the National Congress of Mothers expressed support for a nationally directed and subsidized good roads plan.[5] In the South, the good roads movement came to mean more than just helping the struggling, isolated farmer or stemming rural decline—good roads meant economic development and progress.[6]

Nonetheless, the origins of the good roads movement were not as altruistic as the name or its supporters would imply. The most curious aspect of the movement was its relationship to the new urban recreational bicyclists of the late nineteenth century. These bicyclists would prove to be a powerful, but short-lived force in restarting a drive for national involvement in road building.[7] In 1879, the bicyclists were organized as the League of American Wheelmen (LAW), and by 1888 began to lobby for better roads, since once these cyclists left towns, the roads were generally impassable. Led by Isaac B. Potter, the LAW initially was antagonistic towards farmers. In his work "The Gospel of Good Roads: A Letter to the American Farmer," Potter attempted to demonstrate to farmers the errors of their ways for not supporting the building of modern roads.[8] As a result of cultural and class differences, the cyclists faced initial hostility and lack of support from the farmers. Despite this hostility, bicyclists would continue to agitate for good roads. In this goal they were aided by self-interest and political serendipity.

The enactment of rural free delivery (RFD) in 1896 galvanized rural interests even more than the haranguing of urban bicyclists. Rural residents were brought face to face with the possibility that the RFD routes for which they and their representatives in the farmer's groups had fought would not be realized because of the poor state of rural roads.[9] Ironically, the very railroad industry that the farmers disliked was interested in good roads as well. The railroad industry saw the good roads movement as a way to indirectly increase railroad traffic, by aiding the distribution of goods by national mail-order merchants.[10]

Like many other crusades during the Progressive Era, organized interest groups were involved. The first of these organizations, the National League for Good Roads (NLGR) was cofounded in 1892 by General Roy Stone along with Albert Pope, a bicycle manufacturer. One year later, with the establishment of the Office of Road Inquiry, Stone would be named "Special Agent and Engineer for Road Inquiry," effectively the head of the office. In addition to the bicycle-dominated LAW and the NLGR, there appeared good roads associations in virtually every state. The goal of these organizations, which were joined by leading businessmen and reformers, was straightforward, the creation of state-controlled, or at least state-directed, roads.[11] Many of these organizations had their own publications. The most notable of these organizations was the Southern Good Roads Association, which combined the zeal of Progressivism with the gospel of good roads and economic development. All of these organizations were affiliated with the National Good Roads Association, organized in 1901. Although the American Automobile Association (AAA) was formed in 1902, it was not heavily involved in the good roads movement until much later, after Henry Ford's Model T was introduced in 1914 and the mass automobile market emerged. At that point, autos became an item of middle-class life as opposed to a hobby for the well-to-do, and the AAA discovered a much larger constituency for its services.

National associations of public officials also began to slowly form. The American Association for Highway Improvement (AAHI), established in 1910, worked with national and state legislatures and bureaucrats to create support for funding of good roads. Like the chemists' association, the BPR was intimately involved with the creation of the organization. Under auspices of the director of the BPR, Logan Page, a meeting of officials from state highway departments, representatives from good roads associations, and other interested individuals was held in Washington, DC. Page was duly elected the president of the organization.[12]

The relationship between state officials and the BPR would become even closer when, with the blessing of the BPR, state officials created the American Association of State Highway Officials (AASHO) in 1914. The purpose of AASHO was to "enab[le] full and frank consideration of questions, particularly those of a technical character untrammeled by commercialism or popular prejudices."[13] However, another split would emerge when eastern and some midwestern state and local officials unhappy with AASHO's rural orientation would create the Highway Industries Association in 1918. The road builders and related industries would also begin to organize. The builders were among the first, organizing: the American Road Makers in 1902, the National Quarry Association in 1903, the National Sand and Gravel Producers in 1911, and the National Crushed Stone Association in 1918.[14] Overseeing this sometimes fractious assembly of interests was the Bureau of Public Roads.

Building Roads in the States

Controversy over the state of public roads began during the 1870s.[15] With few exceptions, the building of roads and their maintenance was the responsibility of local government.[16] However, the fiscal and administrative institutions at the local level worked against the adoption of more efficient revenue systems to pay for new roads.[17] With road construction techniques still in their infancy, officials were wary of unduly burdening citizens with road-building projects the results of which would not last beyond a year or two. The split between rural and urban residents was also exacerbated by conflicting views of the true purpose of public roads. Rural interests wanted roads that connected individual farms to markets, while urban interests were more interested in roads that connected major urban centers. The ability of states to address these competing interests varied according to state politics, state resources, and highway bureaucrats.

Some states were successful in promoting a comprehensive highway policy. For example, New York created a state highway department and, in 1909, committed itself to a "state system of highways . . . consisting of state roads, roads constructed jointly by state and county, and town roads with state aid."[18] This commitment was backed by the issue of $50 million in bonds earmarked for the system. Other states, especially those in the South, were less successful. For example, by 1910 only 7% of roads in the South could be classified as improved.[19]

In general there were wide variations among the states in terms of fiscal and bureaucratic capacity (see table 5.1). For example, by 1905, only fourteen states had highway departments, with the majority located in the Northeast.

The states (and year established) were Massachusetts (1893), New Jersey (1894), Connecticut (1895), Rhode Island (1896), New York (1898), Vermont (1898), Pennsylvania (1903), Ohio (1904), Iowa (1904), Illinois (1905), Michigan (1905), Minnesota (1905), New Hampshire (1905), and Washington (1905).[20] Other states lagged behind these early adopters for a number of reasons. In Alabama, for example, the state legislature during the late 1890s twice failed to enact a law that would have instituted centralized state payments for roads, this despite the support of an enthusiastic state governor, railroad reformers, Populist-leaning farmers, and New South promoters.[21]

There were also critical variations in what constituted state highway aid. For example, Iowa in 1904 asserted total state control over highway development. South Dakota offered only educational and advisory services.[22] Some states like Illinois and New Mexico centralized power in a state highway commissioner or engineer overseen by a state highway board.

In many states, the centralizing of control did not occur at once. Although states like Iowa, New York, and Arizona created centralized administrative structures from the beginning, other states like Washington and Nebraska gradually shifted control over road building away from the counties and to the state.[23] Wisconsin, otherwise known for its progressive zeal, did not create a highway department

TABLE 5.1
State Highway Administration, 1916

State	Board/Commission or State Engineer/Commissioner	Highway Department (year established)	State Powers (Advisory and educational or direct delivery)	Aid to Local Governments	Civil Service	Convict Labor
Alabama	B/C	1911	Direct	X		
Arizona	E/C	1913	Direct	X		
Arkansas	B/C	1909	Advisory			X
California	B/C	1895	Direct	X		X
Colorado	E/C	1909	Direct	X		X
Connecticut	E/C	1895	Direct	X		
Delaware	E/C	1903	Advisory			
Florida	B/C	1915	Advisory			
Georgia		1908				X
Idaho	B/C	1905	Direct	X		
Illinois	B/C and E/C	1913	Direct	X	X	
Indiana		1917				
Iowa	B/C and E/C	1904	Direct			
Kansas	E/C	1911	Advisory			X
Kentucky	E/C	1912	Advisory		X	
Louisiana	B/C	1910	Direct	X		
Maine	B/C	1901	Direct	X		
Maryland	B/C	1898	Direct	X		
Massachusetts	B/C	1892		X		
Michigan	E/C	1905	Direct	X		
Minnesota	B/C	1905	Direct	X		
Mississippi	B/C	1915	Advisory			
Missouri	E/C	1907	Direct	X		
Montana	B/C	1913	Direct	X		
Nebraska	B/C	1901	Advisory			
Nevada	E/C	1909				
New Hampshire	E/C	1911	Direct	X		
New Jersey	B/C	1911	Direct	X		
New Mexico	B/C and E/C	1903	Direct	X		
New York	E/C	1891	Direct	X	X	X
North Carolina	B/C	1909	Direct	X		X
North Dakota	B/C	1898	Advisory			X
Ohio	E/C	1904	Direct	X		
Oklahoma	E/C	1911	Direct	X		X

TABLE 5.1 *(cont'd)*
State Highway Administration, 1916

State	Board/ Commission or State Engineer/ Commissioner	Highway Department (year established)	State Powers (Advisory and educational or direct delivery)	Aid to Local Governments	Civil Service	Convict Labor
Oregon	B/C	1913	Advisory			
Pennsylvania	E/C	1903	Direct	X		
Rhode Island	B/C	1902	Direct	X		
South Carolina		1917				
South Dakota	B/C	1911	Advisory			
Tennessee	B/C	1915	Direct	X		
Texas	B/C	1917	Advisory			
Utah	B/C	1909	Direct	X		X
Vermont	E/C	1898	Direct	X		
Virginia	B/C	1906	Direct	X		
Washington	B/C	1905	Direct	X		
West Virginia	B/C	1911	Advisory			X
Wisconsin	B/C	1909	Direct	X	X	
Wyoming	E/C	1911	Direct			X

Source: John Lapp, "Highway Administration and State Aid," *American Political Science Review* 10 (1916): 735–38; Leonard White, *Trends in Public Administration* (New York: McGraw-Hill, 1933): 114.

until 1911, and only provided state aid after a township submitted a petition.[24]

In eight states—Arkansas, Georgia, Kansas, North Carolina, North Dakota, Oklahoma, West Virginia, and Wyoming—the provision of state aid consisted solely of convict labor.[25] Other states—Arizona, California, Colorado, New Mexico, Utah, and the former Confederate states—offered a combination of both convict labor and state funds. Again the South stood apart, in the development of its own peculiar road-building institutions. As the warden of the Colorado system argued, the convict labor system of his state was not to be "confounded with the southern 'contract' camps, where men are sold at auction to highest bidder."[26] In the southern states, convict labor was seen not only as good for business but good for prisoners and for government.[27]

The development of bureaucratic capacity lay not only in the establishment of a highway department, but also in the capacity of a state to invest in public roads.[28] As expected, in terms of overall per capita expenditures there were some regional differences in highway spending, although given the low overall level of expenditures these difference were slight (see table 5.2). Nonetheless, even prior to the enact-

TABLE 5.2
Regional Differences in Per Capita Highway Spending, 1902 and 1915

Region	Year State Agency Created (median)	Mean Spending, 1902	Mean Spending, 1915
East	1901	.007	.06
Midwest	1910	.006	.07
South	1910	.006	.06
West	1909	.005	.07

Source: Leonard D. White, *Trends in Public Administration* (New York: McGraw-Hill, 1933), 114; Jack L.Walker, "The Diffusion of Innovations Among the American States," *American Political Science Review* 63 (1969): 880–99.

ment of the 1916 legislation, there was a tenfold increase in per capita spending on highways between 1902 and 1915. This spending was supplemented by the adoption of new sources of revenues, such as a gasoline tax (first adopted by Oregon in 1919 and by Arizona in 1921) and motor vehicle registration fees. The growing urbanization of the American population and new technology were pushing state and local governments to invest ever more heavily in newer and better roads.

Again intrastate differences developed. Wealthy, urbanized states like New York and New Jersey balanced urban and rural disputes by essentially buying off rural concerns and having the state rather than the farmers pay for the new roads.[29] This strategy, however, was less successful in some midwestern states: "rural opposition to . . . road reforms and the rural commitment to local control were even more pronounced" than in more urban states.[30] For instance, as one official of the Illinois Farm Bureau stated, "[T]here is a growing suspicion . . . that the state highway department is developing into a bureaucracy that has at heart the interests of politicians and tourists rather than those of farmers."[31] Interest groups and their bureaucratic allies had to accommodate both rural and urban interests.

Entrepreneurial Bureaucrats: The Power of Expertise

Entrepreneurial bureaucrats at both the national and state levels also played a role in knitting local highway-building efforts into a comprehensive national plan with a dense network of supporters. At the national level, the responsibility for getting "farmers out of the mud" was assigned to the Department of Agriculture, which established the Office of Road Inquiry (ORI) in 1893.[32] Under its first three directors, General Roy Stone, Martin Dodge, and Logan Page, the ORI (later the BPR) engaged itself in three activities: "build[ing] a reputation for technical knowledge, promot[ing] the gospel of good roads, and utiliz[ing] cooperation to reach those goals."[33]

The BPR engaged in a number of activities in order to build its reputation for technical knowledge, "apolitical" expertise, and professionalism. The agency created a systematized and centralized collection of statistics about the state of roads in the country. It established a new testing facility in 1900 (expanded in 1906), which became the premier research center on road-building techniques. Indeed, as testimony to its status as the primary source of standards, most state standards adopted after 1913 were largely wholesale adoptions of those recommended by the BPR.[34] In addition, a training program for junior civil engineers was begun. While some of these engineers would remain with the BPR, others went to work for state agencies. They became a cadre of experts at both the national and the state level whom the agency was able to meld into an effective bureaucratic interest group.[35] Thus, when the time came to consider legislation expanding the office or its scope, the agency was in a superior informational and strategic position.

The second activity engaged in by the agency was the promotion of the good roads gospel. The agency engaged in a continuous public relations campaign involving the publication and dissemination of thousands of bulletins, circulars, and reports, and the presentation of hundreds of speeches by agency personnel. In one year alone (1912), twenty-seven lecturers from the agency gave speeches in thirty-seven states.[36] Together with the BPR, the rail industry conducted a moving good-roads promotional campaign across rural America.[37] Public relations for the agency were also conducted through its association with a variety of lobbying groups. These associations could much more easily represent the agency's interests to the public; to other, possibly, rival interest groups; and to Congress.[38]

The third activity the agency would engage in was cooperation. One type of cooperation was aiding groups at the state level by providing model legislation for state aid to roads. In addition, the agency played a key role in encouraging the setting up of state highway departments. Like their colleagues in the good roads organizations at the state level, national administrators found it easier to work with a limited number of actors rather than countless local authorities. By aiding in the creation of state agencies, the BPR created and strengthened a set of institutionalized supports for the agency. Alliances were also made with other national government agencies such as the forest program through an agreement to build roads for the national forests; and an agreement with the Post Office in 1906 to aid in inspecting roads for communities that had been rejected for rural free delivery program because of the conditions of their roads.[39]

The public relations and expertise components of the bureau came together in the conduct of numerous demonstration programs. One of these was the "object-lesson construction program." These demonstration projects, done in response to local requests, entailed the building of small sections of roads using the latest techniques. The object-lesson program was particularly popular, starting with two projects in 1897, twenty-nine in 1899, and fifty-seven in 1909 (see table 5.3). Partially as a result of these activities the agency's budget steadily increased from $14,000 in 1901 to $35,000 in 1905 to $279,000 in 1914.

Legislative History

Woodrow Wilson's election in 1912 marked the first time a Democratic president and a Democratic-controlled House shared power since Grover Cleveland's presidency in the 1890s. Democrats gained control of the House in the 62nd Congress (1911–13) for the first time since the 53rd Congress (1893–95). The Democrats also made impressive gains in the Senate, picking up ten seats and narrowing the Republican majority to 7 seats. This new partisan environment created a new window of opportunity for interest groups, their bureaucratic allies, and their congressional patron, Sen. John Bankhead (D-AL) and Rep. Dorsey Shackleford (D-MO).

In March 1912, Shackleford introduced a bill (H.R. 22851) to authorize spending $25 million per year of fiscal surplus to improve and maintain rural postal delivery routes. This bill passed in the House by voice vote, but failed to come up for a vote in the Senate. Shackleford then attached a $500,000 experimental appropriation to the Post Office Appropriation Bill (37 Stat. 551). The rider was approved in the House by a vote of 240 to 86. The appropriation provided matching funds to the states, on a two (national) to one (state) dollar basis, for the "improvement of certain selected post roads." The secretary of agriculture in cooperation with the postmaster general would spend the funds. Both were required to report back to Congress in one year with results and recommendations about the advisability of national aid for improvement of postal roads. The legislation, however, did not specifically allocate to either agency administrative funds for carrying out the act.

The 1912 legislation also authorized the appointment of a Joint Committee on Federal Aid to Post Roads (later cochaired by Shackleford) of five senators and five representatives to investigate and report back

TABLE 5.3
Object Roads Activity, Selected Years

Fiscal Year	Object-Lesson Roads	Agency Appropriations (dollars)
1897	7	8,000
1898	10	8,000
1899[a]	4	8,000
1900	7	8,000
1901	14	14,000
1902	15	14,000
1903[b]	8	30,000
1904	17	35,000
1905	21	35,000
1906	17	35,000
1907	16	70,000
1908	18	70,000
1909	57	87,390
1910	49	116,460
1911	52	116,460
1912	31	160,720
1913	–	202,120
Total	343	1,039,150

Source: *Congressional Record*, 62nd Cong., 3rd sess., vol. 49, pt. 3, February 11, 1913, p. 3000.
[a] ORI became Office of Public Road Inquiries.
[b] Name changed to Office of Public Roads.

to Congress on the issue of national aid to highways. Not surprisingly, in its report submitted to Congress in 1915, the committee endorsed "the need and desirability of Federal aid and its constitutionality."[40]

Although both severely constrained in both size and scope, the 1912 act is notable for three reasons. First, by funding the program through the Post Office, the program broke a lingering constitutional hesitation on the part of Congress over whether the national government ought to be involved in financing roads (that is, whether the national government should expand its scope).

Second, once the notion that the national government could play a role in road building took hold, the primary point of contention was the degree of national involvement and the allocation of monies. Should the national government play the lead role in building highways, reflecting its experience with the Army Corps of Engineers? Highway bureaucrats argued against this possibility; one senior official remarked: "one is staggered by the problem of creating an organization to carry on, from a central office in Washington, the economical maintenance of a million and a quarter odd miles spread from the Atlantic to the Pacific."[41]

The incapacity of a relatively small (approximately 250-person) agency to engage in a massive program of road building was clear. Yet there were fears that simply giving the monies to the states without oversight was a sure recipe for fraud and abuse. This fear was not unwarranted given the degree of patronage and amateur policymaking at the state level, and given the possible negative consequences in terms of reelection of members of Congress. In addition, how could the USDA, the BPR, and their allies ensure that road funds went to farmers and not urban interests? As currently written, the bill could not adequately satisfy these concerns.

In January 1914 (63rd Congress), Shackleford introduced H.R. 11686, a bill for the appropriation of $25 million for rural post roads.[42] The House Rules Committee refused to grant a special rule to consider the Shackleford bill. Debate started on February 6 with one hundred members scheduled to give speeches. Although Republicans stood to benefit from the bill, members such as Rep. Sereno Payne (R-NY) denounced it as a measure that "would break [the] treasury."[43] In February, the bill was passed in the House by a 284 to 42 vote.[44] Despite the considerable support the measure had in the House, it ran into resistance in the Senate. Senators such as Reed Smoot of Utah denounced the bill as "pork for the barrel measure."[45] In the meantime, interest groups and state officials lobbied the Senate for the bill's passage. Indeed, during the year that followed, governors of southern and western states sent telegrams to President Wilson endorsing national aid for highways.

In July, an alternative good roads bill, the "Bourne plan" was reported out of the Senate Committee on Post Offices and Post Roads on an eight to four vote. Under this plan, the national government would issue $500 million in bonds to raise funds for loans to the states. This compromise reflected the diversity of views in the Senate, from those who saw highways as a raid on the Treasury, to those who favored a more national approach. In the latter case, Senator Lane of Oregon proposed that the national government, via the Army Corps of Engineers, actually undertake the construction of highways. In the end, Bourne's compromise died on the floor. The enactment of a national highway bill would have to wait until the next Congress.

In the 64th Congress, the House Committee on Roads (newly appointed) reported out H.R. 7617, a bill introduced by Representative Shackleford, its current chair.[46] The measure—which again proposed $25 million for highway aid—was, according to the *New York Times*, "drawn [so as to] apply to all Congressional districts, thereby making it a vote-getter."[47] The highway bill was not the only distributive measure of the session. The Rivers and Harbor Committee considered a $40 million spending measure, while the Public Buildings Committee was considering an omnibus buildings bill.

To allay concerns about protecting the interests of the states and rural areas, the legislation lodged a considerable amount of control in the hands of the BPR and its state highway department allies. In addition to this implementation power, another innovation was introduced: the attachment of national "strings" to the grants. Under this legislation, grants to states would be conditioned on compliance with the eight-hour labor law (Adams Act), prohibition of convict labor, regulation of hand labor methods, and the requirement that minimum wages be paid to workers.[48] Not everyone was happy with the level of national government administrative requirements in this legislation and in future highway legislation. For example, the *New Republic* condemned the 1916 road bill as "another step in the conversion of state governments into subordinate and parasitic administrative agents in the carrying out of national policies."[49]

Although denounced again as a "humbug and a pork barrel" by Republicans such as Rep. Edmund Platt (R-NY), the highway bill experienced relatively little opposition and passed in the House on a 281 to 81 vote, after an amendment was passed on a voice vote that reduced the national share from 75% to 50% of the funding.[50]

The bill then moved to the Senate, where there was a struggle over committee jurisdiction. Originally the bill had been referred to the Committee on Agriculture, but the Senate Committee on Post Offices and Post Roads, chaired by Sen. John Bankhead (D-AL), claimed and received jurisdiction over the bill after a motion to discharge was approved by forty-two to thirty vote.[51] In March the committee reported out a substitute bill. This bill, according to an early analysis of the program by Thomas McDonald, was "framed by the National Association of Highway Engineers" and provided for more "national supervision and control of the public roads of the United States."[52] The Senate debated this bill for three days and then on April 20 adjourned without reaching a final vote.[53] Bankhead then attempted to get unanimous

TABLE 5.4
Federal Highway Act Grants by Region

Region	Mean	Minimum	Maximum
Northeast	1.10	0.14	3.78
Midwest	1.79	0.25	12.25
South	1.18	0.51	5.28
West	2.13	0.36	6.41
Total	1.56	0.14	12.25

Source: "Nearly $4,000,000 For New York By New Road Law," New York Times, July 9, 1916: 3.

consent to a vote for his measure. Senator Lodge blocked this attempt. However, another vote was taken and Bankhead's bill went forward. A number of alternative funding schemes were voted upon, but in the end, the act passed the Senate by a unanimous vote. In conference committee, the Bankhead bill was substituted for the House bill, and on July 11, the Federal Highway Act of 1916 (39 Stat. 355) became law.

Highway Policy from 1916 through the 1920s

The act appropriated $5 million a year annually in grants-in-aid to the states up to a total maximum of $25 million by 1921. States would match each national dollar with a dollar of their own, thus paying 50% of all project costs. The legislation also included a number of administrative requirements such as requiring states to establish state highway departments or commissions by 1921. Unlike rivers and harbors legislation, the location of road locations and the standards to be used were delegated by Congress to the secretary of agriculture in conjunction with the states. In addition, all other regulations needed for carrying out the provisions of the act were left to the Department of Agriculture (which in turn consulted with the states). Although each state's maximum allotment was determined by formula based on area, population, and miles of rural postal routes, in actuality, the amount of money received by a state was determined by that state's contribution. To protect rural interests, the act also prohibited expenditures in communities of more than 2,500 people.

The funding formula reflected a wide range in monies that would be received by the states (see table 5.4). Overall, the mean per capita grant was $1.56. Western and the midwestern states were winners in this respect with respective mean per capita grants of $1.79 and $2.13. As many of the western states were sparsely settled or contained a high percentage of land owned by the national government, they benefited from a formula that essentially paid for highways by the mile. The South did not do as well as one might have predicted based on the strength of its representation in Congress. This could reflect the reluctance of southern states to engage in any form of government activity, or simply the incapacity of southern state governments to build roads despite this additional infusion of monies.

The Federal Highway Act of 1921 and the First Golden Age of Highways

World War I exposed the fundamental weakness of the nation's road transportation network, and the administrative limitations of the states. Despite the creation of a Railroads' War Board, the rail system proved disastrously inadequate to handle the volume of people and materials being transported or shipped across the country. The roads provided no relief. Beyond the fact that many of the existing roads did not connect major cities, their conditions already marginal, plunged in a muddy quagmire with the onset of spring and heavy truck traffic. The onset of the war limited the number of people and materials available for road building. Of the 527 projects (with 6,249 miles) that had been proposed, only 5 projects (totaling 17.6 miles) had been completed.[54] As the president of the AASHO would state in 1919,

> They [expected] the states which had no highway organizations three or even two years ago . . . to build instantly hundreds of miles of modern roads costing millions upon millions of dollars. In the older States in the highway game, better prepared with organizations and contractors and with some knowledge of materials and construction conditions, they [asked] us to double, triple, or quadruple our annual output of roads.[55]

The battle for the act's reauthorization in 1921 reflected frustration with the states, regional divisions that had largely been dampened by the BPR during the 1916 debate, as well as the continued debate over purpose. Should national funding for roads be for local interests, or should national funding reflect national interest(s)? Northeastern states, with the support of the National Highways Association, pushed for a more unified, nationally directed system. With urban road networks largely in place, these states were hampered by the highway act's restrictions on aid to urban areas.

In addition to these regional divisions, there were intense lobbying efforts from major actors such as the automobile and related industries (organized as the Highway Industries Association [HIA]). With the number of autos on the road in the tens of millions, auto manufacturers and road builders were eager to begin a massive road construction program. To buttress their arguments, these critics pointed to the disastrous experience of World War I.

The pro-nationalization supporters, aided by the National Highways Association, pressed hard for legislation that would reflect the need for a more comprehensive national highway policy. The BPR, however, remained unmoved by these pro-nationalization arguments. In the end, what tipped the debate to the agency's side, and against direct national involvement, was the close relationship its director maintained with the chairs of the Senate and House committees in charge of reporting out the highway legislation, and the ability of the BPR to marshal its supporters now located in state governments across the nation.

The Federal Highway Act of 1921 was a compromise between pronationalization advocates and proponents of continued state control. With the grant system left intact, the national government kept its distance from any notion of taking direct national control. States still matched national funds on a one-to-one basis, and continued to choose the routes that would be funded by the act. This gain in scope, however, was also linked to a broader oversight role given to the Bureau of Public Roads. States were now required to set aside 7% of their nationally funded roads. These roads were required to be connected to other nationally funded roads across county and state lines. Although not as extensive as pro-nationalization advocates had hoped, the "7 percent system" provided the rough beginnings of a truly national highway system.

With the reauthorization of the bill out of the way, the 1920s became the first golden age of highway building in the United States. From 1922 to 1929, thousands of miles of roads were built. Part of this growth was due to the exponential explosion in numbers of cars and trucks on the road. In 1910, approximately 10,000 cars were on the road. By 1920, that would increase to 8 million, and by 1930 it would increase to 23 million. The growth in trucks followed a similar trajectory, with 10,000 registered in 1910, a million in 1920, and 3.4 million by 1929.

In the face of this massive growth in supply of and demand for roads, President Coolidge's calls for restraint in government spending, and in particular curbing the growth of intergovernmental programs, were largely ineffectual. Unlike the Sheppard-Towner Act, highway spending enjoyed widespread, bipartisan appeal. This support was echoed at the state level. By 1929, it was estimated that the majority of the debt held by states was due to highway spending. This debt would later come back to haunt the states with the collapse of the national economy and the onset of the Great Depression. The states, some reluctantly, others desperately, turned to Congress for assistance, especially as the fiscal toll of the Great Depression began to be felt on both citizens and state governments.

The New Deal Highways

The federal highway program was a critical early source of funding for fiscally strapped states. Spending on highways increased from $92 million in 1924 to $285 million in 1936.[56] Initially, this massive increase in spending on highways was not a planned orderly response to economic crisis. Rather it was seen as a stopgap solution to what was seen as a short-term economic problem. Calls from state governors to increase federal funding were resisted by President Hoover and Thomas McDonald, the commissioner of the Bureau of Public Roads. McDonald argued that increased federal aid for highways "would only result in the Federal Government paying more and the State Government less," essentially gutting the intent of the federalist highway system.[57] Thus, besides a concern for the national budget, McDonald's position may have stemmed from a reluctance to have his agency's technocratic focus shifted away from road building to an emergency fiscal rescue measure for the states.

Despite this resistance on the part of the Hoover administration, increasing highway spending became the desperate solution seized upon by state legislators and governors and their national political counterparts. In 1930 Congress authorized the Emergency Construction Act, which advanced $80 million to the states for highway construction, with the funds to be used in lieu of state matching funds. By 1932, with the situation growing more critical, Hoover softened his opposition to emergency spending and acceded to the passage of the Emergency Relief and Construction Act (1932). The act authorized the Reconstruction Finance Corporation to distribute approximately $300 million in relief funds. The RFC was authorized to make loans for self-liquidating public works projects; to provide loans to states building bridges for railroads, railways, or highways; and to assist states in providing relief and work to the needy and unemployed.[58]

The historical legacy of the first New Federalism could be seen in the administration of funds. Congress, in an attempt to limit state discretion over the use of funds (i.e., in order to ensure that funds would be used for public works projects or emergency relief, as opposed to plugging state budget holes), required that states "swear to the necessity of such funds" and certify that state resources "then available and which can be made available" were inadequate.[59] Although control over the funds was given to the governors, the governors were required to file reports with the RFC. Other administrative "strings" were also attached: a prohibition against the use of convict labor, the requirement of a thirty-hour workweek, and employment preference to former service men with dependents. The requirements for highway spending were even more explicit, including the requirement that state highway departments establish minimum wage rates. Despite the promise of help, the response of the RFC was slow, creating complaints from the states about the excessive red tape of Washington. Nonetheless, the increase in highway spending was successful in putting people back to work. By June 1932, approximately 500,000 people were employed on highway projects.

The new Roosevelt administration continued the use of highway spending as a relief and economic stimulus tool. The National Industrial Recovery Act of 1933 appropriated $400 million for road construction in the form of outright grants to the states. The Federal Emergency Relief Administration (FERA) in 1933 continued the federalist legacy of matching grants coupled with administrative oversight. Half of the program's funding ($250 million) was distributed on a three-dollar to one-dollar matching basis, while the other half was distributed at the discretion of the FERA administrator, who moved aggressively to distribute funds to the states.[60] Thus, unlike the RFC, which had taken months to distribute its funds, FERA distributed over $270 million in its first six months. Even more importantly, unlike Hoover's program, the money advanced was in the form of grants, not loans, to the states.

The subsequent "alphabet" programs of the New Deal soon followed the use of FERA as well as NIRA to stimulate economic spending via highway construction. For example, the Public Works Administration (PWA) spent over $1 billion on highways, while the Works Project Administration spent $3.69 billion.[61] It was estimated that from 35% to 45% of all federal workers on relief were on road-building projects.[62] Indeed, the impact of national government spending was so great that at its height, in 1939, 53% of the states' total road expenditures were contributed by the national government.

Ultimately, with the success of highway spending as fiscal stimulus, Roosevelt would argue that highway spending should come under the oversight of the Bureau of the Budget, rather than be accomplished through automatic renewal in Congress. Although Roosevelt would

lose the battle, it did presage the role of highways as an important part
of the fiscal strategy of the national state, as opposed to the original
view of highway building as a response to pressure from agricultural
interest groups. In addition, it also symbolized the end of the Bureau
of Public Roads' preeminence in setting highway policy along with its
state highway department allies.

The Roosevelt administration inaugurated two changes in highway
administration that would later prove significant. Congress in the Hayden-Cartwright Act of 1934 determined that, starting in 1936, the administrative umbrella governing highway building was to encompass
municipal as well as county highway departments, thus weakening
the strong links between the Bureau of Public Roads and state highway
departments. Second, the Hayden-Cartwright Act restricted the national government's contributions to the highway construction programs of states that restricted the use of funds raised from gasoline
and motor vehicle taxes. This was to stop states from using national
highway monies for purposes other than road building or maintenance. Despite this restriction, the legislation also mandated that no
state would in any case lose more than one-third the amount to which
it was entitled.[63] While this change would finally allow nonrural areas
to benefit from national funds, it would also remove funding from
highway out the control of state legislatures and further into the hands
of state and national highway bureaucrats. In the end, this arrangement would also create the basis for future criticism of the intergovernmental system: multiple governments that frequently worked at odds
with each other, producing policy that more often than not was fragmented and disjointed.

Despite this latest development, strong bonds of cooperation still
largely held between the national level and the states. The national
government only rarely threatened to suspend or withdraw funds.
Only in one instance did the Bureau of Public Roads actually withdraw
certification from a state. This happened in 1935, when the governor
of Georgia, Eugene Talmadge, refused to follow national guidelines in
making appointments to the state highway commission.[64]

Nonetheless, cooperation between the national level and the states,
while cordial, was not effective in the view of contemporary critics. By
the 1940s, critics of the highway establishment were arguing that the
bureau had not been forceful in creating a more uniform system of
road building that was capable of handling the new traffic demands
being placed upon it.[65] Not only was the federalist policy structure that
successfully bridged the limited government of the nineteenth century
and the expansiveness of the early twentieth century discredited only
forty years later, the criticism, ironically, was that national bureaucrats

had failed to assert more power. More power would be handed to the BPR and the states with the passage of the Interstate Highway Act. The hegemony of the engineers would come to a decisive end in the 1960s as new movements such as environmentalism spearheaded a citizen revolt against highway building. The age of massive highway building would draw to a close amidst the upheavals of the 1960s and 1970s.

Chapter Six

From Healthy Babies to the Welfare State:
The Sheppard-Towner Act of 1921

> The extent to which the Federal Government
> can legislate in regard to children is limited . . .
> it has nothing to do with legislation directly
> affecting infant mortality, the birth rate,
> physical degeneracy, orphanage, juvenile
> delinquency and juvenile courts, and desertion
> and illegitimacy. There is a dispute as to its
> constitutional power to legislate in regard to
> child labor. The future may see a gradual and
> great extension of federal power. Such I believe
> to be inevitable as well as desirable. The
> country, though large, is by means of
> communication so closely knit together that in
> many things state lines are a hindrance and
> state legislation an obstacle to achieving results.
>   Hon. Herbert Parsons (R-NY), 1909

By 1920, YEARS of experience with intergovernmental policies such as the Pure Food and Drug Act and the Federal Highway Act now provided a model for those interested in expanding the scope of national government. Accordingly, when two prominent Progressive women reformers, Florence Kelly and Lillian Wald, cast about for ways to focus government's attention and funding on the problems of women and children, they used a intergovernmental policy model as their inspiration.[1]

Like the Pure Food and Drug Act and Federal Highway Act, the enactment of the Sheppard-Towner Act in 1921, rested upon the entrepreneurial activities of a national government bureaucracy, allied with state and local officials, and united with a diverse cross-sector and cross-national network of interest groups. In the case of Sheppard-Towner, its bureaucratic champion would be the Children's Bureau.[2] Key to the success of both the Children's Bureau and its legislative offspring, the Sheppard-Towner Act, would be an alliance of women's groups organized at the local, state, and national levels that would comprise a remarkable, for its day, cross-section of political, professional, economic, and ethnic groups.

For the Sheppard-Towner Act, however, the specifics of its conception and death would rest in the hands of political timing and context. Although the act was passed in an era characterized by growing ideological conservatism and reaction to Progressive expansion, as typified by the calls for a return to "normalcy," and renewed Republican Party dominance, the potential of the women's vote can do much to explain its passage.

The enactment of the legislation and its later denouement was critically linked to partisan and electoral calculations surrounding the potential impact of the women's vote, newly established by the ratification of the Nineteenth Amendment in 1920. As they did in the case of the pure food crusade, women's groups mobilized at the local, state, and national levels to persuade national legislators to enact a policy deemed essential to America's well-being *and* to securing the electoral support of women.

In addition to electoral considerations, the enactment of Sheppard-Towner also rested on a sense of familiarity with the structure of the proposed legislation. By the time of its enactment, Congress was more comfortable with the intergovernmental policymaking structure that was becoming characteristic of the first New Federalism. Thus the Sheppard-Towner Act's characteristics—weak national regulatory power coupled with strong state and local control—may have limited its threat to concerned legislators and opposing interests, thus increasing congressional support.

A "Female Dominion": The Establishment of the Children's Bureau

If the national government could create and fund a program examining the effects of the boll weevil on crops, why couldn't the government spend money on a more important national resource, the health of American mothers and their children? This was the argument put forward by Kelley and Wald and echoed by other Progressive female reformers.

Legislation creating the Children's Bureau was enacted in 1912.[3] The establishment of a national Children's Bureau was the result of an intense three-year-long lobbying effort by women's groups such as the General Federation of Women's Clubs and policy groups such as the National Child Labor Committee (NCLC). Organized as both state federations and as local clubs, they proved to be uniquely successful. As in the pure food crusade, from which a number of leaders, such as

Frances Kelley, emerged, they used the techniques of investigation, publicity, and lobbying to push hard for their agenda at the various levels of the political system. This approach dovetailed with their structure because many of them were organized along federated lines. Local and state chapters worked on their own, in conjunction with other chapters, and with the national organization itself.[4]

Although the supporters of the Children's Bureau claimed to be protecting the interests of American families and the nation's future, the legislation faced two important sources of opposition to the creation of the agency. The first source came from groups and legislators who thought that the bureau would promote not just child labor laws, given the NCLC's support, but also an expansion in the powers of the national government over areas that were traditionally deemed under the control of state police powers or the individual family. The second, and in some ways more important source of opposition, was from critics who ridiculed the notion that government bureaucrats, especially if they were single, professional women, could act as a source of expert knowledge on child rearing, health, and hygiene. Because of the dominance of women in the field and in the organization, the Children's Bureau's expertise-based claim over its policy domain would be continually contested by other professional and expert groups (such as physicians) and bureaus (such as the Public Health Service). In this way it differed from the Bureau of Chemistry and the Bureau of Public Roads.

The legislative struggle for the establishment of the Children's Bureau formally began with the 1909 White House Conference on the Care of Dependent Children. This conference, attended by two hundred representatives of various organizations, was followed by House hearings. Despite an initial rush of enthusiasm, Congress did not pass legislation on the matter until three years later.

The legislation creating the Children's Bureau was passed in the House, 177 to 17 (with 190 not voting); and in the Senate on 54 to 20 vote (with 17 not voting).[5] The result of the legislative struggle was the creation of a bureau with the charge "to investigate and report . . . upon all matters pertaining to the welfare of children and child life among all classes of our people." The legislation also enumerated the number (fifteen) and the salaries of the Bureau's staff, and forbade any representative of the bureau to, "over the objection of the head of the family, enter any house used exclusively as a family residence."

Once appointed as bureau head, Julia Lathrop, like Harvey Wiley and General Roy Stone, searched for allies and a mission. Given the bureau's restricted but somewhat ambiguous mandate, Lathrop, in consultation with others, decided to focus on two areas: infant mortality and birth registration.[6] In a speech before the national convention of the General Federation of Women's Clubs, Lathrop argued that this targeted approach would enable the bureau to engage in a process of "intelligent lifesaving."[7]

Despite the less than welcoming political atmosphere, with the creation of the Children's Bureau the primarily women's interest groups, like the pure food groups and the automobile clubs, had achieved a critical milestone of the first New Federalism: the creation of an ally on the inside of national government that could act as a focal point for future policymaking and implementation.

The Creation of an Intergovernmental Network

From its creation in 1912 to the enactment of the Sheppard-Towner Act in 1921, the Children's Bureau, like the USDA's Bureau of Public Roads and the Bureau of Chemistry, engaged in a wide variety of promotional activities in its two focus areas of birth registration and infant mortality. A focus on birth registration was seen as a way to increase constituency contacts and thus was the "lubricant necessary to accomplish the larger purposes of the Bureau."[8] When the bureau's campaign began in 1915, only ten states required birth registrations. After four years, thirteen mores states required birth registrations. Despite these gains, twenty five states did not require registrations.

The drive to lower infant mortality was also conducted via public campaigns. These promotional activities ranged from the holding of baby contests and baby weeks, to the sponsoring of child health conferences.[9] The latter, conducted much in the same way as the good roads "object lesson demonstration roads," relied on a traveling exhibits and experts. In each local area, the bureau—after coordinating with state agricultural extension officials, local public health officials and other local elites—would conduct well-baby conferences with individual mothers and their infants. Another aspect of the bureau's promotional activities, in keeping with its goal to lower infant mortality, was its popular series of baby and childcare pamphlets and publications sent to thousands of women.[10]

The intergovernmental structure of the USDA's extension service was the ideal working model for the work of the Children's Bureau.[11] Institutionalization via an intergovernmental structure would ensure that professional reformers and bureaucrats, inculcated with common values, would implement the right child welfare policy goals.[12] Later, the network of Children's Bureau supporters ensconced at different levels of government, and sharing the same values and goals, would prove to be a valuable tool in sustaining child welfare policy options in the aftermath of Sheppard-Towner's demise, and prior to the New Deal legislation that would resurrect it.

Intergovernmental administrative structures also reflected the imperatives of bureaucratic success in a federalist state: the need to link a national agency with networks of private and public organizations at the state and local levels. According to Lathrop, "[N]ot only would this approach extend the organizational reach of the Bureau, it would also give it a means to lobby Congress effectively for increased appropriations, just as the USDA's networks were able to do so."[13]

Creating State Partners

The bureau's initial goal of developing institutional linkages with the states did seem to be successful. For example, between 1910 and 1915, only five states had created child hygiene departments.[14] Between 1916 and 1920, however, twenty-eight more states created departments. Indeed, as Robyn Muncy argues, the bureau had such "unexpected" power and authority over state agencies, "which acted as the Bureau's subsidiaries," that by 1920, the "Bureau received quarterly reports on budgets, legislation and programs from the state divisions."[15]

Despite this seeming bureaucratic solidarity, the actual power and consent of these state departments varied. For example, Indiana, Nebraska, New York, North Dakota, Oregon, Pennsylvania, South Dakota, and West Virginia were the only states that appropriated or designated funds for permanent staff.[16] Of these eight states, two supplied only token ($500) funds to these agencies. The vast majority of these agencies primarily existed to collect facts, publicize conditions, promote cooperation between state agencies, and report back to either the governor or the state legislature. Finally, twelve states did not create a state department until after 1921 and the enactment of Sheppard-Towner.

In the end, as the cases of both pure food and drug regulation and highway building have shown, national bureaucrats had uneven support from the states. In the case of the Children's Bureau, this unevenness was attenuated by the far weaker and fragmented position child welfare departments held in the state governments.

Indeed, despite its promotional activities and the forging of an intergovernmental policy network, the Children's Bureau was beset by some fundamental weaknesses. Unlike the Bureau of Chemistry or the Office of Road Inquiry, the Children's Bureau was not under a cabinet agency such as the USDA, which was noted for efficiency and professionalism.[17] Instead, because of its roots in the child labor struggle, and to control any attempt at future regulatory power, the Children's Bureau was located within the fairly weak Department of Labor.

In addition to this organizational issue, strategic choices made by Lathrop and her successors foreclosed some of the options available to other national bureaus. For example, after the Children's Bureau was created, to appease critics, and to distance it from further political attack, Lathrop, the new head of the bureau, made a strategic choice to focus on issues less divisive than child labor, such as health and education.[18] Unlike the Bureau of Chemistry, which captured a role for itself in the struggle for pure food and drug legislation, the brief thirteen-month interlude of enforcing the Keating-Owen Child Labor Act of 1916 (until it was the ruled unconstitutional in 1918) did not give the Children's Bureau the institutional leverage that could come from acting as creator and enforcer of regulatory standards. With neither funds nor regulations to offer, the bureau was unable to create a set of strong, parallel, and durable interests in the states, and thus the means to indirectly lobby Congress as the state-level food and drug officials did for the Pure Food and Dug Act, and the state highway departments for the Federal Highway Act.

Nevertheless, despite these shortcomings, the bureau and its allies continued to work for an expansion in services for mothers and children. The establishment of the Children's Bureau created a focal point for further advocacy on the part of women's groups. More importantly, it created and further legitimated a framework for national action, irrespective of whether that action was coordination or supervision.

The Struggle for Sheppard-Towner

In the Children's Bureau's 1917 annual report, Julia Lathrop called for the establishment of a grant-in-aid program for preventive maternal and child health care.[19] In the report Lathrop called for a program of grants to the states. Whereas the intergovernmental strategy was implicit in the establishment of the Children's Bureau, it was explicit in Lathrop's report. Citing the example of the Smith-Lever Act of 1914 (which had extended agricultural extension work), the 1919 annual report argued, "On exactly the same plan of Federal Aid stimulating and standardizing State and local activities, the well-being of mother and child, a basic natural economy, may be secured."[20]

Lobbying for the Sheppard-Towner Act rested upon the interest group support mobilized by and for the Children's Bureau. Under the leadership of the Women's Joint Congressional Committee an impressive array of interest groups was marshaled to support the bill. The following brief list of groups gives a glimpse of the coalition building engaged in by the Children's Bureau and its reformer allies: General Federation of Women's Clubs, National Consumer's League, National League of Women Voters, National Women's Trade Union League, National Congress of Mothers and Parent-Teacher Associations, American Association of University Women, Women's Christian Temperance Union, National Federation of Business and Professional Women's Clubs, National Council of Jewish Women, American Home Economics Association, League of Women Voters, and the Young Women's Christian Association. This coordination of groups was described as "the most widespread and popular lobby that probably has ever visited this city [i.e., Washington, D.C.]."[21] This outpouring of interest group support again flowed along federated (local, state, and national) lines.

Despite widespread support from women's groups and other Progressive groups, opposition came from a number of interest groups. One source of resistance to maternal and child health policy came from those who opposed the feminist agenda behind the act. In particular, anti-suffragists (both women and men) and their groups, such as the National Association Opposed to Woman Suffrage, "having lost one battle . . . determined to lose the war" against expanding the role of women.[22] The brunt of the opposition, however, came from groups like the American Medical Association and its state affiliates, who were hostile not only to the Sheppard-Towner Act, but to any change in health policy not directed by them.[23] Beginning in 1919 throughout the 1920s, the AMA "passed resolutions condemning [the act] . . . as a step toward state or socialized medicine, as a weakening of state and local power, and as an excuse for increased taxation."[24]

Legislative History

A Maternal and Child Health Act was first introduced in Congress in 1918 (Wilson's last term) by Rep. Jeannette Rankin, the first congresswoman.[25] With Wilson's term coming to a painful close, the bill did not even come up for a vote. After Warren Harding's decisive victory over Democratic governor James Cox of Ohio, another bill (H.R. 10925) introduced in the 66th Congress generated little support, and it too died in the House.[26]

However, with the ratification of the Nineteenth Amendment still fresh, and in the face of upcoming congressional elections, the political calculus changed. A window had opened up in the 67th Congress for the passage of some kind of maternal and child health bill. A new bill, S. 1039, would be sponsored by Sen. Morris Sheppard, a Democrat from Texas, and Rep. Horace Mann Towner, a Republican from Iowa.[27]

In many ways, Sheppard and Towner were typical of the new modern Congress. Senator Morris Sheppard was a representative of the solid Democratic South. After serving twelve years in the House, Sheppard was elected to the Senate in 1913, serving until 1941. Politically he was a supporter of prohibition and women's suffrage. The act's sponsor in the House was Representative Towner. Elected to the House in 1912, he served until 1923. On a broader level, Congress was also well through its initial stage of modernization. The norms of seniority, reciprocity, and universalism had been mostly established. The average member spent nearly four terms in office, while turnover decreased to the nearly "modern" rate of 20%.

This greater longevity in Congress had some benefits. Despite the shift in control in Congress and the presidency back to the Republican Party in 1920, Progressive ideals and influence persisted into the early 1920s. More concretely, there was a continued presence in Congress of a coalition of Progressive southern Democrats and western Republicans who acted as a source of support for the Sheppard-Towner Act, as Sheppard's sponsoring of the legislation demonstrated.[28]

In addition to some congressional support for the bill on its own merits, there was an even larger political consideration: the emergence of women as a bloc whose voting patterns were not yet known to legislators, and the strength of the federated women's groups in lobbying national legislators.[29] Few legislators were willing to go against this new unknown electoral force. Despite this support in the House, the act was not without significant and oftentimes heated opposition.[30] As had happened in the creation of the Children's Bureau a decade earlier, members of Congress mocked the idea of "spinsters" and "old maids" having any kind of expertise.[31] Antisuffragists would oppose the legislation, as well as those who raised the argument that the proposed legislation violated constitutional principles of states' rights.[32] One particular provision of the legislation drew the ire of some opponents: that the "services provided under the Act 'be available for all residents of the State' [was] interpreted rightly, as a move toward eliminating racial discrimination."[33] In the end, it was widely acknowledged that if members of Congress had been able to secretly vote on the bill, "it would have emphatically been killed as emphatically as it was finally passed in the open."[34]

The final bill (S. 1039) was passed by large margins in both chambers in 1921.[35] On July 22, the Senate voted, 63 to 7 in the bill's favor. Despite this success in the Senate, the bill remained stuck in the House Committee on Interstate and Foreign Commerce. The chair of the committee, Samuel Winslow, was an "ardent anti-suffragist." Again paralleling their work in the pure food crusade, women's groups mobilized into action. From May through the November, they pressured the Republican Party and Harding into forcing Winslow to discharge the bill. On November 21, the House passed the bill on a 279 to 39 vote. President Harding signed the bill into law on November 23, 1921.

The enactment of Sheppard-Towner required a number of legislative compromises. Urban members of Congress, for example, insisted on a provision that would forbid discrimination against cities. Thus the original language was changed so that the program would encompass rural as well as urban areas. Meanwhile, fiscal conservatives were satisfied in decreasing the proposed funding and automatically ending the program's appropriation at the end of five years. Southerners and social conservatives wrote in requirements that limited the hiring of bureau personnel and the acquiring of facilities, disallowed the payment of benefits or the use of private social service agencies, narrowed the program's beneficiaries, and prohibited agency workers from entering the home of a child without a parent's permission.

The Structure and Implementation of Sheppard-Towner Act

The Sheppard-Towner Act distributed grants on a one-to-one dollar-matching basis to the states. The funds received by the states also included $5,000 lump sum given to all states; $5,000 to each state based on matching state funds, and a subsequent amount based on population (see table 6.1). The total amount available to each state based on each state fully matching its share of funds is shown in the table for fiscal years 1923 through 1927. While many states, like Alabama, Iowa, and Kentucky, took full or partial advantage of this funding over all the years, other states did not. Nine states either did not participate in the program at all (Illinois, and Massachusetts), or participated only sporadically (Connecticut, Kansas, Louisiana, Maine, New York, Rhode Island, Vermont). On a per capita basis, the program would give, in Lathrop's words, a "pitifully small" amount to the states (see table 6.2).

The average per capita amount was approximately three cents per person. By contrast, the highway program allotted over $1.50 per person. There was also less variation among the regions. The Northeast, because of its larger population, did obtain more funds. Again, the average differences between regions were relatively small, less than one cent. Finally, the Children's Bureau was given $50,000 for administra-

TABLE 6.1
Distribution of Funds by State (FY1923–26)

State	U.S. FY 1923–FY1927 Maximum Potential Available Funds	Amounts Granted to States			
		1923	1924	1925	1926
Alabama	$25,837	$25,837	$25,837	$25,837	$25,837
Arizona	12,254	5,000	12,254	12,254	5,000
Arkansas	21,818	6,856	16,818	13,500	14,000
California	33,112	24,279	13,115	15,620	26,730
Colorado	16,337	9,977	9,999	10,000	10,000
Connecticut	19,311	9,656			
Delaware	11,504	11,504	11,504	11,504	11,504
Florida	16,532	8,621	16,532	16,532	16,532
Georgia	29,531	11,000	15,250	28,490	19,270
Idaho	12,913	6,250	7,913	5,692	9,308
Illinois	53,739				
Indiana	29,764	24,995	26,250	25,750	25,000
Iowa	26,214	26,214	26,214	26,214	26,214
Kansas	21,933	12,097			
Kentucky	26,299	26,299	26,299	26,299	26,299
Louisiana	22,130		17,591	22,128	5,000
Maine	15,180				
Maryland	19,777	19,277	19,269	19,165	19,277
Massachusetts	35,982				
Michigan	34,741	34,741	34,741	34,741	34,741
Minnesota	26,100	26,100	26,100	26,100	26,100
Mississippi	22,077	22,077	22,077	22,077	22,077
Missouri	32,958	28,527	21,762	24,000	5,000
Montana	13,702	13,702	13,702	13,702	13,700
Nebraska	18,743	17,662	7,410	11,915	8,845
Nevada	10,522	5,000	10,522	10,522	10,522
New Hampshire	12,988	5,000	12,988	12,988	12,988
New Jersey	31,285	31,285	31,285	31,285	31,285
New Mexico	12,430	12,430	12,236	12,430	12,430
New York	80,042		80,042	80,042	80,042
North Carolina	27,260	27,260	27,260	27,260	27,260
North Dakota	14,363	6,000	6,000	8,300	5,000

TABLE 6.1 *(cont'd)*
Distribution of Funds by State (FY1923–26)

		Amounts Granted to States			
State	U.S. FY 1923–FY1927 Maximum Potential Available Funds	1923	1924	1925	1926
Ohio	48,843	11,900	17,393	26,607	43,843
Oklahoma	23,679	5,000	20,934	23,679	23,679
Oregon	15,283	8,000	15,283	15,283	5,000
Pennsylvania	68,811	68,810	68,811	68,811	68,811
Rhode Island	14,076		5,000	14,076	5,000
South Dakota	14,293	12,844	14,273	14,293	5,000
Tennessee	25,768	18,522	22,411	25,768	15,000
Texas	41,451	32,567	40,689	41,451	35,351
Utah	13,031	6,365	13,000	13,000	5,000
Vermont	12,376		2,775	5,000	5,000
Virginia	25,574	25,574	25,574	25,574	25,574
Washington	19,150	10,000	10,000	10,000	10,000
West Virginia	19,871	5,000	10,000	10,000	19,872
Wisconsin	27,752	27,750	27,752	27,752	27,752
Wyoming	11,311	5,000	11,000	6,600	6,600
Total	$1,190,003	$716,334	$877,221	$923,597	$852,799

Source: U.S. Children's Bureau, "The Promotion of the Welfare and Hygiene of the Maternity and Hygiene," 1927.

Note: Except for Illinois and Massachusetts, blank cells indicate years in which the state did not participate because of state-level legislative or executive issues. Illinois and Massachusetts refused to participate because of opposition to the program.

tive expenses, while the Office of Public Roads had no statutorily defined ceiling on administrative expenses.

The administrative requirements of the act were as follows. The act required that states develop "detailed plans" for carrying out the program. Plans were to be approved by a three-member Federal Board of Maternity and Infant Hygiene and were binding on states accepting the moneys. A state's failure to conform to approved plans was cause for withholding funds. In addition, each state had to establish an agency that would coordinate with the Children's Bureau. Each state agency would be in charge of the creation of subagencies (such as county agencies), which would administer the funds. Unlike the agricultural extension, highway, or vocational education programs also enacted during this period, the board did not have the power to im-

TABLE 6.2
Maternal and Child Health Grants by Region

Region	Mean	Minimum	Maximum
Northeast	0.036	0.003	0.139
Midwest	0.027	0.009	0.175
South	0.021	0.011	0.107
Pacific	0.025	0.004	0.078
Total	0.027	0.003	0.175

Source: Data from Grace Abbott, "Federal Aid for the Protection of Maternity and Infancy," *American Journal of Public Health* 12 (9) (1922): 737–42.

Note: Figures are dollars per capita for FY 1923.

pose national standards, such as merit requirements, on state personnel. Indeed, according to Jane Perry Clark, as a result of these constraints the administrators "were so hesitant to impose their standards on the states" that they were probably they were "probably less familiar with the work of the states than any other federal bureau administering a subsidy law"[36] Unlike the Office of Road Inquiry, the Children's Bureau was limited in its ability to build formal institutional linkages at the state level since states could determine the organizational structure of service delivery.

The act made the receiving of national funds contingent on the approval of the state legislature, or if the legislature was not in session, then on an interim basis, approval by the state governor. The acceptance by the states of the program varied: eleven states accepted by legislative enactment, while thirty-one states accepted by gubernatorial decree.[37] Of these thirty-one states, the following states did not uphold the governor's acceptance: Connecticut, Illinois, Kansas, Louisiana, Vermont, Maine, and Massachusetts. Indeed, Massachusetts went so far as to bring suit against the United States government in *Massachusetts v. Mellon*, arguing the act's unconstitutionality, an argument that the Supreme Court ultimately rejected.

Other aspects of the administrative structure of the act also restricted the building of entrenched state-level interests that characterized the highway program. For example, the act stated that no funds appropriated by any state should be used "for payment of benefits for maternity and infancy or for the purchase or repair of buildings or equipment." In addition, the federal board, usually silent and uninvolved in the running of the program, during the course of the act made two key administrative rulings: that "all infant hygiene work was to be confined to pre-school children," and that "no funds were to be used to subsidize private social or health agencies."[38]

How successful was the bureau in controlling the actions of the state agencies? A generous reading of bureau performance by Robyn Muncy argues that it was largely successful through a strategic use of the agency's "interpretive powers."[39] Indeed, the national board created by Congress to oversee the program "in no way diluted the Bureau's control . . . [the board] simply rubber-stamped the bureau's decisions on states' programs." However, according to Jane Perry Clark, in practice the control and cooperation achieved by the bureau with these state entities was largely illusory since states were "left a free and open field to determine their own lines of conduct" and the bureau "made no very great demands."[40] Indeed this weakness (or "self-effacement" as Clark tactfully called it) on the part of the bureau was due to "the fear of opposition within the states, and to a realization that the subjects of maternal welfare and infant hygiene did not permit rigid standards."

Nevertheless, the act did produce some successes. From 1921 to 1928, the Children's Bureau collected and reported the following statistics: it conducted 183,252 health conferences; established 2,978 permanent prenatal care centers; visited over 3 million homes (by visiting nurses); distributed over 22 million pieces of baby care literature; and presided over significant decreases in infant and maternal death rates.[41] Of course, the meaning of success is limited since in the end, in keeping with the prevailing ethos of localism and state control, the act only addressed those citizens deemed by the states to be eligible for the services provided by Sheppard-Towner.

The End of the Sheppard-Towner Act

Changes in the national political climate would erode the slim core of support for the act, and would ultimately lead to its demise. First, the Senate that convened in 1926 was more conservative than earlier Senates. Of the seventy-four senators who supported the bill in 1921, only thirty-two were still in office by 1927 and three of them were Democrats who changed their support to opposition.[42] These Democratic switchers reflected a deeper problem that had recently emerged within the Democratic Party. With Coolidge's election in 1924, Democrats lost whatever party cohesion they had achieved under Wilson, and began to split again between the southern and rural Democrats and the northern, urban Democrats who supported Al Smith. The 1924 presidential election signaled the emergence of conservative southern Democrats as decisive powers within the weakened party. Allying themselves with conservative Republicans, the southern Democrats sowed the roots of the conservative coalition that would decisively shape social welfare policy in the New Deal and beyond.[43] Outside of the two parties, the Progressive Farmer-Labor bloc also faced challenges both in terms of numbers in the disheartening effect of the Coolidge victory. According to Robyn Muncy, Progressives and congressional Democrats saw the Coolidge victory as a "mandate for [a] generally inactive federal government."[44] Coolidge's budget message to Congress in 1926 underscored the tenuous position of the Sheppard-Towner program and its supporters.

> I have referred in previous budget messages to the advisability of restricting and curtailing formal subsidies to the states. The maternity act offers concrete opportunity to begin this program. The states should be in a position to walk alone along this highway of helpful endeavor, and I believe it is the interest of the states and the federal government to give them the opportunity.[45]

However, all grants were not created equal. Unlike the Sheppard-Towner program, highway grants enjoyed enormous support during this same period. In short, the shift in the political winds between 1921 and 1927 led to a political environment in which "female reformers who had swum in the middle of the stream during the 1910s found themselves stranded on the left bank in the 1920s."[46]

Part of the political vulnerability of the Sheppard-Towner program lay in the institutional weakness of the Children's Bureau. The grassroots movement that had created the bureau and had advocated for the enactment of Sheppard-Towner was not strong enough in this new political environment. Without a strong, easily identifiable, and mobilized constituency at the state level, and without the ability to supply discrete or tangible benefits to draw the support of other powerful, organized groups, the bureau was unable to generate the support enjoyed by the highway program or the food and drug regulators.[47] Thus, although the Children's Bureau had been able to direct policy, its weak support from interest groups at both the national and state levels, and lack of institutional strength within the national state, limited its ability to mobilize the wide-ranging coalition needed for the renewal of the Sheppard-Towner Act.

Despite the successes of the program, and the begrudging acceptance by the states, the Sheppard-Towner Act was due to expire on January 12, 1927. Supporters mobilized again, and after being blocked in the Senate for almost eight months, a renewal bill (H.R. 7555) extending the act for two years was passed in the House by a 218 to 44 vote on April 5, 1926.[48] The renewal bill's large margin of victory in the House somewhat belies the claim that with the evaporation of the "women's vote," support for the program collapsed.[49] Nonetheless, the bill faced sustained opposition within the Senate, where conservative senators conducted a "mini-filibuster" until their demands for the end of the program were met. The bill was blocked for eight months in the Senate until a compromise could be fashioned. During this time, President Coolidge had indicated that while the act should be renewed, the appropriations should be gradually withdrawn.[50] The act was extended for two additional years, but it was scheduled to lapse in June 1929. Efforts to extend the law yet again in 1928 went nowhere, and the Sheppard-Towner Act was allowed to expire.

Toward the New Deal: Maternal and Child Health and the Children's Bureau

The expiration of the Sheppard-Towner Act and the rise of conservative Republican administrations and a Republican-controlled Congress seemed to put an end to the dreams of the Children's Bureau and its supporters. Few advocates of the program could have envisioned the program's resurrection as one of the elements of the Social Security Act of 1935 the centerpiece of America's new welfare state.

The resurrection of an intergovernmental program for maternal and child health partially rested upon a new administration's willingness to expand the nation's commitment to economic security for its citizens.[51] The resurrection of a program for child and maternal health also rested upon the ability of the Children's Bureau to sustain itself during its years in the policy wilderness of the Coolidge and Hoover administrations. The final step of the program's resurrection came from the bureau's ability to strategically leverage the intergovernmental administrative and organizational legacy that emerged from its Sheppard-Towner experience.

The history of the Social Security Act has been recounted in numerous other places; what is of concern in this case study is the role of the Children's Bureau in the formulation of the Social Security Act and more specifically the reemergence of maternal and child health as a goal of policy.

The Fight for Survival

During the Coolidge and Hoover administrations, the energies of the Children's Bureau leadership and its allies were focused on reauthorizing a maternal and child health bill. In addition, the bureau's leadership focused on beating back attempts by opponents of the bureau to either limit its scope or transfer its responsibilities to the U.S. Public Health Service (PHS). Many of the Sheppard-Towner renewal bills introduced in Congress from 1928 to 1932 involved the PHS to some degree.[52] Indeed, Hoover's willingness to support a new maternal and infant health bill rested upon the bureau and its supporters acquiescing to passing the administration of any new program to the PHS. In a 1930 White House conference on child health designed to showcase the Hoover administration's new plans, critical and vocal opposition by the bureau and women's groups blocked an attempt by Hoover to transfer all child health responsibilities to the PHS.[53] Nonetheless, while the battle—control by the Children's Bureau—was won, the war—the passage of a new bill—was lost.

Despite these setbacks, support for the program lingered on at the state level. After appropriations for Sheppard-Towner ended in 1929, legislatures of nineteen states and the Territory of Hawaii appropriated funds equal to or exceeding the combined state and national funds provided under the act. These states were Delaware, Florida, Kentucky, Maine, Maryland, Michigan, Missouri, New Hampshire, New Jersey, New Mexico, New York, North Carolina, North Dakota, Pennsylvania, Rhode Island, South Dakota, Tennessee, Vermont, Virginia, and Wisconsin.[54] This state-level institutional residue was perhaps the most important element in the program's ability to be resurrected in virtually the same form in the Social Security Act of 1935.[55]

During the rest of Hoover's presidency and with the onset of the Great Depression, the Children's Bureau set itself the task of collecting statistics that illuminated the unfolding economic crisis. The bureau collected information on the lapsing of mother's pensions as state after state faced devastating budget shortfalls. The bureau collected relief cost data from the states as well as the impact of cuts in public health spending on child and adolescent health.[56] By the time the Roosevelt administration had taken office, the Bureau had strategically positioned itself to play an important role in setting economic security policy.

The Children's Bureau and the New Deal

Franklin Roosevelt's inauguration would usher in the most sweeping changes in social welfare policy. New ideas and new voices jostled with previously existing institutions and interests. While the urgency of the depression crisis would create opportunities for new policy innovations and the assertion of broader national powers, these innovations and powers were sometimes hastily joined with policy ideas like pensions for the elderly or for mothers that had been percolating at the state level. In the face of these new challenges, the Children's Bureau would have to fight for its right to take part in the new policy landscape that was emerging, and make the case that the policy solutions crafted by Progressives could play a role in the New Deal.

To take part in this new landscape, the Children's Bureau drew upon its perennial weapons: information and people. The bureau gained a seat at the policy table by leveraging the statistical resources that it had amassed during the emerging years of the Great Depression, and by drawing upon a now significant "alumna" network of women who had been involved with the Children's Bureau or allied organizations, and who were now part of the Roosevelt administration.[57] Most notable of the alumna was Frances Perkins, the new secretary of labor, and former colleague (at the New York Consumer's League) of Frances Kelley, one of the earliest advocates for the establishment of a children's bureau. The bureau's network as well as its performance enabled the bureau to have a say in Roosevelt's Committee on Economic Security, established in July 1934.[58]

The statistics collected by the bureau not only allowed it to shape policy, they were also used to administer the $500 million FERA program. Working with FERA administrators, the bureau helped to administer the Child Health Recovery Program (CHRP) initiated in 1933. It was organized along the lines of the Sheppard-Towner program; the bureau used public and private health care and relief organizations to provide children with emergency food and medical care. The organizational structure of CHRP was typically intergovernmental: the bureau employed five physicians, with extensive consultation done with the states; the Civil Works Administration employed approximately two hundred public health nurses at the state level; and, local schools and organizations identified and distributed help to individual children.[59] Until the Security Act in 1935, the CHRP was the only relief program targeted specifically to children.

Nonetheless, despite its organizational and informational resources and the years of programmatic experience under its belt, under the Social Security Act the Children's Bureau did not achieve as much influence over policy as it had hoped.[60] Child welfare (e.g., mother's pensions) was given over to the broader category of relief effort, while the bureau was left with the much narrower domain of maternal and child health and "special needs" (e.g., crippled children's) services. Again, while the Children's Bureau had won an important battle, it had seemingly lost a larger war. Mother's pensions, the focus of much activity on the part of the bureau, were finally going to be nationally funded via the aid to dependent children (ADC) program. The bureau, however, never gained the power to administer ADC. Instead that power would eventually lie in the newly constituted Social Security Board and, given the intergovernmental legacy of the first New Federalism, the states.[61]

The Children's Bureau's New Deal success was Title V of the Social Security Act. Title V authorized grants to states for maternal and child welfare. According to Katharine Lenroot, the chief of the Children's Bureau, the child health part of the Social Security Act was "not merely a revival of the same type of service given from 1922 to 1929 but a program embracing children above the age of infancy and early childhood, as well as maternity and infancy, and stressing particularly the rural areas and the smaller communities."[62]

The new program renewed the vitality of a policy area that had suffered during the depression. In 1928, states had spent approximately $2.8 million on maternal and child health, with $1.02 million coming from the national government. By 1934, states were spending about $1.2 million. Of this amount twenty-two states reported spending half the amount spent in 1928, while nine states spent no money at all on maternal and child health.[63] The new legislation reversed this trend. Approximately $3.8 million was appropriated for maternal and child health, while $2.85 million was appropriated for crippled or physically handicapped children. In addition, $1.5 million was allocated to child welfare services, and $841,000 for vocational rehabilitation.[64]

For the Children's Bureau, the change in policy was equally dramatic. Its staff grew from 143 to 438 in the 1930s. The bureau itself was in charge of allocating $330,000 in 1930. Eight years later, this number would rise to $8.6 million, and by 1940, the number would increase to nearly $10.9 million. The new vigor of the bureau was matched by the alacrity with which states matched funds. Unlike the Sheppard-Towner program, states quickly moved to participate in the maternal and child health program. By 1936, one year after the act's passage, all forty-eight states, Hawaii, Alaska, and the District of Columbia were cooperating with the bureau.

The allocation of the funding also helped to strengthen the bureau's position. Under the legislation, the bureau would distribute a $20,000 base grant to every state, with $2.7 million allotted to states based on a ratio of the number live births in a state versus the national average. These funds would be matched on a fifty-fifty basis with the states. In addition, under Section 502(b), the bureau would receive $980,000 in funding to give direct funds to the state for "assistance in carrying out its State plan." In practice, this additional discretionary funding, later called "Fund B" grants, would increase the bureau's ability to influence state practices.

Administratively, the organization remained the same. The bureau relied on a relatively small field staff to oversee the states and provide special services as needed. The increased power of the bureau came from the state planning requirements included in the legislation. In terms of administrative requirements the position of the Children's Bureau was more enhanced. Under the Sheppard-Towner program, the administrative board was required to approve any plan that was "reasonably appropriate and adequate."[65] Under the new legislation, the standards and requirements were raised to a considerable degree in determining what constituted an adequate state plan. The new legislation provided in part that state plans had to be jointly developed between the state agency and the Children's Bureau.

In general, under the Social Security legislation, state plans were required to provide for

> (1) financial participation by the state; (2) the administration of the plan by the state health agency or the supervision of the plan by the state health agency; (3) methods of administration (other than those relating to selection, tenure of office, and compensation of personnel) as were necessary for the efficient operation of the plan; (4) reports by the state health agency as required by the secretary of labor; (5) the extension and improvement of local maternal and child health services administered by local child-health units; (6) cooperation with medical, nursing, and welfare groups and organizations; and (7) the development of demonstration services in needy areas and among groups in special need.[66]

The state planning requirements had noticeable effects on state administrative structure. Whereas in 1934 prior to the passage of the Social Security Act only thirty-one states had maternal and child health divisions, by 1936, all states and territories now had them. Where only twenty-two of the thirty-four states had full-time directors, now all states had them.[67] More importantly, the Social Security legislation and the significant increases in funding expanded the national, state, and local policy network that had traditionally supported maternal and child health.[68]

The End of the Female Dominion

The Social Security Act proved to be the last high point of the Children's Bureau. By 1946, under the Truman administration, the Children's Bureau would be transferred from the Department of Labor to the Federal Security Agency. As part of the transfer, the bureau lost its ability to administer federal funds. After this decision, the Children's Bureau that remained was a shadow of its former self. Despite this rather ignominious end, the Sheppard-Towner program was emblematic of the time that it emerged from. It was the attempt on the part of bureaucrats, experts, and interest groups to expand the size and scope of the national state. Given the policy alternatives available—intergovernmental policy or nothing at all—these groups supported the creation and the legitimation of national activity. The program also reflected and interacted with the political, institutional, and ideological constraints and opportunities of the period. Republican (and some Democratic) members of Congress struggled to reconcile their aversion to an expanded national state with the opportunities (and possible dangers) of women as a new group of highly mobilized voters. To balance these issues, Congress used intergovernmental policy to create a program that could be easily controlled by Congress and a program that could be easily undone, if need be.

Chapter Seven _____

The First New Federalism and the Governing of a New American State

> The basic political fact of federalism is that it creates separate self-sustaining centers of power and privilege, and profit which may be sought and defended as desirable in themselves, as means of leverage upon elements in the political structure above and below, and as bases from which individuals may move to places of greater influence and prestige in and out of government.
>
> David Truman, *The Governmental Process*

THE PURE FOOD AND DRUG ACT of 1906, the Federal Highway Act of 1916, the Sheppard-Towner Act of 1921—each of these legislative enactments was the product of a unique constellation of political actors operating within a given institutional context. Yet what these three policies shared was quite powerful: each was an attempt to extend the reach of the national government within a disjointed, weak, and fragmented political system. New types of administrative arrangements and procedures were developed to extend this national reach. These new administrative arrangements and procedures would have to pass muster with a judiciary that was reluctant to assent to an overt expansion of governmental power (whether at the national or state level). These new administrative structures would also have to fit the structure and logic of the congressional institutions that created them. Thus, these new administrative structures would reflect Congress's localist orientation, its limited capacity for oversight, and the national bureaucracy's limited ability to implement policy on its own.

While interest group activity and entrepreneurial bureaucrats would all play a role in the development of these policies, they were distinctively shaped by the institutional and partisan arrangements within Congress, and by the presence of a federal system. Far from being "unwieldy" or "messy," as some critics have argued, both federalism and its instrument, intergovernmental policy, reflected basic and sometimes conflicting institutional forces rooted within the American political economy. As the statistical analyses of chapter 3 demonstrated, there was a logic to the enactment and structure of the first New Federalism and the intergovernmental policy instruments created during its emergence that grew out of the American Constitution, and by extension, out of the institutional structures that shape congressional policymaking. It was also rooted within the changing preferences and incentives of actors during the national statebuilding of the Gilded Age and Progressive Era.

During the first New Federalism, decisions about agency structure, scope, and process determined who won and who lost, in the present and in the future. For national legislators, determining wins and losses of administrative structure and procedures was critical to strengthening their representation, whether of their districts, their party, or other interests. More importantly, the choice of administrative structure and procedure could spell the difference between the development of an enacting coalition and the demise of legislation. The development of the intergovernmental policy instruments of the first New Federalism was far from a logical or orderly process. These instruments were chosen in order to balance conflicting interest and demands within a governmental structure whose capacity lagged behind its growing commitments.

Creating a New State: Insights from the Cases

Despite their differences in policy outcomes and administrative arrangements, a number of interesting insights can be drawn from the policies enacted during the first New Federalism. For the case studies in particular, the process of policy development was strikingly similar: entrepreneurial bureaucrats were important in creating and defining the need for policy intervention in all of the areas, while interest groups were critical in the creation of public awareness, educating legislators on the policy and linking public awareness to the political agenda.

Not all entrepreneurial bureaucrats were successful. Some bureaucrats and their agencies, for example, the Bureau of Chemistry (the precursor to the Federal Drug Administration) and the Bureau of Public Roads, were successful in carving out and developing what Theda Skocpol and Kenneth Finegold called "islands of [national] state capacity."[1] Other bureaucracies, such as the Children's Bureau, had their professionalism and autonomy repeatedly challenged by those within and outside of the national government.

The success of interest groups, and the social movements that intersected them, also varied. The good roads movement, one of the assemblage of groups advocating for highway funding, was able to link two very different sectors of the American public: urban automobile enthusiasts and those concerned about the decline of rural America. Similarly, the women's groups that advocated the enactment of the Sheppard-Towner Act were able to link legislators' concerns about the size and influence of the potential women's votes to the enactment of the policy.

The efforts and goals of interest groups and reformers, along with their bureaucratic allies, were not quickly or easily accepted. Among many politicians and citizens there was still wariness, if not outright hostility, to the idea of an active national state. This hostility occurred at the state level as well, where the transition from the nineteenth-century vision of the "well-regulated society" to the centralized bureaucratic structure familiar to today's observers was just beginning to take shape.[2] The need and the desirability for state or local control also played a role in limiting (or expanding, in the case of food and drug regulation) the reach of the national government into the politics and economy of individual states.

In the case studies, bureaucrats at the national and state level, along with interest groups formed by ideological, economic, functional, or regional interests, came together to press for a larger national role. In the case of regulatory policy, such as the Pure Food and Drug Act, conflicting state laws and standards were portrayed as a hazard for both businesses and consumers. In the case of distributive policy, such as the Federal Highway Act, or redistributive policy, such as the Sheppard-Towner Act, the national government was seen as a source of not only expertise but funds that could be leveraged at the state level.

The Impact of Administrative Structures

Government actors, with varying degrees of success, made it a point to build up supportive constituencies through the establishment of satellite interest groups (often under their direct or indirect control), through the establishment of local and state associations and agencies, through alliances with other groups with an interest in the area (e.g., the Grange movement, sanitarians, bicyclists, railroads and automobiles, women's groups), and through the development of working relationships with key congressional supporters.

Having the right administrative structure mattered for those interested in expanding their policy scope, as in the cases of food and drug regulation and of highways, or in protecting their hard-won policy gains, as with the maternal and child health program. In the best-case scenarios of food and drugs and highways, a strong intergovernmental administrative structure enabled the development of networks of interest group support, as well as the development of the administrative capacity necessary to enact desired policy. State-level partners could play a critical role in furthering the expansion of the national agency, or again in consolidating policy gains.

At the state level, in some states intergovernmental policies such as food and drug regulation or highway building were readily embraced (and indeed in some cases, predated national activity), while in other cases, even the lure of national funding could not alleviate concerns over losing local control. Even when states embraced a policy, their ability to implement it varied. In the case of highways, national-level bureaucrats were successful in training a cadre of engineers that would share the same professional ethos. However, sharing the same ethos did not always insulate these state's bureaucratic partners from the particularities of their own state's political and administrative context. Thus for every New York, which adopted a policy early (and implemented it successfully) there was an Alabama, which adopted a policy late or not at all, and with limited administrative capacity. This variation in state capacity, despite national direction, would be called the "Alabama syndrome," and would plague those interested in achieving national goals or standards.[3]

The intersection of administrative structure, institutional configurations, and policy types led to different policy outcomes. For each of the three policies, national legislators carefully developed a working relationship between the national government and the states. This was done through the design of administrative structures such as the national oversight boards like the Federal Board of Maternity and Infant Hygiene, or the state highway departments; and via the selection of administrative procedures such as lodging rule-making ability in the hands of the secretary of agriculture. In the case of the Pure Food and Drug Act, regulation-setting power was fragmented among three agencies in order to reduce the power of the profarmer USDA. At the same time, the regulatory powers of the states were limited out of concern that they would develop standards impossible or very expensive for manufacturers to meet.

The impact of these intergovernmental administrative structures varied. For example, without strong intergovernmental administrative structures at the national level, redistributive policy such as the Sheppard-Towner program was easily attacked at the national level in the face of a very different political context during the mid-1920s. In the case of the Children's Bureau, its inability to build a *durable* federated administrative relationship was one of the reasons for the program's failure to survive a suddenly hostile national political environment. In addition, it did not help that the Children's Bureau was not located within the powerful USDA and thus could not take advantage of the department's strong network of interest groups, state partners, and congressional patrons. Without the national attention spurred by the activities of national and state organized interests, and with the weakening threat of electoral mobilization of women, many states faltered in their commitment to a maternal and child health program. Nonetheless, in some states the program remained functional despite the withdrawal of national support. The endurance of maternal and child health programs at the state level until the appearance of the New Deal illustrates the possibilities of a federal system. Not only are multiple veto points possible, but also multiple policy islands.

Politics and the Shape of Intergovernmental Policy

Politics at the national level also shaped the emergence and development of intergovernmental policy. For example, the rise of sectionally concentrated agricultural movements in the late nineteenth century enhanced the position of the Department of Agriculture and aided in the enactment of intergovernmental policies such as food and drug regulation and highway development, designed to partly address the demands of the agricultural sector. The highway program benefited from the emergence of the Democratic Party after nearly two decades out of power and the party's need to build a broad electoral base.

On the other hand, Republican resurgence, the changing composition of members in both the House and the Senate, and the concomitant collapse of old alliances (between Progressives and Democrats and between farmers and labor) limited the support for and the spread of redistributive programs such as the Sheppard-Towner Act. The rising tide of conservatism during the 1920s demonstrated the precarious position of redistributive policy in a federal system. Politics and political timing played a major role in the enactment of Sheppard-Towner, as they did for pure food and drug legislation and for the highway program. The enactment of Sheppard-Towner took place within the confluence of broader political shifts. It has been argued that the primary political context within which to understand the program's enactment was the emergence and unknown consequence of the women's vote on electoral politics. The program's success proved short-lived when the nonappearance of the women's vote weakened legislators' fear of electoral punishment and thus their support of the program.

Long-term political shifts also played a role in how these policies played out. For example, the elections of the late 1920s produced a House and Senate much more conservative than the Progressive-influenced Congresses that had earlier considered the issue of maternal and child health. However, the impact of the direct election of senators was finally being felt in that Progressive Democrats and Republican senators were able to remain in office despite this conservative trend.

The modernization of Congress, and especially the House, also shaped the character of intergovernmental policy. With the end of the strong reign of House Speaker Joseph Cannon, and the Democrat's shakeup of the committee system in 1911, when the party finally recaptured control of the House, committees such as Public Roads, in addition to traditional prestige committees such as the Interstate and Foreign Commerce Committee, increasingly became the source of intergovernmental policy initiatives.

These initiatives were introduced and lobbied for by a new kind of legislator, one who not only had specialized expertise in a policy area, but also was more likely than ever to be a career member of Congress. Representatives such as William Hepburn and Dorsey Shackleford, and senators such as Porter McCumber and John Bankhead, were largely products of the new modern Congress. Balanced against these policy entrepreneurs was the Republican Party old guard, a coterie of congressmen very much committed to a government limited in scope, albeit attentive to certain special interests such as corporations and the railroads. In the end, even these congressmen gave way to representatives who quietly understood the new customs of a modern American Congress.

Politics and Policy Outcomes

Intergovernmental policy instruments and the first New Federalism reflected and adapted to the institutional structures of the late nineteenth and early twentieth centuries. They did not challenge the judicial boundaries of national-state interaction, or broad-based beliefs in the scope of government activity. Indeed, so adaptively successful were these intergovernmental policy instruments that it was not until the passage of the Sheppard-Towner Act in 1921 that constitutional objections were finally raised by the states, in the cases of *Massachusetts v. Mellon* and *Frothingham v. Mellon*.

In short, the case studies epitomize many of the aspects of Progressivism discussed by historians and political scientists: the growth of new and varied interest groups, the emergence of a professional bureaucracy at the state and national levels, and the political and institutional battles that divided the American political system across region and party. All of these factors contributed to the development of a movement that advocated greater government involvement—whether at the local, state, or national level.

Within the context of the federal structure of the late nineteenth century and early twentieth century, the enactment of any law granting significant powers to the national government over the economy and society was still very much contested. Although, national regulation or fiscal support appeared to some observers to be the only logical alternative, to others the success of states in creating their own regulatory and administrative structures offered a viable and attractive policy alternative. It is instructive that given the conflict and uncertainty of national politics, and the effect of federalism as constraining force, states maintained much of the power with which they had started. Nonetheless, the leverage afforded by intergovernmental policy also benefited the national government. Intergovernmental policy gave it the ability to create a far stronger and centralized state than the institutional, judicial, and ideological limits of the day would have otherwise allowed. The first New Federalism had truly made its mark.

Continuities and Disjunctions: The New Deal and the Second New Federalism

By the end of the New Deal (circa 1938), the scope of the national government had dramatically expanded. Many would argue that this transformation was relatively rapid as a result of a political, ideological, and judicial revolution fueled by the economic and political crisis of the Great Depression. To these observers, the New Deal spelled the end of dualism and the rise of a far more centralized state.

In terms of funding, this seems to be the case. For example, spending on grants-in-aid was only $123 million in 1927. By 1932, spending had risen to $232 million, and to $976 million by 1934.[4] The regulatory scope of the national government also increased, particularly the number of intergovernmental regulations. While twenty-five such regulations were enacted from 1920 to 1929, over thirty were enacted between 1930 and 1939. Nonetheless, the New Deal did reflect a more assertive national government. While pre–New Deal intergovernmental regulations often contained an exemption for intrastate commerce, this exemption largely disappears in the post–New Deal Era.

A closer examination of the three case policies as they played out within the political context of the New Deal shows that there were significant continuities with the first New Federalism. The cases show that in some ways the New Deal revolution simply solidified and expanded a framework for national expansion that had slowly accreted from 1877 onward.

The evidence presented in the case studies suggests that the administrative and organizational structures of the first New Federalism went largely unchallenged. In the case of food and drug regulation, while the debate centered on getting more power in the hands of national regulators, the basic administrative structure of the FDA (including its relationship with state regulators) remained largely unchanged. It was not until much later (the 1950s and 1960s) that the preemption powers contained in the legislation were interpreted to mean a vast expansion in the size and scope of the FDA. In the case of the Bureau of Public Roads, the bureau maintained its close, cooperative, if slightly dominant relationship with the states until the mid-1960s, when the environmentalism and urban renewal backlash forced a reassessment of traditional highway policy. The Children's Bureau was able to dominate its small area of expertise until 1946, when it was stripped of programmatic authority, unable to withstand new political and ideological assaults on its Progressive approach.

In its form—intergovernmental policy instruments—and in its functions, the cooperative federalism of the New Deal reflected a distinctive political, and institutional heritage. This heritage was the fact that the growth of the national government and the emergence of the first New Federalism occurred within a constitutional, political and ideological framework that privileged state interests and favored state control over policy outcomes. When policymakers cast about for solutions to the crisis of the New Deal, a familiar tool—intergovernmental policy—lay before them, ready for deployment. Legislators were comfortable with these administrative structures in that they had examples of how the programs would be administered. Bureaucrats could use these tools to (re)build existing networks of support and expertise in order to implement policy. Thus, public policy of the middle to late twentieth century reflected the political and institutional innovations of the Gilded Age and Progressive Era.

The 1960s and President Johnson's Great Society firmly upended the balancing act between the national government and the states that had been created during the first New Federalism and solidified in the New Deal. With the Great Society, the national government became far more assertive. The intergovernmental regulations and grants enacted during this period reflected a stronger wish to influence and control the activities of the states, while in pursuit of a broader national objective. While the various programs of the Great Society ended during the rise of the Republicans in the 1970s and 1980s, its administrative and electoral legacies live on.

Today, decades after new federalisms were announced by Presidents Nixon and Reagan, we have a national government—and in particular, a Congress—that is still torn between the political and electoral allure of intergovernmental policy, and its disdain for "big government." Congress has partially solved this conundrum by off-shifting costs and administrative responsibilities to the states, while claiming credit for its policy achievements. A clear choice for the efficient administration of policies has yet to be made. As critics of modern federalism repeatedly point out, what should logically be administered and funded at the national level (such as Medicaid) remains a joint national-state endeavor. What should be administered (and funded) at the local level, such as education, has increasingly become part of the national political agenda with the enactment of the No Child Left Behind Act. While national legislators can enjoy the electoral benefits of claiming to reform welfare or strengthen education, states, interest groups, and national bureaucrats engage in a pattern of behavior set forth by their predecessors during the first New Federalism, and embedded within what David Truman called "separate self-sustaining centers of power and privilege" that make up the American federal system.[5]

The persistence of institutional structures and patterns of behavior created during the first New Federalism forces a reconsideration of how researchers understand the processes of change and stability in American national state development. While politics and interests play an important role in the creation of critical junctures, the inherited lines of administrative development can play a powerful role in influencing the path that the American state takes. Yet that path is not paved in stone. The creation of the first New Federalism was a process of optimistic experimentation on the part of many searching for a new relationship between citizens, society, and the state. Rather than seeing the first New Federalism as detour from an idealized definition of government, Americans can instead be inspired. Americans created in the past—and can do so in the future—a political system that accommodated the multitude of interests that comprise the American polity, and that encompassed American governing ideals of efficiency, equality, and responsiveness.

Appendix

IPIs Enacted, 1877–1931

Year	Congress	Public Law or Statute	Title	Instrument	Policy Area	Policy Subarea
1878	45	20 Stat. 37	Contagious Diseases Act	R	REG	SW
1879	45	20 Stat. 467	American Printing House for the Blind	G	RED	EDUC
1879	46	21 Stat. 49	National Board of Health Act	R	REG	SW
1882	47	22 Stat. 58	Regulate immigration	R	REG	GO
1884	48	23 Stat. 31	Animal Industry Act	R	REG	AGR
1886	49	24 Stat. 209	Oleomargarine Act	R	REG	AGR
1887	49	24 Stat. 379	Interstate Commerce Act	R	REG	COM
1887	49	24 Stat. 402	Militia Act	G	DIST	MIL
1887	49	24 Stat. 440	Hatch Experiment Station Act	G	DIST	AGR
1888	50	25 Stat. 450	State and Territorial Homes for Disabled Veterans	G	RED	SW
1890	51	26 Stat. 209	Sherman Antitrust Act	R	REG	COM
1890	51	26 Stat. 313	Wilson Act (regulate liquor)	R	REG	COM
1890	51	26 Stat. 417	Morrill Land Grant Act	G	REG	EDUC
1890	51	26 Stat. 653	Weather Service Organic Act	G	REG	GO
1891	51	26 Stat. 1089	Cattle Inspection Act	R	REG	AGR
1893	52	27 Stat. 445	Limited Liability Act	R	REG	TRANS
1893	52	27 Stat. 449	Federal Quarantine Act	R	REG	SW
1893	52	27 Stat. 531	Safety Appliance Act	R	REG	TRANS
1894	53	28 Stat. 36	Repeal civil rights statute	R	REG	GO
1894	53	28 Stat. 278	National Bank Notes	R	REG	COM
1894	53	28 Stat. 422	Carey Grant (irrigation)	G	DIST	CONS
1896	54	29 Stat. 253	Filled Cheese Act	R	REG	AGR
1897	54	29 Stat. 594	Forest Fire Protection Act	G	DIST	CONS
1899	55	30 Stat. 1151	Rivers and Harbor Act	R	REG	COM
1899	55	30 Stat. 1152	Refuse Act	R	REG	CONS
1898	55	30 Stat. 544	Uniform System of Bankruptcy	R	REG	COM
1900	56	31 Stat. 187	Endangered Species Act (Lacey Act)	R	REG	CONS
1901	56	31 Stat. 1449	Establish National Bureau of Standards	G	REG	GO
1902	57	57–110/32 Stat. 193	Oleomargarine Act	R	REG	AGR
1902	57	57–223/32 Stat. 632	Dairy and Food Products Labeling Act	R	REG	COM
1903	57	57–33/32 Stat. 775	Dick Act	G	DIST	MIL
1903	57	57–49/32 Stat. 791	Cattle Contagious Diseases Act	R	REG	AGR
1903	57	57–103/32 Stat. 847	Elkins Act (antirebate)	R	REG	COM
1903	57	57–133/32 Stat. 943	Safety Appliance Act	R	REG	TRANS
1905	58	58–52/33 Stat. 705	Prohibit Interstate Mailing of Indecent Material	R	REG	COM
1905	58	58–84/33 Stat. 724	Elkins Act (trademarks)	R	REG	COM
1905	58	58–229/33 Stat. 1264	Cattle Contagious Diseases Act	R	REG	AGR
1906	59	59–47/34 Stat. 63	Adams Act	G	DIST	AGR
1906	59	59–219/34 Stat. 232	Federal Employer's Liability Act	R	REG	COM
1906	59	59–243/34 Stat. 299	Quarantine Act	R	REG	SW
1906	59	59–262/34 Stat. 386	Regulate dams	R	REG	COM

Year	Congress	Public Law or Statute	Title	Instrument	Policy Area	Policy Subarea
1906	59	59–337/34 Stat. 584	Interstate Commerce Act Amendments	R	REG	COM
1906	59	59–340/34 Stat. 607	Livestock Transportation Act	R	REG	AGR
1906	59	59–382/34 Stat. 674	Federal Meat Inspection Act	R	REG	AGR
1906	59	59–384/34 Stat. 768	Food and Drug Act	R	REG	SW
1907	59	59–242/34 Stat. 684	Forest Reserve Funds	G	DIST	CONS
1907	59	59–242/34 Stat. 1256	Nelson-Morrill Act	G	DIST	EDUC
1907	59	59–274/34 Stat. 1415	Esch Act (hours of service on railroads)	R	REG	COM
1908	60	60–100	Employer's Liability Act Amendments	R	REG	COM
1908	60	60–136	Forest Highways	G	DIST	TRANS
1908	60	60–145	(Military) Act	G	DIST	MIL
1908	60	60–174	Transportation of Explosives	R	REG	COM
1910	61	61–133	Safety Appliance Act	R	REG	TRANS
1910	61	61–152	Insecticide Act	R	REG	CONS
1910	61	61–218	Commerce Court Act	R	REG	COM
1910	61	61–277	White Slave Traffic Act	R	REG	SW
1911	61	61–383	Boiler Inspection Act	R	REG	TRANS
1911	61	61–435	Weeks Act (conservation of watersheds)	G	DIST	CONS
1911	61	61–505	State Maritime Schools	G	RED	EDUC
1912	62	62–118	White Phosphorous Match Tax	R	REG	COM
1912	62	62–246	Prohibit Interstate Commerce of Prize Fight Films	R	REG	COM
1912	62	62–252	Standard Barrel Act (apples)	R	REG	COM
1912	62	62–275	Nursery Stock/Plant Quarantine Act	R	REG	AGR
1912	62	62–336/62–430	Post Roads Act	G	DIST	TRANS
1913	62	62–398	Webb-Kenyon Act (regulate liquor)	R	REG	COM
1913	62	62–400	Valuation Act	R	REG	COM
1913	62	62–430	"Animal Virus, Serum, Toxin and Antitoxin Act"	R	REG	AGR
1913	62	62–430	Weeks-McClean Migratory Bird Act	R	REG	CONS
1913	63	63–43	Federal Reserve Act	R	REG	COM
1914	63	63–95	Smith-Lever Act	G	DIST	AGR
1914	63	63–203	Federal Trade Commission Act	R	REG	COM
1914	63	63–212	Clayton Antitrust Act	R	REG	COM
1915	63	63–307	"Standard Barrel Act (fruits, vegetables)"	R	REG	COM
1916	64	64–85	National Defense Act	G	DIST	MIL
1916	64	64–156	Federal Aid Road Act	G	DIST	TRANS
1916	64	64–190	U.S. Cotton Futures Act	R	DIST	AGR
1916	64	64–190	U.S. Grain Standards Act	R	DIST	AGR
1916	64	64–190	U.S. Warehouse Act	R	REG	AGR
1916	64	64–228	Standard Barrel Act (limes)	R	REG	COM
1916	64	64–239	Pomerene Bills of Lading Act	R	REG	COM
1916	64	64–248	Standard Baskets Act	R	REG	COM
1916	64	64–249	Interstate Child Labor Act	R	REG	SW
1916	64	64–252	Adamson Act (8-hour day)	R	REG	COM
1917	64	64–347	Smith-Hughes Vocation Education Act	G	RED	EDUC
1917	65	65–37	Waterways Commission	R	REG	TRANS
1917	65	65–82	Johnson Act (Maritime Workmen's Compensation)	R	REG	SW
1918	65	65–106	Daylight Savings Act (Calder Act)	R	REG	COM
1918	65	65–126	Webb-Pomerene Act (export trade)	R	REG	COM
1918	65	65–174	Teachers for Children of Lighthouse Keepers	G	DIST	EDUC
1918	65	65–178	Vocational Rehabilitation	G	RED	EDUC
1918	65	65–186	Migratory Bird Treaty Act	R	REG	CONS

Year	Congress	Public Law or Statute	Title	Instrument	Policy Area	Policy Subarea
1918	65	65–193	Chamberlain-Kahn Act (venereal disease control)	G	RED	SW
1919	65	65–299	Federal Aid Road Act, Act of 1919	G	DIST	TRANS
1919	66	66–40	Calder Act (repeal daylight savings)	R	REG	COM
1920	66	66–152	Transportation Act (Title IV)	R	REG	COM
1920	66	66–236	Fess-Kenyon Vocational Rehabilitation Act	G	RED	EDUC
1920	66	66–242	Military Act	G	REG	MIL
1920	66	66–261	Merchant Marine Act	R	REG	COM
1920	66	66–280	Federal Water Power Act	R	REG	CONS
1920	66	66–400	Transportation of Explosives Amendments	R	REG	COM
1921	66	67–51	Packers and Stockyards Act	R	REG	AGR
1921	67	67–87	Federal Aid Road Act, Act of 1921	G	DIST	TRANS
1921	67	67–97	Sheppard-Towner Maternity Act	G	RED	SW
1922	67	67–146	Agricultural Producers Association Act	R	REG	AGR
1922	67	67–331	Grain Futures Act	R	REG	AGR
1923	67	67–513	Filled Milk Act	R	REG	AGR
1923	67	67–518	National Bank Tax Act	R	REG	COM
1923	67	67–539	U.S. Cotton Standards Act	R	DIST	AGR
1924	68	68–270	Clark-McNary Act (forestry)	G	DIST	COM
1924	68	68–283	Oil Pollution Act	R	DIST	CONS
1925	68	68–401	U.S. Arbitration Act	R	REG	COM
1925	68	68–458	Purnell Act	G	DIST	AGR
1926	69	69–214	Nursery Stock Quarantine Act	R	DIST	AGR
1926	69	69–256	Black Bass Protection Act	R	DIST	CONS
1926	69	69–257	Railway Labor Act	R	REG	COM
1927	69	69–594	European Corn Borer Eradication Act	G	RED	AGR
1927	69	69–639	Banking Act	R	REG	COM
1927	69	69–783	Federal Caustic Poison Act	R	REG	SW
1927	69	69–803	Longshoreman's and Harbor Workers Compensation Act	R	RED	SW
1928	70	70–462	Standard Measures	R	REG	COM
1928	70	70–466	Experiments in Reforestation	G	DIST	CONS
1928	70	70–475	Capper-Ketcham Act	G	DIST	AGR
1928	70	70–669	Hawes-Cooper Act (convict-made goods)	R	REG	SW
1929	70	70–702	George-Reed Vocational Act	G	RED	EDUC
1929	70	70–770	Migratory Bird Conservation Act	G	REG	CONS
1929	71	71–10	Agricultural Marketing Act	R	DIST	AGR
1930	71	71–218	Federal Prison Reorganization Act	R	REG	GO
1930	71	71–325	Perishable Agricultural Commodities Act	R	DIST	AGR
1930	71	71–520	Shore Erosion Protection	G	DIST	CONS
1931	71	71–776	Animal Damage Control Act	G	DIST	AGR
1931	71	71–798	Davis-Bacon Act	R	DIST	COM

Abbreviations

Policy Area		Policy Subarea	
REG	Regulatory	AGR	Agriculture
DIST	Distributive	COM	Commerce
RED	Redistributive	CONS	Conservation
		EDUC	Education
		GO	Government Operations
		MIL	Military
		SW	Social Welfare
		TRANS	Transportation

Notes

Introduction

1. Walter Weyl, *The New Democracy. An Essay on Certain Political and Economic Tendencies in the United States* (New York: Macmillan 1912): 348. Weyl refers to the Progressive movement, not statebuilding per se, but his description is apropos for the latter as well.

2. See Barry Karl's *The Uneasy State: The United States from 1915 to 1945* (Chicago: University of Chicago Press, 1983); also Morton M. Keller, *Affairs of State: Public Life in Late Nineteenth Century America* (Cambridge: Harvard University Press, 1977).

3. For discussion of the impact of the Civil War and nationalism, see Bruce A. Ackerman, *We the People: Foundations* (Cambridge: Belknap Press of Harvard University Press, 1991); and Eric Foner, *Reconstruction: America's Unfinished Revolution, 1863–1877* (New York: Harper and Row, 1988). See Richard F. Bensel, *Yankee Leviathan: The Origins of Central State Authority in America, 1859–1877* (New York: Cambridge University Press, 1990), and *Sectionalism and American Political Development* (Madison: University of Wisconsin Press, 1984).

4. For an overview of the 1920s and the decade's linkage to the New Deal, see Colin Gordon, *New Deals: Business, Labor, and Politics in America, 1920–1935* (New York: Cambridge University Press, 1994); Ellis Hawley, *The Great War and the Search for a Modern Order: A History of the American People and Their Institutions, 1917–1933* (New York: St. Martin's Press, 1979); Marc Eisner, *From Warfare State to Welfare State: World War I, Compensatory State Building, and the Limits of the Modern Order* (University Park: Pennsylvania State University Press, 2000); Morton Keller, *Regulating a New Economy: Public Policy and Economic Change in America, 1900–1933* (Cambridge: Harvard University Press, 1990); Edward Berkowitz and Kim McQuaid, *Creating the Welfare State: The Political Economy of Twentieth-Century Reform* (New York: Praeger, 1980).

5. For discussion of path dependency, see Paul Pierson, "Increasing Returns, Path Dependence, and the Study of Politics," *American Political Science Review* 94(2) (2000): 251–67, "Not Just What, but *When*: Timing and Sequence in Political Processes," *Studies in American Political Development* 14 (Spring 2000): 72–92, and *Politics in Time: History, Institutions and Social Analysis* (Princeton: Princeton University Press, 2004). See also Jacob Hacker, "The Historical Logic of National Health Insurance: Structure and Sequence in the Development of British, Canadian, and U.S. Medical Policy," *Studies in American Political Development* 12 (1998): 57–130. For illustrative discussion of historical institutionalism and issues of timing, sequence, and contingency, see Peter B. Evans, Dietrich Rueschmeyer, and Theda Skocpol, eds., *Bringing the State Back In* (New York: Cambridge University Press, 1985); Sven Steinmo, Kathleen Thelen, and Frank Longstreth, eds., *Structuring Politics: Historical Institutionalism in Compar-*

ative Analysis (New York: Cambridge University Press, 1992); Karen Orren and Stephen Skowronek, "Beyond the Iconography of Order: Notes for a 'New Institutionalism,'" in *The Dynamics of American Politics: Approaches and Interpretations*, ed. Lawrence C. Dodd and Calvin Jillson (Boulder, CO: Westview Press, 1994).

6. For an example of this approach see Robert Higgs, *Crisis and Leviathan: Critical Episodes in the Growth of American Government* (New York: Oxford University Press, 1987).

7. Much like Kenneth Shepsle's notion of structure-induced equilibrium, federalism can be stylized not only as an institutional equilibrium, but also as an equilibrium institution. See Kenneth A. Shepsle, "Studying Institutions: Some Lessons from the Rational Choice Approach," *Journal of Theoretical Politics* 1 (1989): 131–47, and also, "Institutional Equilibrium and Equilibrium Institutions," *Political Science: The Science of Politics*, ed. Herbert F. Weisberg (New York: Agathon Press, 1986).

8. Frank J. Goodnow, *Politics and Administration: A Study in Government* (New York: Russell and Russell, 1900), 28.

9. Stephen Skowronek, *Building a New American State: The Expansion of National Administrative Capacities, 1877–1920* (New York: Cambridge University Press, 1982), 9.

10. Hugh Heclo, *Modern Social Politics in Britain and Sweden* (New Haven: Yale University Press, 1974), 305–6. See also Leonard D. White, *Trends in Public Administration* (New York: McGraw-Hill, 1933).

11. For discussion of executive-centered approaches see Skowronek, *Building a New American State*; as well as Brian Balogh, "Reorganizing the Organizational Synthesis: Federal Professional Relations in Modern America," *Studies in American Political Development* 5 (Spring 1991): 119–72; Ronald N. Johnson and Gary D. Libecap, *The Federal Civil Service System and the Problem of Bureaucracy: The Economics and Politics of Institutional Change* (Chicago: University of Chicago Press, 1994); and Daniel Carpenter, *The Forging of Bureaucratic Autonomy: Reputations, Networks, and Policy Innovation in Executive Agencies, 1862–1928* (Princeton: Princeton University Press, 2001).

12. Polity-centered approaches to American political development are discussed by Theda Skocpol, "The Origins of Social Policy in the United States: A Polity-Centered Analysis," in Dodd and Jillson, *Dynamics of American Politics* and introduction, *Protecting Soldiers and Mothers: The Political Origins of Social Policy in the United States* (Cambridge: Belknap Press of Harvard University Press, 1992).

13. See, for example, Martha Derthick and John J. Dinan, "Progressivism and Federalism" in *Progressivism and the New Democracy*, ed. Sidney M. Milkis and Jerome M. Mileur (Amherst: University of Massachusetts Press, 2002).

14. Christopher Leman, "Patterns of Policy Development: Social Security in the United States and Canada," *Public Policy* 25 (1977): 261–91.

15. See, for example, Luther Gulick, "Reorganization of the State," *Civil Engineering* 3 (August 1933): 420–22; and Harold J. Laski, "The Obsolescence of Federalism," *New Republic* May 3, 1939, 367–69. The view is summarized in W. Brooke Graves, *American Intergovernmental Relations: Their Origins, Historical*

Development and Current Status (New York: Charles Scribner's Sons, 1964), 803–7; and Terry Sanford's *Storm over the States* (New York: McGraw-Hill, 1967).

16. Daniel Elazar, *The American Partnership: Intergovernmental Cooperation in the Nineteenth-Century United States* (Chicago: University of Chicago Press, 1962).

Chapter 1

1. On the primacy of Congress during the Gilded Age and Progressive Era, see Woodrow Wilson, "The Executive," in *Constitutional Government in the United States* (New York: Columbia University Press, 1961). On Congress in the modern era, and theories of its decline, see James L. Sundquist, *The Decline and Resurgence of Congress* (Washington, DC: Brookings Institution, 1981).

2. For overview of the impact of the "interests" on American politics, see William McCormick's "The Discovery That Business Corrupts Politics: A Reappraisal of the Origins of Progressivism," *American Historical Review* 86 (1981): 247–74.

3. Wallace D. Farnham, "'The Weakened Spring of Government': A Study in Nineteenth-Century American History," *American Historical Review* 68 (1963): 662–80.

4. Margaret Susan Thompson, *The "Spider Web": Congress and Lobbying in the Age of Grant* (Ithaca: Cornell University Press, 1985), 73–74.

5. Morton Keller, *Congress, Parties and Public Policy* (Washington, DC: American Historical Association, 1985), 1.

6. For discussion of the "polity"-centered approach, see Skocpol, "Origins of Social Policy."

7. Shepsle, "Studying Institutions," 135. See also Terry M. Moe, "Interests, Institutions, and Positive Theory: The Politics of the NLRB," *Studies in American Political Development* 3 (1987): 236–99, and "The Politics of Structural Choice: Toward a Theory of Public Administration," in *Organization Theory: From Chester Barnard to the Present and Beyond* (New York: Oxford University Press, 1990).

8. Thomas Gilligan, William Marshall, and Barry Weingast, "Regulation and the Theory of Legislative Choice: The Interstate Commerce Act of 1887," *Journal of Law and Economics* 32 (1989): 35–61; Gary Cox and Mathew McCubbins, *Legislative Leviathan: Party Government in the House* (Berkeley and Los Angeles: University of California Press, 1993).

9. For discussion of an "institutional politics" approach, see Samuel Kernell, "Rural Free Delivery as a Critical Test of Alternative Models of American Political Development: A Comment," *Studies in American Political Development* 15 (Spring 2001): 103–12. On transaction costs, see Douglass C. North, *Institutions, Institutional Change, and Economic Performance* (New York: Cambridge University Press, 1990); Kenneth A. Shepsle and Barry R. Weingast, "Structured Induced Equilibrium and Legislative Choice," *Public Choice*, 37 (1981): 503–19, and "Political Preferences for the Pork Barrel: A Generalization," *American Journal of Political Science* 25 (1981): 96–111; Barry R. Weingast and William J.

Marshall, "The Industrial Organization of Congress; or, Why Legislatures, Like Firms, Are Organized as Markets," *Journal of Political Economy* 96 (1988): 132–63; Melissa P. Collie, "Universalism and the Parties in the U.S. House of Representatives, 1921–80," *American Journal of Political Science* 32 (1988): 865–83. For electoral assumption, see David Mayhew, *Congress: The Electoral Connection* (New Haven: Yale University Press, 1974).

10. For discussion of legislative choice of administrative structures and procedures see Kathleen Bawn, "Political Control Versus Expertise: Congressional Choices about Administrative Procedures," *American Political Science Review* 89 (1995): 62–73, and "Choosing Strategies to Control the Bureaucracy: Statutory Constraints, Oversight, and the Committee System," *Journal of Law, Economics and Organization* 13 (1997): 101–26; Randall Calvert, Mark McCubbins, and Barry Weingast, "A Theory of Political Control and Agency Discretion," *American Journal of Political Science* 33 (1989): 588–611; David Epstein and Sharyn O'Halloran, "Administrative Procedures, Information, and Agency Discretion," *American Journal of Political Science* 38 (1994): 697–722, and *Delegating Powers* (New York: Cambridge University Press, 1999); Morris P. Fiorina, "Legislator Uncertainty, Legislative Control, and the Delegation of Legislative Power," *Journal of Law, Economics and Organization* 2 (1986): 33–51; Murray J. Horn, *The Political Economy of Public Administration: Institutional Choice in the Public Sector* (New York: Cambridge University Press, 1995); Murray J. Horn and Kenneth Shepsle, "Commentary on Administrative Arrangements and the Political Control of Agencies: Administrative Process and Organizational Form as Legislative Responses to Agency Costs," *Virginia Law Review* 75 (1989): 499–505; D. Roderick Kiewiet and Mathew D. McCubbins, *The Logic of Delegation: Congressional Politics and the Appropriations Process* (Chicago: University of Chicago Press, 1991); Jonathon Macey, "Organizational Design and the Political Control of Administrative Agencies," *Journal of Law, Economics and Organization* 8 (1992): 93–110; Mathew McCubbins, Roger Noll, and Barry Weingast, "Administrative Procedures as Instruments of Political Control," *Journal of Law, Economics and Organization* 3 (1987): 243–77, and "Structure and Process, Politics and Policy: Administrative Arrangements and the Political Control of Agencies," *Virginia Law Review* 75 (1989): 431–82.

11. For institutionalist approaches to delegation of power in federal systems, see Jonathon Macey, "Federal Deference to Local Regulators and the Economic Theory of Regulation: Toward a Public-Choice Explanation of Federalism," *Virginia Law Review* 76 (1990): 265–91; Robert P. Inman and Daniel L. Rubinfeld, "The Political Economy of Federalism," in *Perspectives on Public Choice: A Handbook*, ed. Dennis C. Mueller (New York: Cambridge University Press, 1997), 73–110; E. Donald Elliott, Bruce A. Ackerman, and John C. Millian, "Toward a Theory of Statutory Evolution: The Federalization of Environmental Law," *Journal of Law, Economics and Organization* 1 (1985): 313–40; Susan Rose-Ackerman, "Does Federalism Matter? Political Choice in a Federal Republic," *Journal of Political Economy* 89 (1981): 152–65. Also see George J. Gordon, "Administrative Discretion in Intergovernmental Context," in *Administrative Discretion and Public Policy Implementation*, ed. Douglas H. Shuvamon and H. Kenneth Hibbeln (Westport, CT: Praeger, 1986).

12. Elisabeth Clemens, *The People's Lobby: Organizational Innovation and the Rise of Interest Group Politics in the United States, 1890–1925* (Chicago: University of Chicago Press, 1997).

13. For discussion of the American state of "courts and parties," see Skowronek, *Building a New American State*.

14. See Samuel Hays, "The Social Analysis of American Political History, 1880–1920," in *American Political History as Social Analysis* (Knoxville: University of Tennessee Press, 1980), 70. For an overview of the Gilded Age and Progressive Era, see also Robert H. Wiebe, *The Search for Order, 1877–1920* (New York: Hill and Wang, 1967), and *Businessmen and Reform: A Study of the Progressive Movement* (New York: Cambridge University Press, 1962); Karl, *The Uneasy State*; Keller's *Affairs of State, Regulating a New Economy,* and *Regulating a New Society: Public Policy and Social Change in America, 1900–1933* (Cambridge: Harvard University Press, 1994); Samuel Hays, *Conservation and the Gospel of Efficiency: The Progressive Era Conservation Movement, 1890–1920* (Cambridge: Harvard University Press, 1959), and *The Response to Industrialism, 1885–1914*, 2nd ed. (Chicago: University of Chicago Press, 1995); Gabriel Kolko, *The Triumph of Conservatism: A Reinterpretation of American History, 1900–1916* (New York: Free Press of Glencoe, 1963).

15. See Hays, *Conservation*, 122–27.

16. Skocpol, *Protecting Soldiers and Mothers*, 3.

17. See John Ferejohn, *Pork Barrel Politics: Rivers and Harbors Legislation, 1947–1968* (Stanford, CA: Stanford University Press, 1974); and R. Douglas Arnold, *The Logic of Congressional Action* (New Haven: Yale University Press, 1990).

18. See Kolko, *The Triumph of Conservatism*; and Wiebe, *The Search for Order* and *Businessmen and Reform*.

19. Quotation from John Tipple, comp., *The Capitalist Revolution: A History of American Social Thought* (New York: Pegasus, 1970), in Higgs, *Crisis and Leviathan*, 115. See also Louis Galambos, *Competition and Cooperation: The Emergence of a National Trade Association* (Baltimore: Johns Hopkins Press, 1966).

20. Wiebe, *The Search for Order*, 164–81.

21. The rise of the experts was partly due to the increasing complexity of business. For example, railroads and national manufacturing firms faced a number of problems due to the scale of their markets (which were *national* in scope) and the complexity of the technology they used. Scientific management became part of the ethos of public administration, resulting in the establishment of municipal research bureaus and aiding in the growth of municipal reform initiatives such as the city manager. For an overview of expertise and science management, see Samuel Haber, *Efficiency and Uplift: Scientific Management in the Progressive Era, 1890–1920* (Chicago: University of Chicago Press, 1964); Martin J. Schiesl, *The Politics of Efficiency: Municipal Administration Reform in America, 1880–1920* (Berkeley and Los Angeles: University of California Press, 1977). See also see Carpenter, *Forging of Bureaucratic Autonomy*; Wiebe, *Businessmen and Reform*; and Hays, *The Response to Industrialism*.

22. For example, many of the leading experts and reformers considered themselves to also be social scientists, believing that "rational measures could

be devised and applied to improve the human condition." See Richard L. McCormick, *The Party Period and Public Policy: American Politics from the Age of Jackson to the Progressive Era* (New York: Oxford University Press, 1986), 271. Indeed the goal of the American Social Science Association was to "apply science, organization and expertise to reform" (Keller, *Affairs of State*, 123). The results from such an approach were particularly notable in the field of public health, where impressive results were achieved. In this area "material achievements . . . provided concrete evidence of the almost unlimited possibilities of change," John D. Buenker, John C. Burnham, and Robert M. Crunden, *Progressivism* (Cambridge: Schenkman, 1977), 19.

23. See Ira Katznelson and Margaret Weir, *Schooling for All: Class, Race, and the Decline of the Democratic Ideal* (New York: Basic Books, 1985); Lawrence A. Cremin, *Transformation of the School: Progressivism in American Education, 1876–1957* (New York: Vintage, 1961); and Arthur F. McClure, James Chrisman, and Perry Mock, *Education for Work: The Historical Evolution of Vocational and Distributive Education in America* (Cranbury, NJ: Associated University Presses, 1985).

24. For conservation movement see Hays, *Conservation*. For maternal education, see Skocpol, *Protecting Soldiers and Mothers*. For education for farmers see Alfred C. True, *A History of Agricultural Education in the United States, 1785–1925* (Washington, DC: United States Department of Agriculture, 1928); and Elizabeth Sanders, *Roots of Reform: Farmers, Workers, and the American State, 1877–1917* (Chicago: University of Chicago Press, 1999). For highways, see Bruce Seely, *Building the American Highway System* (Philadelphia: Temple University Press, 1987); for social work, Roy Lubove, *The Professional Altruist: The Emergence of Social Work as a Career, 1880–1930* (Cambridge: Cambridge University Press, 1965).

25. See Buenker, Burnham, and Crunden, *Progressivism*, 41.

26. McCormick, *Party Period*, 283–84.

27. The idea of grants-in-aid also had a transatlantic appeal. Sydney Webb discusses the idea in *Grants in Aid: A Criticism and a Proposal* (New York: Longmans, Green, 1911). For a general discussion of transatlantic influences on American Progressivism, see Daniel T. Rodgers, *Atlantic Crossings: Social Politics in a Progressive Age* (Cambridge: Belknap Press of Harvard University Press, 1998).

28. Theda Skocpol and Kenneth Finegold, "State Capacity and Economic Intervention in the Early New Deal," *Political Science Quarterly* 97 (1982): 255–78; see also Carpenter, *Forging of Bureaucratic Autonomy*.

29. See Donald Haider, *When Governments Come to Washington: Governors, Mayors, and Intergovernmental Lobbying* (New York: Free Press, 1974); Anne Marie Cammisa, *Governments as Interest Groups: Intergovernmental Lobbying and the Federal System* (Westport, CT: Praeger, 1995); Samuel Beer, "The Modernization of American Federalism," *Publius* 3 (1973): 49–75.

30. See Deil S. Wright, *Understanding Intergovernmental Relations*, 2nd ed. (Monterey, CA: Brooks/Cole, 1982). For overview of American federalism during the middle to late twentieth century see Thomas Anton, *American Federalism and Public Policy* (New York: Random House, 1989); Ballard C. Campbell, *The Growth of American Government: Governance from the Cleveland Era to the Pres-*

ent (Bloomington: Indiana University Press, 1995), and "Federalism, State Action, and 'Critical Episodes' in the Growth of American Government," *Social Science History* 16 (1992): 561–78; Thomas R. Dye, *American Federalism: Competition Among Governments* (Lexington, MA: Lexington Books, 1990); Donald F. Kettl, *The Regulation of American Federalism* (Baton Rouge: Louisiana State University, 1983); Vincent Ostrom, *The Meaning of American Federalism* (San Francisco: ICS Press, 1991); Lawrence J. O'Toole, ed., *American Intergovernmental Relations* (Washington, DC: Congressional Quarterly Press, 1985); Paul Peterson, *The Price of Federalism* (Washington, DC: Brookings Institution, 1995); William H. Riker, *The Development of American Federalism* (Norwell, MA: Kluwer Academic, 1987); David B. Walker, *Toward a Functioning Federalism* (Cambridge, MA: Winthrop, 1981), and *The Rebirth of Federalism* (Chatham, NJ: Chatham House, 1995). This list is by no means definitive; a vast literature exists on American federalism.

31. See Harry N. Sheiber, "American Federalism and the Diffusion of Power: Historical and Contemporary Perspectives," *University of Toledo Law Review* 9 (1978): 640–43.

32. Nevertheless, while the state-led reform movements such as the uniform law movement highlighted the limitations of a state-by-state approach, state policy innovations may have also encouraged various state and national interests and politicians to turn their attention to the national level. State policy innovations that were successful in the eyes of reformers and interest groups encouraged more activity at the state and national levels. This shifting of attention was aided in part by a change in beliefs about the role and ability of the national government, and the frustration of working at the state level. Indeed, the latter frustration may have overshadowed the growing capacity of state governments. On this latter point see William R. Brock, *Investigation and Responsibility: Public Responsibility in the United States, 1865–1900* (New York: Cambridge University Press, 1984).

33. For a discussion of some structural constraints of American federalism, see William Graebner, "Federalism in the Progressive Era: A Structural Interpretation of Reform," *Journal of American History* 64 (1977): 331–57; David Brian Robertson, "The Bias of American Federalism: The Limits of Welfare-State Development in the Progressive Era," *Journal of Policy History* 1 (1989): 261–91; David Brian Robertson and Dennis R. Judd, *The Development of American Public Policy: The Structure of Policy Restraint* (Glenview, IL: Scott, Foresman, 1989); Christopher Howard, "Worker's Compensation, Federalism and the Heavy Hand of History," *Studies in American Political Development*; David A. Moss, *Socializing Security: Progressive-Era Economists and the Origins of American Social Policy* (Cambridge: Harvard University Press, 1996).

34. In addition to the formally organized uniform law movement were the national congresses held by interest groups such as the National Pure Food Congresses between 1899 and 1901, and the National Good Roads Congresses; all of which decried the slow pace of state enactment and issued calls for more coordinated activity at the state and national level.

35. On the uniform law movement see Graebner, "Federalism in the Progressive Era"; and W. Brooke Graves, *Uniform State Action: A Possible Substitute for Centralization* (Chapel Hill: University of North Carolina Press, 1934).

36. See Jack L. Walker, "The Diffusion of Innovations Among the American States," *American Political Science Review* 63 (1969): 880–99. For Justice Brandeis's characterization of a state functioning as a "laboratory of democracy," see *New State Ice Co. v. Liebmann*, 285 U.S. 262, 311 (1932) (Brandeis, J., dissenting).

37. See Brock, *Investigation and Responsibility*; Campbell, *Growth of American Government*; and William J. Novak, *The People's Welfare: Law and Regulation in Nineteenth-Century America* (Chapel Hill: University of North Carolina Press, 1996), for a discussion of nineteenth-century state governance.

38. Holt discusses the midwestern agrarian suspicion of the eastern "monied interests," James Holt, *Congressional Insurgents and the Party System: 1909–1916* (Cambridge: Harvard University Press, 1967), 9. For extensive discussion of sectionalism and its relationship to Gilded Age and Progressive Era policymaking, see Richard Bensel's *Sectionalism and American Political Development* and his *The Political Economy of American Industrialization, 1877–1900* (New York: Cambridge University Press, 2000); and Sanders, *Roots of Reform*. See also Harvey L. Schantz, "Sectionalism in Presidential Elections," in *American Presidential Elections: Process, Policy and Political Change* (Albany: State University of New York Press, 1996); Michael Berkman, *The State Roots of National Politics: Congress and the Tax Agenda, 1978–1986* (Pittsburgh: University of Pittsburgh Press, 1993); and James G. Gimpel and Jason E. Schuknecht, *Patchwork Nation: Sectionalism and Political Change in American Politics* (Ann Arbor: University of Michigan Press, 2003).

39. The emergence of the urban Democrats was important, as they were the basis for the Democrats' resurgence in the industrial Northeast and Midwest in the 1910 midterm elections. Buenker, Burnham, and Crunden argue that these political organizations had the ability to "respond constructively to the demands of urbanites" and especially to the party's urban, ethnic working-class constituents (*Progressivism*, 58). See also David Sarasohn, *The Party of Reform: Democrats in the Progressive Era* (Jackson: University Press of Mississippi, 1989).

40. Not only were the Republican Insurgents suspicious of the eastern "monied" interests and their alleged abuse of corporate power against the people, the Insurgents were also distressed by the growing strength of cities and the slow decline of rural areas (see Holt, *Congressional Insurgents*). Although the Insurgents as a result of their primarily agrarian backgrounds have been described as the heirs of Populism, this comparison underplays the very distinct differences that marked the Insurgent Republicans as different from the Democrats. For the most part, Insurgent Republicans were not, and did not see themselves as, the heirs of Populism. Indeed they made a point of attacking the Democrats and their "Bryanism." For example, Senator Borah of Idaho was the only Republican who supported Bryan's presidential candidacy. At the same time, although the Insurgents saw themselves as Republicans first and foremost, they were not entirely sympathetic to either the regular Republicans or to Roosevelt's "New Nationalism." In fact, their political views could be

"readily distinguished" from Roosevelt's. See Holt, *Congressional Insurgents*; Kenneth W. Hechler, *Insurgency: Personalities and Politics of the Taft Era* (New York: Columbia University Press, 1940); Richard Jensen, *The Winning of the Midwest* (Chicago: University of Chicago Press, 1971); Samuel McSeveney, *The Politics of Depression: Political Behavior in the Northeast, 1893–1896* (Cambridge, MA: Oxford University Press, 1972); Russell Nye, *Midwestern Progressive Politics: A Historical Study of its Origins and Development, 1870–1950* (East Lansing: Michigan State College Press, 1951). For a sharp critique of the Insurgent Republicans and their treatment in the historical literature see David Sarasohn, "The Insurgent Republicans: Insurgent Image and Republican Reality," *Social Science History* 3 (1979): 245–61.

41. There were twelve Insurgents in the Senate, led by Robert La Follette (R-WI), and approximately forty in the House.

42. While Insurgent Republicans disagreed with party regulars on a number of issues such as the tariff, creating a more than a temporary cross-party alliance, e.g., with progressive Democrats, was difficult since the Insurgents were on the whole "enthusiastic [and] committed Republicans" (Holt, *Congressional Insurgents*, 14). Indeed, Holt argues that party loyalty was the result of some of the Insurgents' progressive beliefs, which meant, among other things, independence from political machines. Since they considered Democrats in general to be part of political machines, the Insurgents could not support them. At the same time, some have argued that the growing influence of urban areas further strengthened the animosity of the Republican Insurgents against the Democrats.

43. According to party-centric theorists, centralization—usually meaning greater power accruing to the national government—can only occur when a political party is unified across its varying levels. According to David Brady this centralization only occurs during realignment. See *Critical Elections and Congressional Policy-Making* (Stanford: Stanford University Press, 1988). Inasmuch as realignments are relatively rare, Brady and William Riker are the only ones who have tested this theory. On the role of political parties in a federal system see especially Morton Grodzins, "Centralization and Decentralization in the American Federal System," in *A Nation of States*, ed. Robert A. Goldwin (Chicago: Rand McNally, 1963); William Riker, *Federalism: Origin, Operation, Significance* (Boston: Little, Brown, 1964); David Truman, "Federalism and the Party System," in *Federalism: Mature and Emergent*, ed. Arthur W. MacMahon (Garden City, NY: Doubleday, 1955); Julius Turner and Edward Schneier Jr., *Party and Constituency: Pressures on Congress*, rev. ed. (Baltimore: Johns Hopkins Press, 1970).

44. See Lynn Dumneil, "The Insatiable Maw of Bureaucracy": Antistatism and Education Reform in the 1920," *Journal of American History* 77 (1990): 499–524.

45. For a discussion of intergroup coalition building during the late nineteenth and early twentieth centuries, see Sanders, *Roots of Reform*; and Clemens, *The People's Lobby*.

46. See Melvin I. Urofsky, "State Courts and Protective Legislation during the Progressive Era: A Re-evaluation," *Journal of American History* 72 (1985): 63–91; see also Howard Gillman, *The Constitution Besieged: The Rise and Demise*

of Lochner Era Police Powers Jurisprudence (Durham, NC: Duke University Press, 1993). See also William J. Novak's "The Legal Origins of the Modern American State," in *Looking Back at Law's Century*, ed. Austin Sarat, Bryant Garth, and Robert Kagan (Ithaca, NY: Cornell University Press, 2002).

47. See David L. Shapiro, *Federalism: A Dialogue* (Evanston, IL: Northwestern University Press, 1995), 29.

48. See *Pollock v. Farmer's Loan & Trust Co.*, 157 U.S. 429 (1895), invalidating the national income tax; and *United States v. E.C. Knight*, 156 U.S. 1 (1895), which ruled that mining or manufacturing, even when the product would move in interstate commerce, was not covered under the commerce clause; as well as cases such as *Lochner v. New York*, 198 U.S. 45 (1905). *Lochner* invalidated a New York State law that set maximum working hours for bakery workers. Other key decisions during the era of the first New Federalism included *United States v. Delaware and Hudson Co.*, 213 U.S. 1 366, 408 (1909), which overturned the Federal Employers Liability Act of 1906; *Adair v. United States*, 208 U.S. 161 (1908) and *Coppage v. Kansas*, 236 U.S. 1 (1915), invalidating the prohibition of contracts that made nonmembership in a trade union a condition of employment. For a more extensive discussion of these issues, see Shapiro, *Federalism*, 29–32.

49. *United States v. Shauver*, 214 Fed. 154 (1914) overturned the Migratory Bird Treaty Act of 1913; while *Hammer v. Dagenheart*, 247 U.S. 251, 276 (1918) invalidated the Interstate Child Labor Act (1916).

50. Charles Beard, *An Economic Interpretation of the Constitution* (1913); and Frank Goodnow, *Social Reform and the Constitution* (New York: Macmillan, 1911).

51. See Barry Friedman, "Everyone's Doing Congressional Historiography: Where Are the Historians?" *Social Science History* 24 (2000): 333–48, and "Legislative Findings and Judicial Signals: A Positive Political Reading of *United States v. Lopez*," *Case Western Reserve Law Review* 46 (1996): 757–800; and Gillman, *The Constitution Besieged*.

52. Elihu Root, Roosevelt's conservative secretary of state, gave a notable speech in 1907 in which he argued that national sentiment was rising because of the increasing common ties between the people through the "workings of free trade among the states" and "the development of travel and communication." See Elihu Root, *How to Preserve the Local Self-Government of the States: A Brief Study of National Tendencies*, Authorized and correct edition (New York: Brentano's, 1907).

53. See for example, John Burgess, "The American Commonwealth," *Political Science Quarterly* (March 1886): 9–35, and Simon N. Patton, "Decay of State and Local Government," *Annals*, July 1890, 26–42.

54. Graves, *American Intergovernmental Relations*, 799. For Progressive Era critiques, see Stephen Leacock, "The Limitations of Federal Government," *Proceedings of the American Political Science Association* 5 (1908): 37–52.

55. There has been some disagreement over the influence of Croly on Theodore Roosevelt. Eric Goldman emphasizes the influence of Croly's *Promise* on Roosevelt; while Edward Stettner argues that the influence was much less significant, and that there were important differences between the two men. See

Eric Goldman, *Rendezvous with Destiny: A History of Modern American Reform* (New York: Knopf, 1952); and Edward A. Stettner, *Shaping Modern Liberalism: Herbert Croly and Progressive Thought* (Lawrence: University Press of Kansas, 1993). On Croly, see Charles Forcey, *The Crossroads of Liberalism: Croly, Weyl, Lippman, and the Progressive Era, 1900–1925* (New York: Oxford University Press, 1961); Richard Hofstadter *The Progressive Movement, 1900–1915* (Englewood Cliffs, NJ: Prentice-Hall, 1963), and *The Age of Reform: From Bryan to F. D. R.* (New York: Alfred A. Knopf, 1955).

56. Herbert Croly, *The Promise of American Life* (New York: Macmillan, 1912), 274–75. See also his *Progressive Democracy* (New York: Macmillan, 1915).

57. It is not clear whether Croly's stance is based on ideology or recognition of the limitations on national power posed by the Supreme Court (Croly, *Progressive Democracy*, 240).

58. Croly, *Progressive Democracy*, 241. Croly also described the " 'great American drift,' the tendency for Americans to believe that the nation's problems would automatically solve themselves." He argued that this lethargy would lead to a struggle among powerful groups for their private gain and leave the public interest unguarded. Thus he made a plea for a "strong assertion of the national will to overcome the disruptive tendencies in America" (Croly, *Promise of American Life*, 115).

59. Burgess, "The American Commonwealth."

60. A number of biographers suggest that in his early state government career, Wilson made a strategic "conversion" to Progressivism. On the political career of Woodrow Wilson, see Arthur Link, *Woodrow Wilson and the Progressive Era: 1910–1917* (New York: Harper and Row, 1963); and Sarasohn, *The Party of Reform*. According to Lewis Gould, as governor of New Jersey, Wilson oversaw the enactment of legislation dealing with "direct primary, corrupt practices, utility regulation and workmen's compensation laws." Lewis L. Gould, *Reform and Regulation: American Politics from Roosevelt to Wilson*, 2nd ed. (New York: Alfred A. Knopf, 1986), 161.

61. Gould, *Reform and Regulation*, 160.

62. Gould, *Reform and Regulation*, 183.

63. *World's Almanac* (1912), 140.

64. This discussion of the income tax relies heavily on Ben Baack and Edward Ray, "The Political Economy of the Origin and Development of the Federal Income Tax," in *The Emergence of the Modern Political Economy: Research in Economic History, Supplement 4*, ed. Robert Higgs (Greenwich, CT: JAI Press, 1985); Susan Hansen, *The Politics of Taxation: Revenue without Representation* (Westport, CT: Praeger, 1983); Randolph E. Paul, *Taxation in the United States* (Boston: Little, Brown, 1965); Sidney Ratner, *Taxation and Democracy in America* (New York: John Wiley and Sons, 1942); Sven Steinmo, *Taxation and Democracy: Swedish, British and American Approaches to Financing the Welfare State* (New Haven: Yale University Press, 1993); Charles Stewart, "The Federal Income Tax and the Realignment of the 1890s," in *Realignment in American Politics: Toward a Theory*, ed. Bruce A. Campbell and Richard J. Trilling (Austin: University of Texas Press, 1980); John Witte, *The Politics and Development of the Federal Income Tax* (Madison: University of Wisconsin Press, 1985).

65. See Higgs, *Crisis and Leviathan*, 97–103.

66. Research is divided as to whether the state expansion possibilities of the income tax were fully in the minds of national legislators. Baack and Ray, for example, argue that legislators were quite aware of the distributive implications of enacting the income tax. Despite this claim, a number of others have stated that there was no evidence of this intent on the part of national legislators. Holt, for one, argues that "few of the insurgents or their allies in the Democratic Party were thinking of the great spending programs. . . . Their concern was not with revenue but with the redistribution of wealth and the equalization of burdens." For this argument and their supporting evidence, see Baack and Ray, "Federal Income Tax," and "Special Interests and the Adoption of the Income Tax in the United States," *Journal of Economic History* 45 (1985): 607–25. For Holt, see *Congressional Insurgents*, 10–11.

67. Discussion of the direct election of senators relies on William H. Riker, "The Senate and American Federalism," *American Political Science Review* 49 (1955): 452–69. See also Ronald F. King and Susan Ellis, "Partisan Advantage and Constitutional Change: The Case of the Seventeenth Amendment," *Studies in American Political Development* 10 (1996): 69–102; C. H. Hoebeke, *The Road to Mass Democracy: Original Intent and the Seventeenth Amendment* (New Brunswick, NJ: Transaction, 1995); James R. Sopp, "Federalist Claims and Empirical Findings: The Case of Indirect Election of the U.S. Senate and the Decline of States' Rights," presented at the Annual Meeting of the American Political Science Association, Washington, DC, August 28–31, 1997.

68. See George Haynes, *The Election of Senators* (New York: Henry Holt, 1906), and *The Senate of the United States* (New York: Russell and Russell, 1938). See also King and Ellis, "Partisan Advantage."

69. See Robert Jay Dilger, *National Intergovernmental Programs* (Englewood Cliffs, NJ: Prentice-Hall, 1989):129.

70. Riker, "Senate and American Federalism," 466.

71. The states that were exceptions included Utah, which ratified in 1937, New Mexico (1938), Rhode Island (1947), and Connecticut (1955).

72. See Sarasohn, *The Party of Reform*.

73. Haider, *Governments Come to Washington*, for example, argues that the governorship increasingly becomes a dead-end job.

74. In light of recent American political developments, including the tendency of candidates to run as outsiders—against Washington and the "Beltway"—since President Jimmy Carter's administration, governors have been more successful than senators in winning the presidency.

75. On postgubernatorial careers, see Thad Beyle and J. Oliver Williams, eds., *The American Governor in Behavioral Perspective* (New York: Harper and Row, 1972); Sopp, "Federalist Claims" Dilger, *National Intergovernmental Programs*; and Hoebeke, *Road to Mass Democracy*.

76. Eric Schickler, *Disjointed Pluralism: Institutional Innovation and the Development of the US Congress* (Princeton: Princeton University Press, 2001), 3.

77. See Mayhew, *Congress*, 13–18.

78. See most notably Nelson Polsby and his associates' early discussion of congressional modernization. Nelson W. Polsby, "The Institutionalization of the U.S. House of Representatives," *American Political Science Review* 62 (1968):

144–68; and Nelson W. Polsby, Miriam Gallagher, and Barry Rundquist, "The Growth of the Seniority System in the U.S. House of Representatives," *American Political Science Review* 63 (1969): 787–807.

79. U.S. Census, *Historical Statistics of the United States, Colonial Times to 1970*, Series Y 189–98: Congressional Bills, Acts and Resolutions: 1789–1970 (Washington, DC: GPO, 1975).

80. These rules "established that the Speaker could count for a quorum, and for the first time instituted the reduced quorum of 100 in Committee of the Whole. They also eliminated the privilege of the motion to recess and to fix the day in which to adjourn. The changes further permitted the Speaker to exercise discretion in recognition and to rule out dilatory motions, the definitions of which have expanded over the years. In addition, they permitted public bills to be introduced through the 'hopper.' " http://www.house.gov/rules/jcoc2g.htm.

81. For this quotation and following, see Polsby, "Institutionalization of House," 145.

82. On rotation see Samuel Kernell, "Toward Understanding 19th Century Congressional Careers: Ambition, Competition and Rotation," *American Journal of Political Science* 21 (1977): 669–93. Also see Douglas Price, "Careers and Committees in the American Congress," in *The History of Parliamentary Behavior*, ed. William O. Ayedolotte (Princeton: Princeton University Press, 1977), and "The Congressional Career: Then and Now," in *Congressional Behavior*, ed. Nelson W. Polsby (New York: Random House, 1971).

83. For figures on incumbency see Stuart Rice, *Quantitative Methods in Politics* (New York: Alfred A. Knopf, 1928).

84. For the following numbers on congressional staffing see Polsby, "Institutionalization"; Polsby, Gallagher, and Rundquist, "Growth of Seniority System"; and U.S. Historical Census, Series Y 308–17: Paid Civilian Employment of the federal Government: 1816–1970. For general discussion of growth in congressional staff, see Harrison W. Fox and Susan Webb Hammond, *Congressional Staffs: The Invisible Force in American Lawmaking* (New York: Free Press, 1977); and Michael Malbin, *Unelected Representatives: Congressional Staff and the Future of Representative Government* (New York: Basic Books, 1980).

85. See "All For the Sake of Kansas: Senator Benson Given a Messenger Because Each of His Republican Colleagues Has One," *Chicago Daily Tribune*, June 6, 1906, 2.

86. For discussion of growth of congressional staff in the late nineteenth and early twentieth centuries, see Lindsay Rogers, "The Staffing of Congress," *Political Science Quarterly* 56 (1941): 1–22; Lauros G. McConachie, *Congressional Committees* (New York: Thomas Y. Crowell, 1898); and George B. Galloway, *The Legislative Process in Congress* (New York: Thomas Y. Crowell, 1953). The Appropriation Act of 1856 provided for a clerk for the House Ways and Means Committee and the Senate Finance Committee.

87. As Elisabeth Sanders argues, "[I]n the territorially based American legislature, ideas had to find geographic vessels. Proposals that might have been generated elsewhere were seized upon by regional politicians" (*Roots of Reform*, 3).

88. On the link between congressional modernization and changes in the federal system see Campbell, *Growth of American Government*; as well as John E. Chubb, "The Political Economy of Federalism," *American Political Science Review* 79 (1985): 994–101, and "Federalism and the Bias for Centralization," in *The New Direction in American Politics*, ed. John E. Chubb and Paul E. Peterson (Washington, DC: Brookings Institution, 1985).

Chapter 2

1. Austin McDonald, "Federal Subsidies to the States," Ph.D. diss., University of Pennsylvania, 1923, 1; and also McDonald, "Recent Trends in Federal Aid to the States," *American Political Science Review* 25 (1931): 628–34; Paul H. Douglas, "The Development of a System of Federal Grants-in-Aid," *Political Science Quarterly* 35 (1920): 522–44.

2. This voluntary aspect of grants-in-aid was reaffirmed in *Massachusetts v. Mellon*, 262 U.S. 447, which was decided with *Frothingham v. Mellon* (1923). Ultimately, the Court dismissed objections to the program, ruling that "no State was obliged to accept [a] grant unless it chose to do so."

3. See V. O. Key, *The Administration of Federal Grants to States* (Chicago: Public Administration Service, 1937); and Jane Perry Clark, *The Rise of a New Federalism: Federal-State Cooperation in the United States* (New York: Columbia University Press, 1938).

4. *Bruce Jacobs, The Political Economy of Organizational Change: Urban Institutional Responses to the War on Poverty* (New York: Academic Press, 1981); Walter Williams, *The Implementation Perspective* (Berkeley and Los Angeles: University of California Press, 1980); and Helen Ingram, "Policy Implementation through Bargaining: The Case of Federal Grants-in-Aid," *Public Policy* 25 (1977): 499–526.

5. The debate over the pure food bill reflected the attempt to fragment power and control state regulatory activity. The House bill authorized the secretary of agriculture to "determine standards and wholesomeness of food products," and to call on the standards committees of the Association of Agricultural Chemists (the state chemist group), the Association of State Dairy and Food Departments, "and other such experts as [the secretary] deemed necessary," Oscar Anderson, "The Pure-Food Issue: A Republican Dilemma, 1906–1912," *American Historical Review* 61 (1956): 569–70. The first provision was dropped in conference committee at the insistence of the Senate, which got a provision that essentially left the setting of standards up to the courts, thus increasing the burden of proof for state or national regulators. See James H. Young, *Pure Food: Securing the Federal Food and Drugs Act of 1906* (Princeton: Princeton University Press, 1989), 161.

6. Examples of this type of federalist regulatory activity included the Oleomargarine Act of 1886 and the Filled Cheese Act of 1896.

7. According to one report, from 1789 to 1876 approximately forty intergovernmental policies were enacted. These policies included regulations regarding boat pilots, the placement of lighthouses, and early quarantine laws. Of the forty enacted, half were enacted from the 37th to the 44th Congresses (1861–

76). ACIR, *Federal Statutory Preemption of State and Local Authority: History, Inventory and Issues* (Washington, DC: Advisory Commission on Intergovernmental Relations, 1992).

8. See Elazar, *The American Partnership*; and also Henry N. Scheiber, "Government and the Economy: Studies of the 'Commonwealth' in Nineteenth-Century America," *Journal of Interdisciplinary History* 3 (1973): 135–51.

9. For definitions of policy types, see Theodore Lowi, "American Business, Public Policy, Case-Studies, and Political Theory," *World Politics* 16 (1964): 677–715.

10. Lowi, "American Business" 691. Paul Peterson's definition of redistribution is also helpful; he defines redistributive policies as those that "reallocate societal resources from the 'haves' to the 'have-nots.' " See Peterson, *The Price of Federalism*, 17; and also his work with Barry R. Rabe and Kenneth K. Wong, *When Federalism Works* (Washington, DC: Brookings Institution, 1986).

11. In this section I define policy rather narrowly, focusing on the concrete goal of an act. For example, an act providing funds for highway construction is defined as transportation policy, while an act setting standards for the size of barrels used in interstate shipping is defined as commerce. Other acts are harder to place. For example, should an act providing for state homes for veterans be counted as military policy or social welfare policy? Since state homes have no bearing on the behavior or performance of the military, I defined the act as social welfare policy. While the classification scheme may not be perfect, it enables us to gain a sense of how these federalist policy instruments were distributed across the policy spectrum.

12. The social welfare programs for veterans underscores the important distinction policymakers would make between deserving clients, such as veterans, and the undeserving poor. See Skocpol, *Protecting Soldiers and Mothers*.

13. Deil S. Wright, *Federal Grants-in-Aid: Perspectives and Alternatives*, 2d ed. (Washington, DC: American Enterprise Institute, 1973); and also Harry N. Scheiber, "The Conditions of American Federalism: An Historian's View," in O'Toole, *American Intergovernmental Relations*.

14. Mathew McCubbins and Talbot Page, "A Theory of Congressional Delegation," in *Congress: Structure and Policy*, ed. Mathew McCubbins and Terry Sullivan (New York: Cambridge University Press, 1987), 409. For a more extensive discussion of the "new economics of organization" see Oliver E. Williamson, *The Economic Institutions of Capitalism* (New York: Free Press, 1985). See also Mathew D. McCubbins and Thomas Schwartz, "Congressional Oversight Overlooked: Police Patrols versus Fire Alarms," *American Journal of Political Science* 28 (1984): 165–79; McCubbins, Noll, and Weingast,"Administrative Procedures as Instruments" and "Structure and Process"; Calvert et al., "A Theory of Political Control and Agency Discretion."

15. In the modern era, administrative procedures also included overarching instruments such as the Administrative Procedures Act of 1947, which constrains overall agency decision-making. See Joel Aberbach, *Keeping a Watchful Eye* (Washington, DC: Brookings Institution, 1990).

16. Collectively, these administrative design features are known as "hardwiring" and "deckstacking." See McCubbins, Noll, and Weingast, "Administrative Procedures as Instruments"; and Macey, "Organizational Design."

17. McCubbins and Schwartz identify interest group monitoring and direct congressional oversight as "police patrols" and "fire-alarms." Investigations of agencies might occur at the behest of interest groups that monitor agencies for behavior and actions that may be in conflict with the group's concerns and interests. See McCubbins and Schwartz, "Congressional Oversight Overlooked"; as well as Lawrence Dodd and Richard Schott, *Congress and the Administrative State* (New York: Macmillan, 1979).

18. See Randall Calvert, Mark J. Moran, and Barry Weingast, "Congressional Influence over Policymaking: The Case of the FTC,"in McCubbins and Sullivan, *Congress*.

19. See Key, *Administration of Federal Grants to States*, 373.

20. Although separating these instruments into "grants" or "regulations" is a way to make the complexity of legislation easier to understand it does mean that some nuance can be lost. For example, a few intergovernmental regulations such as the Migrant Bird Treaty Act of 1918 not only set out national standards, but also encouraged the adoption of state laws through the offer of national funds for state administration. In this case, the line between grants-in-aid and regulation became less clear. I have dealt with this definitional problem in two ways. First, I referred to a number of secondary sources, notably ACIR's 1992 compilation of intergovernmental regulations for confirmation on whether or not an act was primarily regulatory in nature. For legislation not on this list, I examined the text of the act. If an act primarily referred explicitly to the status or role of the states vis-à-vis the regulation, it was coded as an intergovernmental regulation.

21. The U.S. Office of Management and Budget defines grants-in-aid as "resources provided by the federal government in support of a state or local program of governmental service to the public." See ACIR, *Categorical Grants: Their Role and Design* (Washington, DC: ACIR, 1975), 4. Excluded from this definition are payments to nonprofit organizations, administrative expenses, or payments for services rendered. Also excluded from OMB's definition are programs in which "private, non-profit institutions of higher education are eligible to receive funds without the action on the part of a subnational governmental unit." This exclusion holds even if public institutions are eligible. Only if the program exclusively provides aid to public institutions of higher education, or if state and local governments have a role in the grant process, is it included. In addition, payments to states for activities conducted in support of federal activities are not included. Finally, programs that are designed for a particular grantee (e.g. a bridge) or circumstance (one state, a tribe, or a limited area) are excluded. The following sources were used to identify grants-in-aid: W. Brooke Graves, *American Intergovernmental Relations*; United States Senate, *Catalog of Federal Aids to State and Local Governments*, Subcommittee on Intergovernmental Relations, 88th Cong. 2d Sess. (Committee Print, 1964); ACIR, *Categorical Grants: Their Role and Design* (Washington, DC: ACIR, 1975); and White, *Trends in Public Administration*. The U.S. *Statutes at Large* was used to identify additional grants missed in the secondary sources above, and to exclude grants that simply increased funds of a preexisting

grant, but had no other administrative or substantive effect on the performance of grant recipients.

22. The text of the Hatch Act states that "in order to secure, as far as practicable, uniformity of methods and results in the work of said stations, it shall
be the duty of the United States Commissioner [now Secretary] of Agriculture
to furnish forms, as far as practicable, for the tabulation of results of Investigation or experiments; to indicate from time to time such lines of Inquiry as to
him shall seem most important, and in general, to furnish such advice and
assistance as will best promote the purpose of this act. It shall be the duty of
each of said stations annually, on or before the first day of February, to make
to the governor of the State or Territory in which it is located a full and detailed
report of its operations, including a statement of receipts and expenditures, a
copy of which report shall be sent to each of said stations, to the said Commissioner [now Secretary] of Agriculture, and to the Secretary of the Treasury of
the United States."

23. U.S. Census, *Historical Statistics of the United States: Colonial Times to 1970*
(Washington, DC: U.S. Government Printing Office, 1975)

24. Universalism is defined as coalitions "well in excess of minimal winning
size and often approaching unanimity." See Shepsle and Weingast, "Political
Preferences." See also Collie, "Universalism"; Ferejohn, *Pork Barrel Politics*; and
Robert M. Stein and Kenneth M. Bickers, *Perpetuating the Pork Barrel: Policy Sub-
systems and American Democracy* (New York: Cambridge University Press,
1995).

25. See Ingram, "Policy Implementation through Bargaining."

26. Some have argued that because of these requirements, highway grants
were "the first sort of federal aid to be thoroughly supervised and administered. Advance examination of projects, detailed progress reports, audits of expenditures, careful examination of the finished work to ensure that plans had
been followed and that there was proper maintenance—all the techniques of
good administration were utilized." James A. Maxwell, *Fiscal Impact of Federalism in the United States* (Cambridge: Harvard University Press, 1946), 187; see
also ACIR, *Categorical Grants*, 17.

27. The decision rules for coding regulations were as follows. A statute was
counted as intergovernmental regulation if the text of the statute contained
language preempting state or local government authority. Not included were
recodifications or minor amendments to a preexisting preemption, or rules
attached to a preexisting grant-in-aid. However, included were amendments
to an act that produced a substantive expansion of a preexisting preemption.
The following ACIR sources were used to identify intergovernmental regulations: *Regulatory Federalism: Policy Process, Impact and Reform* (1984); *Federal Statutory Preemption of State and Local Authority: History, Inventory and Issues* (1992);
Federal Preemption: The Silent Revolution (1992); also used were Graves, *American Intergovernmental Relations*; and United States *Statutes at Large* from 1877 to
1931.

28. In some cases, states have been authorized to exercise primary regulatory responsibility "provided that state standards are at least as high and are
enforced." ACIR, *Federal Statutory Preemption*, iii. Other types of partial pre-

emptions included transfer of authority to the states. For example, the Whole-sale Meat Act grants the secretary of agriculture the authority to "transfer responsibility to a state that has enacted an inspection law consistent with federal standards" (ACIR, *Federal Preemption*, 17). A third type of intergovernmental regulation is the enactment of a requirement that state or local governments comply with a national standard if that government receives national funding. This type of regulation is more popularly known as a "mandate."

29. ACIR found five exceptions where state and local governments may have a voice: when state/local assistance is needed in case of emergency or to enforce a federal ban at the state level, the states in some instances are allowed to set standards for its own activities; limited turn back of regulatory authority to states authorized in some instances; the promotion of interstate compacts; the granting of gubernatorial petitions; and the granting of state vetoes over administrative decisions in some instances.

30. For a broad overview of the basis for increased congressional power vis-à-vis the states, see Shapiro, *Federalism*, and ACIR's *Regulatory Federalism*.

31. V. O. Key, *Administration of Federal Grants*, notes that matching grants that require a significant state contribution are associated with less national control and less administrative supervision; see also Ingram, "Policy Implementation through Bargaining," for discussion of national administrators.

32. See Milton Conover, "National, State, and Local Cooperation in Food and Drug Control," *American Political Science Review* 22 (1928): 910. This is not to say that the latter power is insignificant. In *Weigle v. Curtice Brothers Company*, 248 U.S. 285, 288, the Supreme Court held that "the fact that a food or drug might be condemned by Congress if it passed from state to state, does not carry it an immunity of food and drugs making the same passage, that it does not condemn. . . . When objects of commerce get within the sphere of state legislation, the state may exercise its independent judgment and prohibit what Congress did not see fit to forbid."

33. The act also prohibited expenditures in communities of more than 2,500 people.

34. The Federal Highway Act of 1921 required that state departments of highways have "adequate powers and [be] suitably equipped and organized to discharge to the satisfaction of the Secretary of Agriculture the duties required by law."

35. This situation was not the case with other intergovernmental policies such as the agricultural extension, highway, or vocational education programs also enacted during this period.

36. The federal board made two key administrative rulings: (1) "all infant hygiene work was to be confined to pre-school children," and (2) "no funds were to be used to subsidize private social or health agencies." Clark, *Rise of the New Federalism*, 145 no. 22, quoting *The Promotion of the Welfare and Hygiene of Maternity and Infancy*, U.S. Children's Bureau Publication No. 156 (1925), 3.

37. McDonald, "Federal Subsidies," 221.

38. For discussion of bureaucratic discretion, see Epstein and O'Halloran, *Delegating Powers*: Calvert, McCubbins, and Weingast, "Theory of Political Control"; and Carpenter, *Forging of Bureaucratic Autonomy*.

39. Applying traditional principal-agent theory, and in particular the concept of delegation, to the relationship between the national government and the states is difficult because under the Constitution, the direct power of the national government over the states is limited via the Tenth Amendment. On the other hand, both the commerce clause and the "necessary and proper" clause have served as the basis for national government expansion. As a result of these conflicting constitutional cues, in the American federal system it is not clear which entity is the principal and which one is the agent. Second, even if national government is assumed to be the principal, its power over its agent, the states, is not absolute. Thus a sharing—rather than a delegation—of power is a more accurate description of the relationship between the national government and the states. Readers should thus note that when talking about delegation in the federal context, I am really talking about sharing.

40. For discussions of discretionary "floor" see Bawn, "Political Control Versus Expertise" and in particular, Epstein and O'Halloran, "Administrative Procedures."

41. A score of 1 was given for each characteristic possessed by an individual policy instrument. The results were then summed with scale construction confirmed by reliability analysis. The equation for the national discretion scale: NATIONAL DISCRETION = Delegation—(Delegation × Constraints).

42. This is not to say that Congress would always get the balance of power right. Several intergovernmental policies such as the Migratory Bird Treaty Act (1913) and the Interstate Child Labor Act (1916) would be declared unconstitutional.

43. While redistributive, regulatory, and distributive intergovernmental policy areas may all seem to be characterized by a certain degree of decentralization, there is nonetheless a difference in the quality of that decentralization. Distributive policy is more likely to resemble contractual arrangements between the national level and its agent; agreement over the goals is mutual, while the performance of the agent is visible and measurable. Redistributive policy often has multiple, conflicting goals. In addition, the attainment of some of these goals cannot be measured. As a result, redistributive and regulatory policy is more likely to resemble a multilevel administrative arrangement. The greater the complexity, the harder national legislators will attempt to control the range of policy outcomes. In turn this may lead to greater attempts to centralize via rules as opposed to structure. In sum, decentralization may be preferred for distributive policy while centralization is preferred for redistributive and regulatory policy.

44. In some ways, this is the premise of many demand-side theories of American federalism. Demand for intergovernmental policy comes from state and local governments that attempt to maximize their benefits. The findings from a vast array of studies suggest that states, localities, and interest groups are all somewhat successful in translating their demands for national government goods into grants. The capacity of states and localities to play the "grants" game is an important factor in the distribution of grants. See Michael Rich, "Distributive Politics and the Allocation of Federal Grants," *American Political Science Review* 83 (1989): 193–213, and his *Federal Policymaking and the*

Poor: National Goals, Local Choices, and Distributional Outcomes (Princeton: Princeton University Press, 1993). Indeed, it is argued that the ability of these actors to extract goods from the national government can overwhelm the national government's ability to control policy outcomes, its own bureaucracy, or even the actions of states themselves. The "flypaper" effect, noted by policy analysts in the 1970s, demonstrated that bureaucrats are able to retain intergovernmental aid for themselves rather than passing the aid along to citizens in the form of more private goods as desired by the donor government. See P. Courant, E. Gramlich, and D. Rubinfeld, "The Stimulative Effects of Intergovernmental Grants: Or Why Money Sticks Where It Hits," in *Fiscal Federalism and Grants-in-Aid* (Washington, DC: Urban Institute, 1979); Wallace E. Oates, *Fiscal Federalism* (New York: Harcourt Brace Jovanovich, 1972), and *The Political Economy of Federalism* (Lexington, MA: Lexington Books, 1977). In a similar vein, a study by Richard Nathan and his associates of state policymaking in the wake of Reagan budget cutting in the early 1980s vividly illustrated the power of state-level interest groups and bureaucrats to keep nationally funded programs at near equivalent levels of funding. Richard Nathan, Fred C. Doolittle, and Associates, *The Consequences of Cuts: the Effects of the Reagan Domestic Program on State and Local Governments* (Princeton: Princeton Urban and Regional Research Center, distributed by Princeton University Press, 1983).

45. E. E. Schattschneider, *The Semi-Sovereign People* (New York: Holt, Rinehart, and Winston, 1960).

46. A second assumption is that the supply of intergovernmental policy stems from the actions of a unitary national actor (sometimes "Congress" but usually, the "president"). The emphasis of the federalism research literature on the presidency is based primarily on the steady expansion in presidential power during the twentieth century; the president's titular control over the administrative branch; and the fact that the president, unlike Congress, is a relatively unitary actor.

47. Mayhew, *Congress,* 129.

Chapter 3

1. Funding for the study was inserted into the Agricultural Appropriation Act of 1894, by Representatives Allan Durburow (D-IL) and Clarke Lewis (D-MS). The act was approved by Congress and signed by President Benjamin Harrison on March 3, 1894, his last day in office.

2. Stone's official title was Special Agent and Engineer for Office of Road Inquiry (ORI). Prior to the ORI, Stone had been elected general vice president and acting secretary of the National League of Good Roads, at its first meeting in 1892. See his speech, "National Aid to Road Building," *Good Roads*, September 1892.

3. Another obstacle was the constitutionality of road building itself. Although there was provision for post roads in Article 1, Section 8 of the Constitution, President Andrew Jackson's decisive veto of the Maysville Road Turnpike in 1830 seemingly closed the door on national involvement in the building of roads. See United States Department of Transportation, *America's Highways*

1776–1976 (Washington, DC: U.S. Government Printing Office, 1976), 22–23. The constitutional case that settled the roads issue was *Wilson v. Shaw*, 204 U.S. 24 (1907), in which the court determined that under its constitutional right to regulate interstate commerce, Congress had the power to construct interstate highways.

4. See Kernell, "19th Century Congressional Careers"; Charles H. Stewart III, *Budget Reform Politics: The Design of the Appropriations Process in the House of Representatives 1865–1921* (Cambridge: Cambridge University Press, 1989); Price, "Careers and Committees."

5. For discussion of Shackleford's career see William Rufus Jackson, *Missouri Democracy: A History of the Party and its Representative Members, Past and Present; with a Vast Amount of Informative Data* (Chicago: S.J. Clarke, Inc., 1935).

6. After being defeated for reelection to the House in 1906, Bankhead was appointed by the Alabama state governor to fill out the term of Senator John Tyler Morgan, who had died. Bankhead was subsequently reelected in 1908 (60th Congress) to the Senate. Bankhead was also the last Confederate veteran to serve in Congress, and the grandfather of actress Tallulah Bankhead.

7. Indeed, Bankhead's policy leadership derived in part from his prior non-congressional activities, when he served as vice president of the Alabama Good Roads Association, and vice president of North Alabama Good Roads Association. During his years in the Senate, Bankhead was also president of the United States Good Road Association, the only southern-based association. According to Howard Preston, the connection between Bankhead and the association was tenuous and fraught with complications, Howard Preston, *Dirt Roads to Dixie: Accessibility and Modernization in the South, 1885–1935* (Knoxville: University of Tennessee Press, 1991).

8. According to Stewart (1992), this committee was highly ranked (fourteenth out of fifty-five) from the 62nd to the 65th Congresses. Charles Stewart III, "Committee Hierarchies in the Modernizing House, 1875–1947," *American Journal of Political Science* 36 (1992): 835–56.

9. Staff was assigned to the Senate Post Office and Post Roads Committee in 1861, along with Commerce, Foreign Relations, Judiciary, Military Affairs, Naval Affairs, and Pensions. See Rogers, "The Staffing of Congress," 3.

10. For effect of malapportionment and the rural bias of congressional delegations see Turner and Schneier, *Party and Constituency.*

11. On party divisions, see Benjamin Ginsberg, "Elections and Public Policy," *American Political Science Review* 70 (1976): 41–49; James Sundquist, *Dynamics of the Party System*, rev. ed. (Washington, DC: Brookings Institution, 1983); Brady, *Critical Elections*; and Bensel, *Political Economy.*

12. In addition to Holt, *Congressional Insurgents*, see Sarasohn's "The Insurgent Republicans" and *The Party of Reform: Democrats in the Progressive Era*. See also Anne Firor Scott, "A Progressive Wind from the South, 1906–1913," *Journal of Southern History* 29 (1963): 53–70; and Dewey Grantham, "Southern Congressional Leaders and the New Freedom, 1913–1917," *Journal of Southern History* 13 (1947): 439–59.

13. See Schantz, "Sectionalism in Presidential Elections." For aggregative methods of determining sectionalism see Riker, *Federalism*; and William Alex-

ander Jr., "The Measurement of American Federalism," in Riker *Development of American Federalism*.

14. See Samuel Kernell and Michael McDonald, "Congress and America's Political Development: The Transformation of the Post Office from Patronage to Service," *American Journal of Political Science* 43 (1999): 792–811. See also Mayhew, *Congress*; Polsby, "Institutionalization."

15. See Price, "The Congressional Career," 35–36; and David Rothman, *Politics and Power: The United States Senate, 1869–1901* (Cambridge: Harvard University Press, 1966).

16. Of course, as some have cautioned, making the assumption that nineteenth-century legislators are driven by electoral imperatives may be problematic. Nonetheless, given that this electoral connection assumption forms the basis of most analyses about the modern Congress and given that this study focuses on the emergence of the modern Congress and its linkage to federal structure, we might expect that member turnover is related in some way to the enactment of IPIs. Polsby, Gallagher, and Rundquist, "Growth of Seniority System," argue that although the safety of seats was not the primary concern of national legislators during this period, the issue was growing in salience. See also, Barbara Sinclair, "Coping with Uncertainty: Building Coalitions in the House and Senate," in *The New Congress*, eds. Thomas Mann and Norman Ornstein (Washington, DC: American Enterprise Institute, 1981).

17. See for example, Gary Jacobson, "Running Scared: Elections and Congressional Politics in the 1980s," in McCubbins and Sullivan, *Congress*, as well as Mayhew, *Congress*.

18. Elizabeth Sanders quoting Haney (1910), in *Roots of Reform*, 182. For recent discussion of the Post Office, the development of administrative capacity, and the role of Congress see Carpenter's *Forging of Bureaucratic Autonomy*; and Richard John, *Spreading the News: The American Postal System from Franklin to Morse* (Cambridge: Harvard University Press, 1995).

19. See Epstein and O'Halloran, *Delegating Powers*; and Richard Bensel, "The Origins of the Discretionary State: Political Insurgency and Statutory Articulation, 1895–1917," presented at the Annual Meeting of American Political Science Association, 1981.

20. Two policy areas, military and transportation, were not analyzed because of the small number of cases. Education was folded into the social welfare category.

21. Bureaucratic drift can be defined as the concern that administrative agencies will act in ways contrary to the interests of legislators. The reasons for bureaucratic drift are many, ranging from capture of the agency by interest groups, to the development of asymmetrical information favoring bureaucrat preferences, to imperfect monitoring by elected officials. See Macey, "Organizational Design"; and McCubbins, Noll, and Weingast, "Administrative Procedures as Instruments."

22. This suggests that the models should be a system of simultaneous equations: NATIONAL DISCRETION = $a_0 + a_1$RepParty + a_2PartyVoting + a_3SectDiv + a_4DivGovt + a_5Member Turnover + a_6LegStaff + a_7STATE DISCRETION + a_7DeficitYr + a_8Trough + a_9X + u_1 STATE DISCRETION = $\beta_0 + \beta_1$RepParty + β_2PartyVoting

+ β_3SectDiv+ β_4DivGovt+ β_5Member Turnover + β_6LegStaff + β_7NATIONAL DIS-
CRETION + β_7DeficitYr + β_8Trough + β_9Z + u_2, where a_9X and β_9Z are the identification variables needed to estimate the equations. Hausman specification
tests, however, leads me to reject the hypotheses that NATIONAL DISCRETION
and STATE DISCRETION are simultaneous equations.

23. In other words, each Y_i can be included in the estimates without concern
that the u_i and Y_i are correlated.

24. Many of the observations of the dependent variable are in the "0" category, while the rest of the observations are continuously distributed. This suggests that the data may be censored; thus estimating these equations using OLS
would lead to estimates that are biased as well as inconsistent. Thus a Tobit
model is appropriate. See William H Greene, *Econometric Analysis*, 2nd ed.
(New York: Macmillan, 1993); and Damodar Gujarati, *Basic Econometrics* (New
York: McGraw-Hill, 1995).

25. IPIs from the policy areas of national resources and transportation were
combined to increase the sample size needed for statistical analysis. Nonetheless, the small size of the sample (N = 13) suggests that the estimates are not
wholly reliable. While the estimates are provided in table 3.3, I primarily discuss the findings from the other policy areas in the text.

26. See Skocpol and Finegold, "State Capacity."

27. Grant McConnell, *Private Power and American Democracy* (New York:
Knopf, 1966), 7. Indeed McConnell argues that "[f]arm policy had been taken
into the possession of the private organization." *Decline of Agrarian Democracy*
(New York: Atheneum, 1969), 235.

Chapter 4

1. The disagreement among groups was not simply based on economic self-
interest. A number of authors trace support for pure food laws among rural
midwesterners back to the Populist era. See Sanders, *Roots of Reform*; and Mary
Summers, "Putting Populism Back In," *Agricultural History* 70 (1996): 395–414.
Lorine Swainston Goodwin's *The Pure Food, Drink, and Drug Crusaders, 1879–
1914* (Jefferson, NC: McFarland, 1999) has been instrumental in bringing back
into focus the importance women's groups played in articulating the need and
lobbying for the enactment of pure food and drug laws. For discussion of the
role of urban reformers and the rise of public health as an important item on
the progressive agenda see Michael Okun, *Fair Play in the Marketplace: The First
Battle for Pure Food and Drugs* (De Kalb: Northern Illinois University Press,
1986); as well as Thomas Pegram, "Public Health and Progressive Dairying in
Illinois," *Agricultural History* 65 (1991): 36–50; and R. James Kane, "Populism,
Progressivism, and Pure Food," *Agricultural History* 38 (1964): 161–66. For
other comprehensive histories see Young, *Pure Food*; Oscar Anderson, *The
Health of a Nation: Harvey E. Wiley and the Fight for Pure Food* (Chicago: Univer-
sity of Chicago Press, 1958), and "The Pure-Food Issue: A Republican Di-
lemma, 1906–1912," *American Historical Review* 61 (1956): 550–73; and Peter
Temin, *Taking Your Medicine: Drug Regulation in the United States* (Cambridge:
Harvard University Press, 1980).

2. Like other works, I use the shortened phrase *pure food* to stand in for the more general (and more cumbersome) phrase "pure food, drink and drugs."

3. According to William Novak, *salus populi* is from "*salus populi suprema lex est* (the welfare of the people is the supreme law)" (*The People's Welfare*, 9). On the role of local and state governments in enforcing food and drug laws see also Brock, *Investigation and Responsibility*; and Wendy E. Parmet, "From Slaughter-House to Lochner: The Rise and Fall of the Constitutionalization of Public Health," *American Journal of Legal History* 40 (1996): 476–505.

4. George A. Akerlof, "The Market for 'Lemons': Quality Uncertainty and the Market Mechanism," *Quarterly Journal of Economics* 84 (1970): 488–500.

5. Duffy, *The Sanitarians*; Okun, *Fair Play*; Pegram, "Public Health and Progressive Dairying in Illinois."

6. Oleomargarine was invented in 1869 by a French chemist, Hippolyte Mège-Mouriès; received an American patent in 1873, and began production that year by the New York firm, Oleo-Margarine Manufacturing Company. For general discussion of enactment of oleomargarine laws at state and national level, see Ruth Dupré, "If It's Yellow, It Must Be Butter: Margarine Regulation in North America Since 1886," *Journal of Economic History* 59 (1999): 353–71; Henry Bannard, "The Oleomargarine Law: A Study of Congressional Politics," *Political Science Quarterly* 2 (1887): 545–57; R. Alton Lee, *A History of Regulatory Taxation* (Lexington: University Press of Kentucky, 1973); and Gerry Strey, "'The Oleo Wars': Wisconsin's Fight Over the Demon Spread," *Wisconsin Magazine of History* 85 (Autumn 2001): 3–15.

7. The Oleomargarine Act, 24 U.S. Stat. 209. Further, the legislation also called for oleomargarine producers to mark and stamp their product in various ways. This was in keeping with state regulations, which also required distinctive markings (US Senate 1900–01).

8. The court further states that "'[i]n conferring upon Congress the regulation of commerce, it was never intended to cut the states off from legislating on all subjects relating to the health, life, and safety of their citizens, though the legislation might indirectly affect the commerce of the country. Legislation, in a great variety of ways, may affect commerce and persons engaged in it without constituting a regulation of it within the meaning of the Constitution.' . . . And it may be said, generally, that the legislation of a state, not directed against commerce or any of its regulations, but relating to the rights, duties, and liabilities of citizens, and only indirectly and remotely affecting the operations of commerce, is of obligatory force upon citizens within its territorial jurisdiction, whether on land or water, or engaged in commerce, foreign or interstate, or in any other pursuit" (p. 472, L. ed. p. 227, *Inters. Com. Rep.* p. 600, *Sup. Ct. Rep.* p. 158).

9. See Milton Conover, "National, State, and Local Cooperation in Food and Drug Control," *American Political Science Review* 22 (1928): 910–28. Also Pegram, "Public Health and Progressive Dairying in Illinois"; and Brock, *Investigation and Responsibility*.

10. See Conover, "National, State, and Local Cooperation," 919.

11. See Ilyse D. Barkan, "Industry Invites Regulation: The Passage of the Pure Food and Drug Act of 1906," *American Journal of Public Health* 75 (1985): 20.

12. See US Senate, 1899–1900, 529–30.

13. See Kane, "Populism, Progressivism, and Pure Food," 161.

14. According to Young (*Pure Food*, 198–99), "[Sullivan] unearthed the 'red clause' that proprietary advertisers had come to insist upon in their contracts with newspapers . . . requiring the cancellation of all advertising should the state in which the newspaper was located enact a law to restrict or prohibit the manufacture or sale of proprietaries. Cheney [a manufacturer of a proprietary medicine, Halls Catarrh Cure] boasted of how he had used the clause in Illinois to energize newspapers into defeating a tax on patent medicines threatened by the legislature. Cheney's fellows learned the lesson quickly, and 'muzzle-clauses' proliferated. Sullivan secured pictures of such contracts, and also of letters sent to the press by proprietary producers when danger threatened. Hence, Sullivan showed how patent medicine manufacturers used their power over the press to prevent state regulation of their products. This revelation of this type of 'corruption'—the inappropriate influence of business over state government regulation due to business's superior power or political influence—may have helped fuel consumer demand for federal food and drug regulation." The actual article written by Mark Sullivan was "The Patent Medicine Conspiracy against the Freedom of the Press," *Colliers*, November 4, 1905.

15. See Graebner, "Federalism in the Progressive Era"; and Campbell, *Growth of American Government*.

16. *Congressional Record*, 49th Cong., 1st Sess., 5040–41.

17. *Journal of Proceedings of the National Pure Food and Drug Congress Held in Columbian University Hall, Washington, D.C.* (Washington, DC, 1898); *Report of the Proceedings of the Second Annual Convention of the National Pure Food and Drug Congress* (Washington, DC, 1899); "President's Address, Third Annual Pure Food and Drug Congress of 1900," *Science*, March 23, 1900, 1. See also Young, *Pure Food*, 125–27.

18. Conover, "National, State, and Local Cooperation," 927.

19. See Kolko's *Triumph of Conservatism*; but also Wood, "Strategic Uses of Public Policy 1985."

20. The countries banning American products were Great Britain, France, Greece, Turkey, Italy, Austria, and Germany. See *Congressional Record* 59th Cong., 1st sess. 40: 8900; also Kolko, *Triumph of Conservatism*, 98–107; and Barkan, "Industry Invites Regulation," 23.

21. Brosius introduced H.R. 9154 on March 15, 1898 (see *Congressional Record*, 55th Cong., 2nd sess., 2844). The following year, in December 1899, Brosius introduced H.R. 2561 (see *Congressional Record*, 56th Cong., 1st sess., 151, 3006).

22. See *Journal of Proceedings of the National Pure Food and Drug Congress*, 34–39. See also "President's Address, Third Annual Pure Food and Drug Congress of 1900," *Science*, March 23, 1900, 441–43.

23. See Charles Rosenberg, "Science, Technology, and Economic Growth: The Case of the Agricultural Experiment Station Scientist, 1875–1914," *Agricultural History* 45 (1971): 1–20; also Rosenberg, "The Adams Act: Politics and the

Cause of Scientific Research," *Agricultural History* 38 (1964): 3–12; Leonard D. White, *The Republican Era, 1869–1901* (New York: Macmillan, 1958), 248–52.

24. Porter argues that scientists in southern states were much more amenable to local control, Jane M. Porter, "Experiment Stations in the South, 1877–1940," *Agricultural History* 53 (1979): 84–101.

25. Kane, "Populism, Progressivism, and Pure Food," 162–64.

26. Indeed even this solidarity may have been the result of self-interest. Rosenberg argues that the creation of "dairy interest groups" was in large part the result of the work of early state experiment personnel who urged Wisconsin farmers to adopt dairying, as opposed to other types of production, as a "remunerative and stable response to a changing market" ("Science, Technology," 8).

27. Ladd was elected with the support of the Nonpartisan League. He was expelled from the Republican Party in 1924 for his support of Robert La Follette's presidential campaign in 1924. See Kane, "Populism, Progressivism, and Pure Food," 161–66; also Fred B. Linton, "Ladd of North Dakota," *Food, Drug, Cosmetic Law Journal* 7 (1952): 314–21; Ladd Family papers, http://www.lib.ndsu.nodak.edu/ndirs/collections/manuscripts/politics/Ladd/.

28. Young, *Toadstool Millionaires*, 229.

29. Alan I. Marcus, "Setting the Standards: Fertilizers, State Chemists, and Early National Commercial Regulation, 1880–1887," *Agricultural History* 61 (1987): 47–73; William Horwitz, "The Role of the AOAC in the Passage of the Federal Food and Drugs Act of 1906," *Food, Drug and Cosmetic Law Journal* 11 (1956): 77–85.

30. See Horwitz, "The Role of the AOAC," 78–80.

31. James Harvey Young suggests that most of these state officials were political appointees, and thus were more sympathetic to their own state's particular economic interests. Others "may have been jealous of Wiley's rising stature and fearful of the impact of a national law" on their fiefdoms (*Pure Food*, 179–81).

32. See also High and Coppin, "Wiley and the Whisky Industry"; 294.

33. Kolko, *Triumph of Conservatism*, 108; see also Young, *Pure Food*.

34. See High and Coppin, "Wiley and the Whiskey Industry"; and Carpenter, *Forging of Bureaucratic Autonomy*, 257–66. Also Clayton Coppin, "James Wilson and Harvey Wiley: The Dilemma of Bureaucratic Entrepreneurship," *Agricultural History* 64 (1990): 167–81.

35. According to Kane, Secretary Wilson's decentralization plans would have "stripped Wiley's bureau . . . of much its importance" ("Populism, Progressivism," 162). Wiley had a difficult relationship with James Wilson, the USDA secretary, for much of Wiley's tenure. According to Wiley, Wilson "had the greatest capacity of any person I ever knew to take the wrong side of public questions" (*An Autobiography*, 190).

36. Wiley came to the position with a strong background in chemistry as well as a deep familiarity with the issues of pure food; he obtained a medical degree from Indiana Medical College in 1871, and subsequently a bachelor's degree in chemistry from Harvard University. As a chemistry professor at Purdue University, he spent time at the Imperial Food Laboratory in Germany;

and he assisted the Indiana State Board of Health with studies of sugar adulteration. See Young, *Pure Food*, 100–103.

37. On this point, see Marc T. Law and Gary D. Libecap, "Corruption and Reform? The Emergence of the 1906 Pure Food and Drug Act and the 1906 Meat Inspection Act," International Centre for Economic Research (ICER) Working Paper No. 20/2003, 19n.6. See also Anderson, *The Health of a Nation*.

38. In order of publication dates, in 1887 the first three appeared: "Dairy Products," "Spices and Condiments," and "Fermented Alcoholic Beverages, Malt Liquors, Wine and Cider"; in 1889 the fourth and fifth reports, "Lard and Lard Adulterations" and "Baking Powders"; in 1892 the sixth and seventh reports, "Sugar, Molasses and Syrup, Confections, Honey and Beeswax," and "Tea, Coffee and Cocoa Preparations"; in 1893, the eighth report, "Canned Vegetables." The ninth report, "Cereal and Cereal Products," was issued in 1898, and the tenth and last report, "Preserved Meats," appeared in 1902. See Department of Agriculture, Bureau of Chemistry, Bulletin 13, "Foods and Food Adulterants."

39. See Anderson, *Health of a Nation*, 122–23; Barkan, "Industry Invites," 20–21; Wood, "Strategic Use," 405.

40. See also "Year of Food Laws," *Nation*, June 28, 1906; "Food Adulteration Scares," *Independent*, May 16, 1901, 1148–50; "The Exaggeration of Food Adulteration," *Independent*, January 5, 1905, 49–51; and Young, *Pure Food*, 151–57.

41. See Bureau of Chemistry, Department of Agriculture, *Food Definitions and Standards; Prepared by Committee on Food Standards, Association of Agricultural Chemists* (Washington, DC, 1903). See also Anderson, *Health of A Nation*, 142; and Young, *Pure Food*, 161–62.

42. 9 U.S. Stat. 237 (June 26, 1848).

43. 22 U.S. Stat. 451 (March 3, 1883).

44. This was actually the first of three acts passed by Congress. The first was 26 U.S. Stat. 414 (August 30, 1890); the second included stricter ante- and postmortem inspections of all livestock including hogs, 26 U.S. Stat. 1089 (March 3, 1891). The third act was included in Department of Agriculture Appropriations, 28 U.S. Stat. 727 (March 2, 1895). See Young, *Pure Food*, 130–33.

45. 32 U.S. Stat. 728 (July 1, 1902).

46. For comprehensive overview of this early stage, see Thomas A. Bailey, "Congressional Opposition to Pure Food Legislation, 1879–1906," *American Journal of Sociology* 36 (July 1930): 52–64; and Young *Pure Food*, 40–123.

47. A number of sources from the era reflect this belief. For example, *World's Work*, an influential periodical, published three articles blaming the "special interests" for blocking pure food legislation. See Edward Lowry, "The Senate Plot against Pure Food," *World's Work* 10 (1905): 6215–17; and Henry Beach Needham, "The Senate of Special Interests," *World's Work* 11 (January 1906): 7060–65 and (February 1906): 7206–11.

48. Indeed, Margaret Thompson argues that especially for senators, the definition of constituent was elastic and ambiguous. While some senators were beholden to the state legislatures, parties, or machines that elected them, other senators were "insufficiently grateful" and independent. Still others "adopted"

constituencies (e.g., issues such as veteran's or education) that did not directly reflect a senator's geographic base (*Spider Web*, 132–36).

49. See Thompson, *Spider Web*, 84.

50. Thus, Kane claims that though "none of the Congressmen who carried the brunt of the pure-food fight were Populists or progressives," all were "westerners long acquainted with the urgent demands of farmers for reform and regulation" ("Populism, Progressivism, and Pure Food," 165). See also Okun, *Fair Play*; Pegram, "Public Health and Progressive Dairying in Illinois," 1985; and Keach Johnson, "Iowa Dairying at the Turn of the Century: The New Agriculture and Progressivism," *Agricultural History* 45 (1971): 95–110.

51. According to one estimate, the Committee on Manufactures was a relatively low-status committee, with an overall ranking of 55th on a committee attractiveness rankings scale. However, the committee's status did rise, from 44th (from the 45th–53rd Congresses) to 33rd (54th–61st Congresses). See Stewart, "Committee Hierarchies."

52. See Wiley, *An Autobiography*, 224.

53. For example, the Paddock bill, which passed the Senate in March 1892, did not come up for vote in the House. Among the bill's provisions was a requirement that labels could not say ingredients were present if they were not, or list only certain substances and leave others off the list. See Young, *Pure Food*, 95–99; Bailey, "Congressional Opposition," 58.

54. The mean term in office rises to 3.1, if the time series begins with the 55th Congress (Class of 1896) and ends with the 60th Congress (1906). In general, by 1910 turnover decreases to an average of 20%, while the mean term in office increases to 3.6 terms (see Stewart, "Committee Hierarchies").

55. For summary information on members of congress, see United States Congress, *Biographical Directory of the United States Congress, 1774–1989, the Continental Congress, September 5, 1774, to October 21, 1788, and the Congress of the United States, from the First through the One Hundredth Congresses, March 4, 1789, to January 3, 1989, inclusive*(Washington D.C.: GPO, 1989) See *Biographical Directory* for information on Hepburn, 1203; on McCumber, 1478; and Heyburn, 1208.

56. According to one biography, Heyburn was considered a loyal Republican. Given his opposition to national oversight of natural resources, he was a highly unlikely supporter of pure food legislation. See Rufus George Cook, "A Study of the Political Career of Weldon Brinton Heyburn through his First Term in the United States Senate, 1852–1909," master's thesis, University of Idaho, 1964.

57. According to Young, "Mason was a maverick who truly seemed interested . . . he had no qualms about opposing popular causes or about championing not yet popular one" (*Pure Food*, 140). See "Investigation of Adulteration of Foods," 56th Congress, 1st sess., 1900, S. Rept. 516, or see "Adulteration of Foods," 56th Congress, 2nd sess., February 6, 1901, S. Doc. 141.

58. See U.S. Senate, *Adulteration of Articles of Food: A Tabulated Statement Prepared by the Agriculture Department for the Senate Committee on Manufactures Showing the Adulteration of the Most Common Articles of Food Consumed in the*

United States. Senate Document No. 181, 57th Congress, 1st Session, v. 4234, 1902.

59. U.S. House of Representatives, *Hearings before the Committee on Interstate and Foreign Commerce of the House of Representatives on the Pure-Food Bills* (57th Congress, 1st sess., 1902).

60. *Congressional Record,* 57th Cong., 2nd sess., 445–58.

61. *Congressional Record,* 57th Cong., 2nd sess., 1724–29, 2647, 2964–67.

62. *Congressional Record,* 58th Cong., 3rd sess., 126–29, 190–95, 3843–55.

63. See Goodwin, *Pure Food, Drink and Drug Crusaders,* 242.

64. See for example, William Randolph Hearst, "The Kind of Law That Cannot Be Passed," *New York Evening Journal,* January 9, 1906, editorial page.

65. Roosevelt communicated his support for legislation to address adulteration in the food, beverage, and drug industries, in his annual message to Congress. See Roosevelt, "Message to the 59th Congress," *Congressional Record,* 1st sess., 102.

66. *Congressional Record,* 59th Cong., 1st sess., 894–98; January 18, 1906, 1216–19.

67. Hepburn was reportedly mystified at this action. See Sullivan, *Our Times,* 2:533–34; also Young, *Toadstool,* 238.

68. See David Graham Phillips, *The Treason of the Senate,* 2nd ed. (Chicago: Quadrangle Books, 1964).

69. For statements of southern opposition, see *Congressional Record,* 59th Cong., 1st sess., 2720–21.

70. Senate, *Congressional Record,* 59th Cong., 1st sess., 1129–35, 1906, 1923, 2652–57, 2773.

71. Senate, *Congressional Record,* 59th Cong., 1st sess., 2654–55.

72. Among the senators not voting were Thomas Platt (NY), Orville Platt (CT), Henry Lodge (MA). Senate, *Congressional Record,* 59th Cong., 1st sess., 2773.

73. Among the numerous articles, see "Pure Food Bill Doped by Lobby?" *Chicago Daily Tribune,* May 24, 1906, 1.

74. See "Fear Cannon's Tactics will Defeat His Party," *New York Times,* June 4, 1906, 9.

75. Some researchers suggest that this delay reflected sectional and economic concerns over the impact of proposed legislation. For example, on the latter issue Barkan argues that with pure food legislation seemingly inevitable, large food industries were more interested in delaying the date on which the law would take effect than in blocking its enactment. She suggests that prior to the enactment of the law in 1906, the food, beverage, and drug industries systematically dumped goods that they would be unlikely to be able to sell under the new regulations (Barkan, "Industry Invites Regulation," 18–20).

76. For *New York Times* editorials and Cannon's rebuttal see Letter to the Editor, "Mr. Cannon and Pure Food: Congressman Olcott Denies that Bill has been Held Back by the "Czar," June 7, 1906, 6; "Mr. Cannon and the Speaker," June 6, 1906, 8; "The Pure Food Bill," June 8, 1906, 8.

77. See Mrs. Walter McNab Miller, "Report of the Pure Food Committee," *Consumer's Reports*, June 1906; also Goodwin, *Pure Food, Drink and Drug Crusaders*, 247–49.

78. *Congressional Record*, 59th Cong., 1st sess., 8889.

79. "Views of the Minority on Pure Food Bill," *Congressional Record*, 59th Cong., 1st sess., 8910–15.

80. Anderson, "The Pure Food Issue," 569–70.

81. *Congressional Record*, 59th Cong., 2nd sess., 1906, 9067–76.

82. See *Congressional Record*, 59th Cong., 1st sess., 1217, 2655, 2663, 2724, 9496, 9738.

83. The best accounts of the administration of the Pure Food Law prior to the enactment of the FCDA are Anderson, "Pure Food Issue"; James Harvey Young, "Pure Food and Drug Regulation Under the USDA, 1906–1940," *Agricultural History* 64 (1990): 134–42; "From Oysters to After-Dinner Mints: The Role of the Early Food and Drug Inspector," *Journal of the History of Medicine and Allied Sciences* 42 (1987): 30–53, and "Food and Drug Enforcers in the 1920s: Restraining and Educating Business," *Business and Economic History*, 2nd ser., 21 (1992): 119–28. See also Gustavus Weber, *The Food, Drug and Insecticide Administration: Its History, Activities, and Organization* (Baltimore: Johns Hopkins University Press, 1928); Paul B. Dunbar, "Memories of Early Days of Federal Food and Drug Law Enforcement," *Food, Drug and Cosmetic Law Journal* 14 (1959): 334–47; Charles O. Jackson, *Food and Drug Legislation in the New Deal* (Princeton: Princeton University Press, 1970); Ole Salthe, "State Food, Drug, and Cosmetic Legislation and Its Administration," *Law and Contemporary Problems* 6 (1939): 151–64; Lauffer T. Hayes and Frank J. Ruff, "The Administration of the Federal Food and Drugs Act." *Law and Contemporary Problems* 1 (1933): 16–35. The inaugural edition of *Law and Contemporary Problems* "The New Food, Drug, and Cosmetic Legislation" (Durham, NC: 1933), was particularly helpful.

84. This right was affirmed in *Weigle v. Curtice Brothers Company*, 248 U.S. 285 (1919). The Court stated that "the fact that a food or drug might be condemned by Congress if it passed from state to state, does not carry an immunity of food and drugs, making the same passage that it does not condemn. . . . When objects of commerce get within the sphere of state legislation the state may exercise its independent judgment and prohibit what Congress did not see fit to forbid" (Conover, "National, State, and Local Cooperation," 910). In short, the Court upheld a local statute that banned a product that was not banned under the national law. The reasoning was that the local law applied only to retail sales within the state. Therefore, the law did not interfere with interstate commerce.

85. See Alice Lakey, "Report of the Food Committee," *The Consumer's Control of Production: The Work of the National Consumer's League*, Tenth Report, March 2, 1909, 53; see also Mrs. Walter McNabb Miller, "Report of the Pure Food Committee," *Consumer's Reports*, June 1906.

86. Paul Pierce, "Seek Reform in State Food Laws," *Washington Post*, July 17, 1906, 7; also "Pure Food Cause Given Big Boost," *Chicago Daily Tribune*, July

17, 1906, 4; "Steps for Uniform Standard Taken by Pure Food Convention," *Chicago Daily Tribune*, July 12, 1906.

87. See Lakey, "Report of the Food Committee," 53.

88. For following discussion of Wiley's battles, see Anderson, "The Pure Food Issue," 562, 558, 564–67; see also Young, *Pure Food*; and Lakey, "Report of the Food Committee."

89. Conover, "National, State, and Local Cooperation," 921–25.

90. See *Federal Food, Drug and Cosmetic Law Administrative Report 1928*, 679–80. Another perspective, and more prevalent in the political science literature, is that the relationship was that of agency capture. See Pendleton Herring, "The Balance of Social Forces in the Administration of the Pure Food and Drug Act," *Social Forces* 13 (1935): 358–66, for an early analysis from this perspective.

91. See Hayes and Ruff, "The Administration of the Federal Food and Drugs Act," 18n.12. In 1927, the agency was briefly named the Food, Drug and Insecticide Administration (Department of Agriculture Act of January 18, 1927, 44 Stat. 1002–3).

92. See Hayes and Ruff, "The Administration of the Federal Food and Drugs Act," 26, citing *Manual of Procedure for Guidance of City and State Health, Food and Drug Officials* (Department of Agriculture, 1919).

93. The office would later be renamed the Office of Cooperation of the Food and Drug Administration.

94. According to Hayes and Ruff, regulatory announcements did not exactly have the force of law; they were advisory rather than mandatory ("The Administration of the Federal Food and Drugs Act," 20).

95. Indeed, "Resort to disciplinary action has seldom been required" (Hayes and Ruff, "The Administration of the Federal Food and Drugs Act," 19). See also Dunbar, "Memories of Early Days of Federal Food and Drug Law Enforcement."

96. Charles O. Jackson's *Food and Drug Legislation in the New Deal* is the definitive secondary account of the passage of the FDCA; also Charles Wesley Dunn's *Federal Food, Drug, and Cosmetic Act, A Statement of Its Legislative Record* (New York, 1938). See also David F. Cavers, "The Food, Drug, and Cosmetic Act of 1938: Its Legislative History and Its Substantive Provisions," *Law and Contemporary Problems* 6 (1939): 2–42; Daniel Carpenter and Gisela Sin, "Crisis and the Emergence of Economic Regulation: The Food, Drug and Cosmetics Act of 1938," working paper, 2002; and more recently, Gwen Kay, "Healthy Public Relations: The FDA's 1930s Legislative Campaign," *Bulletin of the History of Medicine* 75 (2001): 446–87.

97. The original bill endorsed by Tugwell (S. 1944) went down to resounding defeat in the fall of 1933. Given the existing law, the "Tugwell bill" called for a substantial increase in national government regulatory power. A number of provisions in the bill would have given considerable discretionary power to agency officials (Jackson, *Food and Drug Legislation*, 24–38).

98. Jackson, *Food and Drug Legislation*, 63.

99. Copeland kept his seat even after failing to get Roosevelt's endorsement for reelection. Senator Hubert Stephens of Mississippi, who had received

FDR's endorsement, was defeated, thus opening up the chairmanship for Copeland (Jackson, *Food and Drug Legislation*, 76).

100. According to James Patterson, Copeland ranked tenth in antiadministration votes out of the thirty-five conservative Democrats identified by the author as members of the Conservative Coalition. See James Patterson, *Congressional Conservatism and the New Deal: The Growth of the Conservative Coalition in Congress, 1933–1939* (Louisville: University of Kentucky Press, 1967).

101. See Jackson, *Food and Drug Legislation*, 55.

102. Jackson, *Food and Drug Legislation*, 43–48. See also Kay, "Healthy Public Relations," 449–51.

103. Kallet and Schlink's book focused on the questionable marketing and advertising tactics of the food, drug, and cosmetic industries. See Arthur Kallet and F. J. Schlink, *100,000,000 Guinea Pigs* (New York: Consumer's Research, 1936); as well as Ruth Lamb, *American Chamber of Horrors* (New York: Farrar and Rinehart, 1936).

104. For evidence of Wiley's growing disenchantment see his *History of a Crime against the Food Law* (Washington, DC: H. W. Wiley, 1929), and his *An Autobiography* (Indianapolis: Bobbs-Merrill, 1930).

105. Indeed Roosevelt ordered the FDA to assume a lower profile when new legislation was proposed in 1934 (Jackson, *Food and Drug Legislation*, 57).

106. According to Jackson, there were 14 women's organizations involved in shaping policy: American Association of University Women, American Dietetic Association, American Home Economics Association, American Nurses' Association, Girls Friendly Society, Homeopathic Medical Fraternity, Medical Women's National Association, Young Women's Christian Association, National Congress of Parents and Teachers, National Council of Jewish Women, National Women's Trade Union League, District of Columbia Federation of Women's Clubs, Women's Christian Temperance Union (Jackson, *Food and Drug Legislation*, 198 n. 74).

107. Ruth Lamb dedicated her book *American Chamber of Horrors* to the "gallant group of women who have been holding the front line trenches in the consumers' war for pure foods, drugs, and cosmetics."

108. Consumer's Research was founded in 1929 and reported a membership of 45,000 by 1933. For a discussion of the consumer groups, see James F. Corbett, "The Activities of Consumers' Organizations," *Law and Contemporary Problems* 1 (1933): 61–66. For further discussion of the group, see also Jackson, *Food and Drug Legislation*, 109.

109. The food, drug, and cosmetic industries proclaimed the proposed legislation was "anti-NRA and defeating of its self-regulatory principles" (Jackson, *Food and Drug Legislation*, 33). This is ironic, given the vehement opposition of many other parts of American industry to the NRA.

110. The wide discretionary power granted to the USDA was not the only thing that worked against the enactment of the Tugwell-Copeland bill(s). There were significant divisions between and within industries that would be affected by the proposed legislation. The food and prescription drug industry were generally more amenable to the overall notion that a new law was needed. The patent drug industry and cosmetic industry feared that they had everything to lose

and nothing to gain in any new legislation. Trying to write legislation that would satisfy these disparate industries proved too difficult. Each time a compromise was seemingly at hand, a new objection would crop up.

111. This was the concern that producers had expressed during the debate over the Pure Food and Drug Act in the early 1900s. As the current law stood, even basic issues that were key to national marketing were not covered in the act. For example, under the 1906 law, labels were not required to state the weight or measure. The only requirement was that a contents statement, *if used*, must be truthful. Indeed, widespread concern over the possible costs of conflicting state weight and measure laws had led food manufacturers to support the Gould Amendment in 1913. The amendment would enforce some measure of uniformity in labeling by requiring that the net contents of a product be declared (with tolerances for reasonable variations) on package labels.

112. New York City was also prepared to enact a sweeping drug statute, dubbed the "little Tugwell bill." See Jackson, *Food and Drug Legislation*, 114–15; Salthe, "State Food, Drug, and Cosmetic Legislation and Its Administration," and Jack Johannes, "Need for Suitable State Legislation," *Food Drug Cosmetic Law Quarterly* 4 (1949): 187–92.

113. See Johannes, "Need for Suitable State Legislation," 191.

114. Jackson, *Food and Drug Legislation*, 129.

115. Jackson, *Food and Drug Legislation*, 151–74; and Carpenter and Sin, "Crisis and Emergence." See also James Harvey Young, "Three Southern Food and Drug Cases," *Journal of Southern History* 49 (1983): 3–36. The official report was Henry A. Wallace, *Report of the Secretary of Agriculture on deaths due to Elixir Sulfanilamide-Massengill*, U.S. Congress, Senate Documents 124, 75th Cong., 2nd sess. (1937).

116. A long-standing major sticking point that blocked the gaining of full industry support behind S. 5 was the fear of increasing the USDA's regulatory powers. This was ultimately resolved (although not to the FDA's liking) by transferring oversight of advertising practices to the Federal Trade Commission. For full accounts of the legislative battle, see Jones, *Food and Drug Legislation*; and Cavers, "The Food, Drug, and Cosmetic Act of 1938."

117. The Copeland bill was designated S. 5. The House bill H.R. 9341 was passed in early June 1938 and incorporated into the Senate bill.

118. S. 1077 passed the House on January 12, 1938. It was passed by the Senate on March 14, 1938, and signed into law on March 21, 1938.

119. The following description of the FDA's organizational structure and responses from the states is from Charles Crawford, "The Administration of the Federal Food, Drug and Cosmetic Act," *Food Drug Cosmetic Law Quarterly* 1 (1946): 9–19. See also, Suzanne White Junod, "The Class of '39: Implementing the 1938 Food, Drug, and Cosmetic Act," *Journal of the Association of Food and Drug Officials of the United States* 52 (4) (1988): 10–25.

120. Only six states required the mandatory adoption of national standards: Indiana, Missouri, New Jersey, Utah, Vermont, and Wyoming. Fifteen states allowed for discretionary adoption of national standards: Arkansas, California, Connecticut, Florida, Louisiana, Nevada, New Hampshire, New York, North Carolina, North Dakota, Oklahoma, Oregon, Tennessee, Virginia, Washington,

West Virginia. See Franklin M. Depew, "State Food Standards," *Food Drug Cosmetic Law Journal* 4 (1949): 375–90. For a discussion of laggard, or "non-uniform" states see Johannes, "Need for Suitable State Legislation."

121. See William A. Quinlan. "The Sullivan Case: Does It Offer a Third Basis of Federal Power over Intrastate Commerce?" *Food Drug Cosmetic Law Quarterly* 3(4) (1948): 532–51.

Chapter 5

1. This chapter relies heavily on the following works: Stephen B. Goddard, *Getting There: The Epic Struggle Between Road and Rail in the American Century* (New York: Basic Books, 1994); Seely, *Building American Highway System*; United States Department of Transportation, *America's Highways: 1776–1976* (Washington, DC: U.S. Government Printing Office, 1976). There is also a series of articles on the history of the highway program by Robert Weingroff in *Public Roads* magazine, published by the U.S. Department of Transportation, Federal Highway Administration (http://www.fhwa.dot.gov/infrastructure/publicroads.htm). For older accounts see Charles L. Dearing, *American Highway Policy* (Washington, DC: Brookings Institution, 1941); W. Stull Holt, *The Bureau of Public Roads: Its History, Activities and Organization* (Baltimore: Johns Hopkins Press, 1923); Phillip Mason, "The League of American Wheelmen and the Good Roads Movement 1890–1905," master's thesis, American University, 1957; and Frederic L. Paxson, "The Highway Movement, 1916–1935," *American Historical Review* 51 (January 1946): 236–53. For regional accounts see Howard Lawrence Preston, *Dirt Roads to Dixie: Accessibility and Modernization in the South, 1885–1935* (Knoxville: University of Tennessee Press, 1991); Hal S. Barron, *Mixed Harvest: The Second Great Transformation in the Rural North, 1870–1930* (Chapel Hill: University of North Carolina Press, 1997); and "And the Crooked Shall Be Made Straight: Public Road Administration and the Decline of Localism in the Rural North, 1870–1930," *Journal of Social History* 26 (1992): 81–103; Paul S. Sutter, "Paved with Good Intentions; Good Roads, the Automobile, and the Rhetoric of Rural Improvement in the *Kansas Farmer*, 1890–1914," *Kansas History* 18 (1995–96): 284–99; Ballard Campbell, "The Good Roads Movement in Wisconsin, 1890–1911," *Wisconsin Magazine of History* 49 (1966): 273–93; Kenneth Earl Peters, *The Good-Roads Movement and the Michigan State Highway Department, 1905–1917* (Ann Arbor: University of Michigan Press, 1972); and Michael R. Fein, "Public Works: New York Road Building and the American State, 1880–1956," Ph.D. diss., Brandeis University, 2003.

2. For discussion of early-nineteenth-century internal improvement debates, see Carter Goodrich, *Government Promotion of American Canals and Railroads* (New York: Columbia University Press, 1960); John Lauritz Larson, *Internal Improvement: National Public Works and the Promise of Popular Government in the United States* (Chapel Hill: University of North Carolina Press, 2001); and Elazar, *The American Partnership*. For original discussion, see Alexander Hamilton, *Report on Manufactures*; and Albert Gallatin, *Report of Roads and Canals* (1806).

3. Seely argues that "to a surprising degree, the government efforts and policies [adopted by these governments] were the product of the federal highway

engineer's vision of what roads should be and do" (*Building American Highway System*, 7).

4. William L. Bowers, "Country Life Reform, 1900–1920: A Neglected Aspect of Progressive Era History," *Agricultural History* 45 (1971): 211–21; and Clayton Ellsworth, "Theodore Roosevelt's Country Life Commission," *Agricultural History* 34 (1960): 155–72.

5. Seely, *Building American Highway System*, 33–35. See also Wayne E. Fuller, "Good Roads and Rural Free Delivery of Mail," *Mississippi Valley Historical Review* 42 (1955): 67–83.

6. According to Preston, the development of good roads was the "third god [along with education and industrial development] in the trinity of southern progress" (*Dirt Roads to Dixie*, 3).

7. For history of LAW, see Mason, "League of American Wheelmen."

8. Isaac B. Potter, *The Gospel of Good Roads: A Letter to the American Farmer* (New York: League of American Wheelmen, 1891). For an example of Potter's message see "Our Common Roads," *Century Magazine*, April 1892, 803–21.

9. See Fuller, "Good Roads and Rural Free Delivery of Mail."

10. The rail industry would later oppose highway funding, rightly seeing it as a threat to its interests. See Goddard, *Getting There*, 46–47; Seely, *Building American Highway System*, 18–20; and Dearing, *American Highway Policy*, 226–57.

11. For discussion of state-level good roads organizations, see Department of Transportation, *America's Highways*, 41–43. For a specific example, see *Brief History of the Washington State Good Roads Association* (Seattle: Washington State Good Roads Association, 1939).

12. See Logan Page, Director, U.S. Office of Public Roads and Rural Engineering, Address to Pan-American Road Congress, 1915. The AAHI would later change its name to the American Highway Association. See Department of Transportation, *America's Highways*, 77–79.

13. See *American Association for Highway Improvement, Papers, Addresses, and Resolutions Before the American Road Congress* (Baltimore: Waverly Press, 1912), 52, in Department of Transportation, *America's Highways*, 79. See also Seely, *Building American Highway System*.

14. Paxson, "The Highway Movement," 238–40.

15. See Barron, "And the Crooked"; Preston, *Dirt Roads to Dixie*.

16. Work on roads was done via a road tax in which able-bodied males were required to give a certain amount of labor (either in person or in cash). Rural areas favored this system for a number of reasons. First, there was a "deep-seated commitment to local government that held sway in the countryside" (Barron, "And the Crooked," 84). This localism was reinforced by the place the road system held in the social system of rural life. Barron argues that communal work on highways "gave the people of the neighborhood a chance to get together and discuss the questions of the neighborhood, town and nation" (quoting Frederic G. Howes, "History of the Town of Ashfield, Franklin County, Massachusetts, from its Settlement in 1742 to 1910" ["And the Crooked," 98 n. 5). Second, rural residents preferred the older system because switching to a cash system would be to the detriment of farmers. A switch to

a system of payments based on property taxes penalized land-rich but cash-poor farmers, and it especially penalized those farmers whose land abutted roads. See also, Department of Transportation, *America's Highways*, 35–39.

17. For example, counties in the South "wishing to upgrade their roads by special taxation or bonded indebtedness had to organize local referenda . . . it was because of this cumbersome process that road improvement measures failed more often than they passed" (Preston, *Dirt Roads to Dixie*, 24).

18. White, *Trends in Public Administration*, 106; see also Fein, "Public Works."

19. Preston, *Dirt Roads to Dixie*, 37.

20. Department of Transportation, *America's Highways*, 65.

21. Preston, *Dirt Roads to Dixie*, 75.

22. White, *Trends in Public Administration*, 114; and John Lapp, "Highway Administration and State Aid," *American Political Science Review* 10 (1916): 735–38.

23. For New York State see Fein's "Public Works"; for Washington State, see Washington State, Department of Transportation, *Forty Years with the Washington State Department of Highways* (n.d.); Arizona, Department of Transportation, *Good Roads Everywhere: A History of Road Building in Arizona* (May 2003); George E. Koster, *A Story of Highway Development in Nebraska* (Lincoln: Nebraska Department of Roads, 1997); and Emory Johnson, "Improvement of Country Roads," *Annals of the American Academy*, September 1894, 121–23.

24. Barron, "And the Crooked," 91.

25. For contemporary discussions of good roads and convict labor see Charles Henry Davis, "Good Roads and Convict Labor," *Proceedings of the Academy of Political Science in the City of New York* 4 (January 1914): 1–5; Joseph Hyde Pratt, "Convict Labor in Highway Construction," *Annals of the American Academy of Political and Social Science* 46 (March 1913): 78–87; Sydney Wilmot, "Use of Convict Labor for Highway Construction in the North," *Proceedings of the Academy of Political Science in the City of New York*, 4 (January 1914): 6–68.

26. See Thomas J. Tynan, "Prison Labor on Public Roads," *Annals of the American Academy of Political and Social Science* 46 (March 1913): 57–60.

27. Lichtenstein suggests that the BPR was not totally comfortable with the concept of convict labor. See Alex Lichtenstein, "Good Roads and Chain Gangs in the Progressive South: 'The Negro Convict is a Slave,' " *Journal of Southern History* 59 (1993): 85–110. The BPR produced its own report on convict labor in 1914, with only modest support for the practice. See J. E. Pennybacker, H. S. Fairbank, and W. F. Draper, *Convict Labor for Road Work*, USDA, Bulletin No. 414. See also Jane Zimmerman, "The Penal Reform Movement in the South During the Progressive Era, 1890–1917," *Journal of Southern History* 17 (1951): 462–92.

28. The development of capacity did not mean immunity from corruption. New York State was rocked by a series of corruption scandals from 1911 to 1916 (see Fein, "Public Works," 56–58).

29. See Barron, "And the Crooked"; and Fein, "Public Works."

30. Barron, "And the Crooked," 90–91; see Sutter, "Paved with Good Intentions," 292–93, for discussion of Kansan ambivalence.

31. Barron, "And the Crooked," 96.

32. The Agricultural Appropriation Bill of 1893 included an appropriation of $10,000, and directed the secretary to "make inquiries regarding public roads [and] to make investigations for a better system of roads" (Department of Transportation, *America's Highways*, 44).

33. Seely, *Building American Highway System*, 13. See also Daniel Carpenter's discussion of the importance of "reputation building" as a means of increasing bureaucratic autonomy in his *Forging of Bureaucratic Autonomy*, and "State Building through Reputation Building: Coalitions of Esteem and Program Innovation in the National Postal System, 1883–1913," *Studies in American Political Development* 14 (2000): 121–55).

34. See *Congressional Record*, 62nd Cong., 3rd sess., 3000. This is not to say that the agency worked alone; it worked with a number of new groups that had also organized, such as the American Society for Testing Materials (ASTM) in 1899.

35. Department of Transportation, *America's Highways*, 44–52, 75.

36. Seely, *Building American Highway System*, 35; Department of Transportation, *America's Highways*, 76.

37. The BPR's relationship with the newly formed American Automobile Association (AAA) was still tentative and uncertain. See Goddard, *Getting There*; Department of Transportation, *America's Highways*, 48–50.

38. The most serious organized rival to the BPR and its allies was the National Highways Association, established (in 1911) and largely funded by Charles Henry Davis, an early investor in Henry Ford's company. Davis agitated for a "broad and comprehensive system of National Highways, built, owned, and maintained by the National Government." See Richard F. Weingroff, "Good Roads Everywhere: Charles Henry Davis and the National Highways Association," DOT, http://www.fhwa.dot.gov/infrastructure/davis.htm.

39. Congress passed legislation authorizing rural free delivery in 1896. The legislation required that rural delivery would only be established "along reasonably good roads and that the carrier need not go out on his route unless the roads were in fit condition to travel" (Department of Transportation, *America's Highways*, 80). See also Seely, *Building American Highway System*, 27; and Fuller, "Good Roads and Rural Free Delivery of Mail."

40. Department of Transportation, *America's Highways*, 86.

41. Seely, *Building American Highway System*, 41.

42. For debate see *Congressional Record*, 63rd Cong., 2nd sess., 3101–4182.

43. "Payne Scents Pork in Good Roads Bill," *New York Times*, February 8, 1914, 2.

44. *Congressional Record*, 63rd Cong., 2nd sess. 51, 3291–92.

45. "Senators on Roads: Several Express Their Views to Three A's on Federal Aid," *New York Times*, April 19, 1914, 8.

46. For debate see *Congressional Record*, 64th Cong., 1st sess., 1057–2100, 2101–3112.

47. "Pork Barrel' Fight Faced By Congress," *New York Times*, December 26, 1915, 21.

48. Department of Transportation, *America's Highways*, 83.

49. *New Republic*, February 1916, 263.
50. *Congressional Record*, 64th Cong., 1st sess., 1536–1537.
51. *Congressional Record*, 64th Cong., 1st sess., 2335.
52. Macdonald, "Federal Subsidies to the States," 55–56.
53. See *Congressional Record*, 64th Cong., 1st sess., 6494–6504.
54. See Department of Transportation, *America's Highways*, 91–99; and Richard Weingroff, "For The Common Good: The 85th Anniversary of a Historic Partnership," *Public Roads* 64 (March–April 2001): 30–46.
55. Department of Transportation, *America's Highways*, 104.
56. See U.S. Census, *Historical Statistics*, Series Q 64–68: Mileage and Cost of Federal-Aid Highway Systems, 1917–1970; and U.S. Bureau of Public Roads, *An Economic and Statistical Analysis of Highway-Construction Expenditures* (Washington, DC: GPO, June 1935).
57. See James Patterson, *The New Deal and the States: Federalism in Transition* (Princeton: Princeton University Press, 1969), 29.
58. The legislation also required that the RFC report to Congress, on a monthly basis, the identity of all new borrowers of RFC funds. This requirement would actually exacerbate the looming bank crisis facing the United States.
59. Patterson, *The New Deal and the States*, 32.
60. According to Patterson, a number of states were in such dire fiscal straits that even the $3 to $1 matching contribution was beyond them (Patterson, *The New Deal and the States*, 65). In general, funds were disbursed only to states that applied, and with the approval of the national administrator. The law allowed for varying types of state control. In general, the types and amounts of relief spending, as well as the organization of state relief agencies, were functions kept under state control. Nonetheless, under certain circumstances the national administrator could assume control of state administrations.
61. The CWA was a quasi-IPI, in that the national administrator selected the state administrators for the program. In practice, most of the state FERA administrators were handed CWA duties as well. The WPA program, by contrast, was almost purely nationally administered. Control and administration for the overall program rested in the hands of WPA administers, while state and local governments were allowed a limited role in proposing, administering, and financing individual projects. Again, like the CWA, often the existing state (national) FERA administrator was also given control over a state's WPA program. Nationalization did not necessarily mean greater efficiency. Because there were no state requirements, or means for influencing state actions, states felt free to simply delegate all relief responsibilities to the WPA, and in some instances actively block WPA efforts. See Patterson, *The New Deal and the States*, 80; also U.S. Works Project Administration, *Final Report in the W.P.A. Program, 1935–43* (Washington, DC: GPO, 1946).
62. A study by the BPR would show that highway spending provided over 3.6 million man-years of direct job employment, and over 6 million man-years in ancillary services and spending. BPR, *An Economic and Statistical Analysis of Highway-Construction Expenditures*; and Seely, *Building American Highway System*, 91.

63. According to Clark, state highway departments supported the tax requirement in order to preserve their budgets in the face of overall state budgetary cutbacks and diversion of funds (Clark, *The Rise of a New Federalism*, 150).

64. In 1933, Talmadge on assuming office purged all state agencies, including the state highway department. Talmadge also diverted state highway funds to other uses, counting on the federal aid to take up the slack. The PWA attempted to force Talmadge to accept a "supervisory engineer" appointed by Washington who would oversee PWA road projects in Georgia. Talmadge, however, was able to get the PWA to back down. By 1935, the Federal Roads Bureau attempted to freeze funds to Georgia in order to force Talmadge to reorganize the department up to the bureau's standards. Again, Talmadge was able to ultimately prevail. Indeed, Harry Hopkins's ongoing battles with Talmadge in other New Deal policies precipitated the "federalization," or centralizing, of FERA in June 1934. See Michael S. Holmes, *The New Deal in Georgia: An Administrative History* (Westport, CT: Greenwood Press, 1975), 175–76.

65. See Mark H. Rose and Bruce Seely, "Getting the Interstate System Built: Road Engineers and the Implementation of Public Policy, 1955–1985," *Journal of Policy History* 2 (1990): 23–55. See also Seely, *Building American Highway System*; and Dearing, *American Highway Policy*.

Chapter 6

1. According to researchers Robyn Muncy, J. Stanley Lemons, and Theda Skocpol, while discussing the lack of public health information about children, Kelley and Wald saw an article describing the government's plan to investigate the damage caused by the boll weevil. That it was for insects and not for individuals offended their reformist sensibilities; nonetheless the program provided a model for their proposed legislation. Florence Kelley made the case of a national commission in her book *Some Ethical Gains Through Legislation* (New York: Macmillan, 1905). See Robyn Muncy, *Creating a Female Dominion in American Reform, 1890–1935* (New York: Oxford University Press, 1991), 39; J. Stanley Lemons, "The Sheppard-Towner Act: Progressivism in the 1920s," *Journal of American History* 55 (1969): 776–86; and Theda Skocpol, *Protecting Soldiers and Mothers*, 483. See also Herbert Parsons, "Establishment of a National Children's Bureau," in "Race Improvement in the United States," *Annals of the American Academy of Political and Social Science* 34 (1) (1909): 48.

2. For the discussion of the Sheppard-Towner Act, I draw heavily from the following works: Joseph B. Chepaitis, "Federal Social Welfare Progressivism in the 1920s," *Social Service Review* 46 (June 1972): 213–29, and "The First Federal Social Welfare Measure: The Sheppard-Towner Maternity and Infancy Act, 1918–1932," Ph.D. diss., Georgetown University, 1968; Molly Ladd-Taylor, *Mother-Work: Women, Child Welfare, and the State, 1890–1930* (Urbana: University of Illinois Press, 1994); J. Stanley Lemons, *The Woman Citizen: Social Feminism in the 1920s* (Charlottesville: University Press of Virginia, 1990), and "The Sheppard-Towner Act: Progressivism in the 1920s"; Kriste Lindemeyer, *"A Right to Childhood": The U.S. Children's Bureau and Child Welfare, 1912–46* (Ur-

bana: University of Illinois Press, 1997); Richard Meckel, *"Save the Babies":
American Public Health Reform and the Prevention of Infant Mortality, 1850–1929*
(Baltimore: Johns Hopkins University Press, 1990); Gwendolyn Mink, *The
Wages of Motherhood* (Ithaca: Cornell University Press, 1995); and Edward D.
Schlesinger, "The Sheppard-Towner Era: A Prototype Case Study in Federal-
State Relationships," *American Journal of Public Health* 57 (1967): 1034–40.

3. In addition to works cited in previous notes, see the following for specific
accounts of the creation of the Children's Bureau: Jacqueline K. Parker and
Edward M. Carpenter, "Julia Lathrop and the Children's Bureau: The Emer-
gence of an Institution," *Social Service Review* (March 1981): 60–77; Martha M.
Eliot, "The Children's Bureau: Fifty Years of Public Responsibility for Action in
Behalf of Children," *American Journal of Public Health* 52 (1962): 576–91; William
Schmidt, "The Development of Health Services for Mothers and Children in
the United States," *American Journal of Public Health* 63 (1973): 419–27; Dorothy
Bradbury, *Four Decades of Action of Children: A Short History of the Children's Bu-
reau* (Washington, DC: GPO, 1956).

4. For discussion of the federated structure of women's organizations see
Skocpol, *Protecting Soldiers and Mothers*, 314–72; and Goodwin, *The Pure Food,
Drink and Drug Crusaders*, 131–51.

5. For debate and votes, see *Congressional Record*, 62nd Cong., 2nd sess.,
1573–1579.

6. Infant mortality was also an issue that was intimately familiar to Lathrop
due to her prior experience at Hull House. In addition, her own professional
background and networks exposed her to current thinking in European circles
on the role of public health as prevention. See Parker and Carpenter, "Julia
Lathrop," 64; and Rodgers, *Atlantic Crossings*, 237–41.

7. Julia Lathrop, "The Children's Bureau," address before the Biennial Meeting of the General Federation of Women's Clubs, San Francisco, July 5, 1912,
reprinted in *The American Journal of Sociology* 18 (1912): 318–30.

8. See Parker and Carpenter, "Julia Lathrop," 68.

9. These contests, to modern eyes, were not entirely benign. The purposes
of these contests, and to some extent the movement as a whole, was the maintenance of racial (Anglo-American) purity and order against the threats of
what supporters argued were serious mental and physical degeneracy deriv-
ing from new eastern and southern European immigrants. See Linda Gordon,
"Black and White Visions of Welfare: Women's Welfare Activism, 1890–1945,"
Journal of American History 78 (1991): 559–90.

10. See Ladd-Taylor, *Raising a Baby the Government Way: Mothers' Letters to
the Children's Bureau, 1915–1932* (New Brunswick: Rutgers University Press,
1986).

11. According to Skocpol, "Lathrop repeatedly invoked parallels between
the USDA and the Children's Bureau, and not only for rhetorical purposes. It
is fascinating that Lathrop modeled aspects of her statebuilding work for
women and children on this unusually well-articulated part of the otherwise
weak U.S. federal administration of the early twentieth century" (*Protecting
Soldiers and Mothers*, 486).

12. See Muncy, *Creating a Female Dominion*, 107–9; also Ladd-Taylor, *Mother-Work*, 177–80. See Jacqueline Parker, "Women at the Helm: Succession Politics at the Children's Bureau," *Social Work* 39 (1994): 551–59.

13. See Skocpol, *Protecting Soldiers and Mothers*: 487; Muncy, *Creating a Female Dominion in American Reform*: 100; Parker and Carpenter, "Julia Lathrop," 68–69.

14. United States Children's·Bureau, *Promotion of the welfare and hygiene of maternity and infancy: The Administration of the act of Congress of November 23, 1921, for fiscal year ended June 30, 1929* (Washington, DC: GPO, 1931).

15. Muncy, *Creating a Female Dominion*, 99–101. Skocpol disagrees with this interpretation. She suggests that Muncy "greatly overestimates the Bureau's capacity" (*Protecting Soldiers and Mothers*, 683 n. 9).

16. See Emma O. Lundberg, "State Commissions for the Study and Revision of Child-Welfare Laws," United States Children's Bureau, U.S. Department of Labor, Publication No. 131 (Washington, DC: GPO, 1924).

17. Although the bureau was successful in creating, in Robyn Muncy's words, a "female dominion" of professional women at both the national and state level, this was not enough to stave off the combined attacks of the United States Public Health service and the male-dominated AMA. See Sheila M. Rothman, *Woman's Proper Place: A History of Changing Ideals and Practices, 1870 to the Present* (New York: Basic Books, 1978), 126–52.

18. Parker and Carpenter, "Julia Lathrop," 62–66.

19. U.S. Children's Bureau, *Annual Report for 1917* (Washington, DC, GPO).

20. U.S. Children's Bureau, *Annual Report for 1919* (Washington, DC, GPO).

21. For this oft-cited quote, see Lemons, "The Sheppard-Towner Act," 779; and Muncy, *Creating a Female Dominion*, 106. Both authors cite the following article: Charles A. Selden, "The Most Powerful Lobby in Washington," *Ladies Home Journal*, April 1922, 95.

22. Chepaitis, "The First Federal Social Welfare Measure," 219.

23. See Key, *The Administration of Federal Grants to States*, 15.

24. Chepaitis, "The First Federal Social Welfare Measure," 219–20. For the AMA's position, see "The Sheppard-Towner Bill" (Editorial), *Journal of the American Medical Association (JAMA)* 76 (May 28, 1921): 1503–4; and "The Sheppard-Towner Bill—Public Health or Politics?" *JAMA* (February 11, 1922): 435.

25. For Rankin's bill (H.R. 12634), see *Congressional Record*, 65th Cong., 2nd sess. 1918, 8599–8600; and United States Congress, House Committee on Labor, *Hearings: Hygiene of Maternity and Infancy, H.R. 12634*. 65th Cong., 3rd sess., 1919.

26. United States Congress, House, *Hearings: Public Protection of Maternity and Infancy, H.R. 10925*, 67th Cong., 3rd sess. 1921.

27. See United States Congress, House, *Protection of Maternity and Infancy: H Rept. 467 to Accompany S. 1039*, 67th Cong., 1st sess., 1921. Also *Hearings on H.R. 2366, a Bill for the Public Protection of Maternity and Infancy.* 67th Cong., 1st sess., 1921.

28. For general discussion on this point see Lemons, "The Sheppard-Towner Act"; and Muncy, *Creating a Female Dominion in American Reform*. See also

David Burner, *The Politics of Provincialism: The Democratic Party in Transition, 1918–1932* (New York: Alfred A. Knopf, 1970).

29. For discussion of strength of women's lobby see Skocpol, *Protecting Soldiers and Mothers*, 505. Cheryl Logan Sparks and Peter R. Walniuk, "Enacting Mothers' Pensions: Civic Mobilization and Agenda Setting or Benefits of the Ballot?" *American Political Science Review* 89 (1995): 710–30 criticize Skocpol's interpretation). See also Anna L. Harvey, *Votes Without Leverage* (New York: Cambridge University Press, 1998).

30. This is contrary to Skocpol's claim that the act encountered no virulent opposition, since it was not passed as part of "emergency" war legislation (*Protecting Soldiers and Mothers*, 501). For debate see *Congressional Record* 67th Cong., 1st sess., 172, 525, 4207, 4215–17, 7916, 7921–26, 7940–43, 8022, 8036–37, 8052–53, 8115, 8154, 8178.

31. For remarks on "old maids" and "spinsters" see *Congressional Record*, 67th Cong., 1st sess., 4207, 4215–17, 8759.

32. See *Congressional Record*, 67th Cong., 1st sess., 7916, 7932, 7936, 7984, 7997.

33. See Schmidt, "Development of Health Services," 421.

34. See Muncy, *Creating a Female Dominion*, 106; and Lemons, "The Sheppard-Towner Act," 779.

35. For votes see *Congressional Record* 67th Cong., 1st sess., 8036–37, 8052–53.

36. Clark, *The Rise of a New Federalism*, 146, quoting Austin McDonald, "Federal Subsidies to the States," 221.

37. The governor of Maine vetoed the legislature's acceptance of the Sheppard-Towner Act, while New York State's governor, Nathan Miller (who had defeated Alfred E. Smith in 1920) threatened to veto any legislation dealing with the act. Miller would be defeated by Smith in New York's next gubernatorial election. Smith, with the support of the New York League of Women Voters, in turn would get the legislature to approve of the state's participation in the program in 1923 (see Lemons, "The Sheppard-Towner Act," 782).

38. Clark quoting "The Promotion of the Welfare and Hygiene of Maternity and Infancy," U.S. Children's Bureau Publication No. 156 (1925), 3.

39. See Muncy, *Creating a Female Dominion*, 107–8.

40. For this assessment of the bureau, see Clark, *The Rise of a New Federalism*, 207.

41. Lemons, "The Sheppard-Towner Act," 785–86. See also Grace Abbott, "The Federal Government in Relation to Maternity and Infancy," *Annals* 151 (September): 92–101.

42. The Democrats were Peter Gerry (D-RI), Carter Glass (D-VA), and David Walsh (D-MA). For discussion of the changed political climate, see Chepaitis, "Federal Social Welfare Progressivism in the 1920s," 222–23; and Lemons, *The Woman Citizen*, 157.

43. See Burner, *The Politics of Provincialism*. For a discussion of the influence of Southern members of Congress on New Deal legislation, in addition to Patterson, *Congressional Conservatism and the New Deal*, see David W Brady and Charles Bullock III, "Is There a Conservative Coalition in the House?" *Journal*

of Politics 42 (1980): 549–59; Ira Katznelson, Kim Geiger, and Daniel Kryder, "Limiting Liberalism: The Southern Veto in Congress, 1933–1950," *Political Science Quarterly* 108 (1993): 283–306; and Robert Lieberman, *Shifting the Color Line: Race and the American Welfare State* (Cambridge: Harvard University Press, 1998).

44. Muncy, *Creating a Female Dominion*, 130; Burner, *The Politics of Provincialism*, 29–30.

45. "President Coolidge's Budget Message to Congress," *New York Times*, December 9, 1926, 26.

46. Muncy, *Creating a Female Dominion*, 129.

47. Molly Ladd-Taylor agues that the Children's Bureau in fact enjoyed widespread grassroots support because of its direct connection (via correspondence and pamphlets) with millions of (white and nonwhite) working-class women. These women, however, were not politically strong enough to overcome the virulent opposition to Sheppard-Towner. See Ladd-Taylor, "Women's Health and Public Policy," in *Women, Heath and Medicine in America*, ed. Rima D. Apple (New York: Garland, 401–2.

48. See United States Congress, House, Committee on Interstate and Foreign Commerce, *Hearing on H.R. 7555: Extension of Public Protection of Maternity and Infancy Act*; 69th Cong., 1st sess. 1921. For debate in House and Senate on extension, see *Congressional Record* 69th Cong., 1st sess., 12918–52; *Congressional Record* 69th Cong., 2nd sess., 79, 1113, 1119, 1215–18, 1413, 1425, 1468, 1481, 1485–87, 1503–4, 1553–5, 1571–72, 1583–85.

49. See Chepaitis, "Federal Social Welfare Progressivism in the 1920s," 222.

50. Schlesinger, "The Sheppard-Towner Era," 1038.

51. See *Social Security in America, The Factual Background of the Social Security Act as Summarized from the Staff Reports to the Committee on Economic Security*, U.S. Committee on Economic Security, Social Security Pub. No. 20, 1937.

52. Muncy, *Creating a Female Dominion*, 146–50.

53. The White House Conference on Child Health and Protection (November 19, 1930). Not only would any new program be administered by the PHS, it would also be (in keeping with Hoover's voluntarist stance) funded by private donations and the states.

54. See Abbott, "The Federal Government in Relation to Maternity and Infancy," 95.

55. For a Reagan-era example of this type of policy institutionalization at the state level, see Nathan et al., *The Consequences of Cuts: the Effects of the Reagan Domestic Program on State and Local Governments*.

56. Kriste Lindemeyer argues that the bureau "acted as one of the country's best sources of social welfare statistics" (*"A Right to Childhood,"* 171).

57. Muncy, *Creating a Female Dominion*, 150–57.

58. For a discussion of the creation of the Social Security Act, see Edwin E. Witte, *The Development of the Social Security Act* (Madison: University of Wisconsin Press, 1963); William E. Leuchtenberg, *Franklin D. Roosevelt and the New Deal* (New York: Harper and Row, 1963); also Suzanne Mettler, *Dividing Citizens: Gender and Federalism in New Deal Public Policy* (Ithaca, NY: Cornell University Press, 1998); Russell Hanson, "Federal Statebuilding During the New

Deal: The Transition from Mother's Aid to Aid to Dependent Children," in *Changes in the State: Causes and Consequences*, ed. Edward S. Greenberg and Thomas F. Mayer (New York: Sage, 1990).

59. According to Lindemeyer, the impact of CHRP was limited since the bureau did not have the funds for more personnel, and states were loath to contribute additional monies to a health care program (*"A Right to Childhood,"* 178).

60. The bureau advocated a "whole child" approach, which argued that all the aspects of a child's life, from health to family income, needed to be considered in order to ensure a healthy childhood. See Lindemeyer, *"A Right to Childhood,"* 179–95; and also Bradbury, *Four Decades*.

61. An important war over the status of mother's aid was also lost. Mother's aid was considered charity relief as opposed to insurance or an earned benefit (like veteran's pensions). Thus, many have argued this was the basis of the United States' two-tiered social insurance system. For a broad overview of this argument, see Skocpol, *Protecting Soldiers and Mothers*; Mettler, *Dividing Citizens*; and Margaret Weir, Anna Shola Orloff, and Theda Skocpol, *The Politics of Social Policy in the United States* (Princeton: Princeton University Press, 1988). On the other hand, the battle for outlawing children's labor was partially won with the passage of the Fair Labor Standards Act of 1938, which regulated child labor. The act was applicable only to establishments that produced goods that were shipped across state lines. Again the enforcement of the statute was given to the Children's Bureau; and again, like the Social Security Act, significant exceptions were carved out in terms of the law's coverage.

62. See Katharine F. Lenroot, "Maternal and Child Welfare Provisions of the Social Security Act," *Law and Contemporary Problems* 3 (1936): 253–62.

63. Lindemeyer, *"A Right to Childhood,"* 188.

64. The lion's share of Social Security funding, however, was for Title I (Grants to states for old age assistance), which was allocated $49.75 million; Title III (unemployment compensation), allocated $49 million; and Title IV (Aid to Dependent Children), allocated $24.75 million.

65. Clark, *The Rise of a New Federalism*, 207.

66. Key, *The Administration of Federal Grants to States*, 65 n. 58.

67. See *Twenty-fourth Annual Report of the Secretary of Labor, 1936* (Washington, DC), 117–21.

68. This is not to say that there was perfect harmony within this network. V. O. Key, for example, reported a "certain coolness among the state health officers towards the Children's Bureau," probably reflecting long-standing rivalry and hostility between the Children's Bureau and the traditional medical establishment. Despite this coolness, Key argued that Congress should have merged the general grants for public health and the grants for maternal and child health on the grounds of administrative simplicity and policy. Though there may have been good strategic, administrative, and political reasons for not placing the maternal and child health grants under the USPHS in 1921, the USPHS of 1937 was "far removed" from the USPHS of 1921 (Key, *Administration of Federal Grants*, 211).

Chapter 7

1. Skocpol and Finegold, "State Capacity."
2. For discussion of "well-regulated" society, see Novak, *The People's Welfare*.
3. For discussion of "Alabama syndrome," see James Sundquist, *Making Federalism Work* (Washington, DC: Brookings Institution, 1969), 271; and also Clark, *The Rise of a New Federalism*.
4. U.S. Census, *Historical Statistics of the United States*, 1975.
5. David Truman, *The Governmental Process* (New York: Knopf, 1951), 123.

Index

AAA (American Automobile Association), 119, 205n.37
AASHO (American Association of Highway Officials), 119
Adair v. United States, 178n.48
ADC (aid to dependent children), 152–53, 212n.64
administrative capacity, 8–9, 159
Administrative Procedures Act (1947), 183n.15
administrative procedures/structures, definition of, 45–46, 183n.15
agency design/personnel, 46
Agricultural Appropriation Act (1894), 188n.1
Agricultural Appropriation Bill (1893), 205n.32
Agricultural Appropriations Act (1903), 99
aid to dependent children (ADC), 152–53, 212n.64
Alabama syndrome, 159
Aldrich, Nelson, 100, 103, 104
"alphabet" programs, 133
AMA (American Medical Association), 142
American Association for Highway Improvement (AAHI; *later named* American Highway Association), 119, 203n.12
American Association of Highway Officials (AASHO), 119
American Association of State Highway Officials, 24
American Association of University Women, 142, 200n.106
American Automobile Association (AAA), 119, 205n.37
The American Chamber of Horrors (Lamb), 111
American Dietetic Association, 200n.106
American Highway Association (*formerly* American Association for Highway Improvement), 119, 203n.12
American Home Economics Association, 142, 200n.106

American Medical Association (AMA), 142
American Nurses' Association, 200n.106
American Printing House for the Blind, 6, 43
American Public Welfare Association, 24
American Road Makers, 119
American Society for Testing Materials (ASTM), 205n.34
Animal Industry Act (1884), 48
antisuffragists, 142, 143–44
AOAC (Association of Official Agricultural Chemists), 24, 94–95, 96–97, 105, 106, 110
appropriations process, for reward/punishment, 46
Arizona, 120, 122, 123
Arkansas, 122, 201n.120
Army Corps of Engineers, 63, 127–28
Association of American Dairy, Food and Drug Officials, 97, 108, 110, 194n.31
Association of Official Agricultural Chemists. *See* AOAC
ASTM (American Society for Testing Materials), 205n.34
automobiles, 119, 158

Bankhead, John, 62–63, 64, 70, 125, 128–29, 161, 189nn.6–7
Bankhead, Tallulah, 189n.6
Bankruptcy Act (1898), 42
Barkan, Ilyse D., 197n.75
Beard, Charles, 29
Bensel, Richard, 71–72
Beveridge, Albert, 103
bicyclists, 118
Bigelow, W. D., 85
Biologics Control Act (1902), 99
birth registration, 138–39
Board of Food and Drug Inspection, 107–8
BOC (Bureau of Chemistry). *See* Bureau of Chemistry
boll weevils, 137, 207n.1
Bourne plan, 127–28

PRINCETON STUDIES IN AMERICAN POLITICS:
HISTORICAL, INTERNATIONAL, AND COMPARATIVE PERSPECTIVES

Series Editors
Ira Katznelson, Martin Shefter, and Theda Skocpol

Governing the American State: Congress and the New Federalism, 1877–1929
by Kimberley S. Johnson
*What a Mighty Power We Can Be: African-American Fraternal Groups and the
Struggle for Racial Equality* by Theda Skocpol, Ariane Liazos, and
Marshall Ganz
Filibuster: Obstruction and Lawmaking in the U.S. Senate
by Gregory Wawro and Eric Schickler
When Movements Matter: The Townsend Plan and the Rise of Social Security
by Edwin Amenta
Disarmed: The Missing Movement for Gun Control in America
by Kristin A. Goss
Shaping Race Policy: The United States in Comparative Perspective
by Robert C. Lieberman
*How Policies Make Citizens: Senior Political Activism and the American
Welfare State* by Andrea Louise Campbell
*Managing the President's Program: Presidential Leadership and Legislative
Policy Formulation* by Andrew Rudalevige
*Shaped by War and Trade: International Influences on American Political
Development* edited by Ira Katznelson and Martin Shefter
Dry Bones Rattling: Community Building to Revitalize American Democracy
by Mark R. Warren
*The Forging of Bureaucratic Autonomy: Reputations, Networks, and Policy
Innovations in Executive Agencies, 1862–1928* by Daniel P. Carpenter
*Disjointed Pluralism: Institutional Innovation and the Development of
the U.S. Congress* by Eric Schickler
*The Rise of the Agricultural Welfare State: Institutions and Interest
Group Power in the United States, France, and Japan*
by Adam D. Sheingate
*In the Shadow of the Garrison State: America's Anti-Statism and Its Cold
War Grand Strategy* by Aaron L. Friedberg
*Stuck in Neutral: Business and the Politics of Human Capital
Investment Policy* by Cathie Jo Martin
Uneasy Alliances: Race and Party Competition in America
by Paul Frymer
*Faithful and Fearless: Moving Feminist Protest inside the Church
and Military* by Mary Fainsod Katzenstein
*Forged Consensus: Science, Technology, and Economic Policy in
the United States, 1921–1953* by David M. Hart